Abode of Divinities

Abode of Divinities

Toward a Universal Philosophy,
Science, and Spirituality

Frank Ignace Babatoundé ALAPINI

Cosmic Harmony and Happiness Publishing

E-mail: cosmicharmony12@gmail.com

ISBN: 978-0-615-44499-4

The three strangest things on this earth consist in three observations:
1- Most humans still do not have absolute proofs that a Creator God or gods exist or not; some only believe, others doubt, still others deny
2-Something is really wrong with the human and the world condition
3- Humanity has not yet found a philosophy for all to be truly happy

However,

Anybody who understands the need for a philosophical and spiritual upgrading can use the content of this book and the one that follows it to guide him/herself and society better than with the use of astrology passing through a global transitional period toward cosmic harmony and happiness

CONTENTS

Preface

The Adventures of Seeker: Episode 1

IN a time when Darkness was reigning on earth, was born in the

country of Houédjè, a boy named Seeker who would engage in a legendary quest for the good of humankind. Early, around the age of ten, he became aware of the heavy presence of Darkness and could not help but dislike it.

Next, he discovered that many of the sages, seers, medicine-men, kings, and other people of the land did not like Darkness either. Seeker saw that those people of good will were striving to bring Light into the country.

Some of them advertised a form of light received from ancient times, but others who have been in contact for a long time with the vast and renowned country of Houéfon showed a different kind of light. Still others, well aware of the habits of the Sinkun people from far in the north brought forth another light.

In the village of Seeker, all the three lights were in use and helped people to see. But many times there were stories telling how some men and women of the village could not find their way in the Darkness and how accidents happened to them.

The community was sad that Zinflougan, the King of Darkness and his evil servants, the lègbas, could still harm people making families, friends, and all compassionate inhabitants unhappy. Some accidents happened in the family of Seeker too and even to himself personally.

Seeker noticed at first that each of the three lights was useful to clearing away some specific aspects of Darkness and that they also had common features. But it was obvious to him that there were still many aspects of Darkness that needed to be dissipated.

Hence, he thought, certainly as many others who were concerned in their hearts, that it will be a good thing if he could come into contact with a light so brilliant that there will be no obscurity left where Zinflougan could hide and commit his crimes.

He had heard from peoples from all lands that Mahu is "He-Who-Owns-Lights-and-Delights". Seeker acknowledged that the better the light, the better the delight. So, he addressed a supplication to Mahu from the bottom of his heart. He asked Mahu to help him find where that Ultimate Light was.

Mahu heard him, smiled and said: 'Here is another who wants something that he probably cannot handle'. Addressing Seeker who was now a teenager, Mahu asked 'Don't you know that those to whom I have given those lights you found not entirely satisfactory had had to go through terrible ordeals to show their worthiness to handle them? Don't you know that anybody who engages in that quest has to undergo the painful ordeal of purification by fire and that many had died or became insane because they were stubborn enough not to give up in time? Do you know what awaits you if you keep holding such a desire?'

Seeker however did not hear those worrisome questions. Mahu used extraordinary powers to store the message in the heart of the teenager knowing he will decipher it when he is ready. He took some of the Sacred-Oil-of-Heaven and spoke on it while gazing at it.

Strange rays of light came out of his eyes and entered the precious oil at the same time when the words pronounced were being recorded in it. He then poured one drop of the potion on the heart of Seeker which began to beat more slowly. The strengthening nature of the operation is well known to those who people the heavens.

Mahu then told Bubba, the watcher in charge of Seeker: 'Your job is going to be harder from now on. Take good care of him and beware of Zinflougan and those who follow him!' They always try to prevent all those who walk the path Seeker is taking from succeeding. Don't help him too much and in case you really need some back up, you know you can count on the rest of the heavenly population that works for good.

'Thank you oh INCOMPARABLE-LORD-OF-THE-WORLDS. I have always been eager to have a mission like this' replied Bubba to Mahu.

Unaware of these events in the High Places, Seeker began his quest.

He was convinced that there should be somewhere on earth a group of light bearers who would have what he was looking for. Whenever he finds a group of light bearers, he asks them questions about the nature of their light and how much Darkness it can dissipate. Each group claimed its light to be the most powerful possible with great properties. But Seeker was not as certain as they were.

After meeting several of those groups, he came into contact with a particular group who claimed its light is not old but results from the combination of the strengths of all the other lights plus some new amazing properties. The light looked indeed brilliant in the eyes of Seeker and he thought it could have the kind of result he was looking for. For 44 great cycles of Houénoukon, he used that light.

Although he was able to see a lot of quality to it; his practice of the science of dissipating darkness convinced him more and more that something additional was needed. Since he did not know where else to go look, he decided not only to have a closer look at all existing lights, but to engineer light himself with the help of Mahu. He knew Mahu is the central person he will have to deal with more directly in order to have the appropriate blueprint.

Seeker who was now a man made a new prayer of determination to Mahu: 'Please, Lord-of-Lights-and-Delights assist me directly, heart to heart and mind to mind to come up with the kind of light I'm searching. It is good that I know of the good aspects of the existing lights. What I need now is that you help me find that something which I feel is missing. I do not want to continue seeing so much useless suffering in the world that you made with your bear hands and which should manifest your glory. I also know you can use other people to help me. If it happens that I make a mistake in the engineering process, please use someone to put my finger on it or tell me directly.'

Mahu was aware of all the difficulties Seeker has faced so far during his journey. He was more excited about his quest, now that he had come so far. It was in the interests of the Lord-of-Lights-and-Delights that Seeker succeeds. He was even more concerned than the young man. How long the engineering process will take, Seeker did not know.

In one of the oldest book of wisdom, it is written that Mahu was curious about how the first walker he made would name things. In another book of wisdom, it is added that Mahu actually taught the first walker the names of things. Seeker was convinced that this was the first task in any engineering process. He knew that in all important traditions, the name of things are not mere names but elements of the Word of Mahu that give precious information about their natures, functions, and places in the universe.

He was sure that the first step should be to make the necessary clarifications about the nature of Mahu himself as well as that of Zinflougan and their respective courts; so that when the people of the world hear their names, all the right ideas come into their minds and the appropriate feelings into their hearts.

When he thought he was at the end of that first step, he brought the result to all walkers and was willing to know if some have discovered the same light he found and if it would be useful.

Dear reader, whether you are convinced of the existence of Mahu or not, read this book with all the critical sense of your mind and all the love you have in your heart.

For sure, there will be a second episode of 'The Adventures of Seeker.'

Rev. Dr. Frank Ignace Babatoundé ALAPINI: M.D., M.Div.

New York, April 2012

Introduction

Thinking and consciousness

THE philosopher René Descartes considered as the 'Father of Modern Philosophy' is most famous for the statement '*I think, therefore I am*' that he made in his book *Discourse on Method; and, Meditations*. Following him, several other modern and post-modern thinkers have declared as a quick Google search shows: '*I think, therefore I'm not*' or '*I think, therefore I'm an atheist*' or '*I think, therefore I'm conservative*' and also '*I think, therefore I'm explanation.*'

This ability to think is according to Blaise Pascal, also a philosopher and younger contemporary of Descartes, the faculty in which dwells all the dignity of human beings. When people think, most of the time, they search for the meaning of life; they do not miss asking themselves, at least once in a lifetime, ultimate philosophical questions such as: '*What is the meaning of existence?*', '*What is the origin of the world?*', '*Is there an afterlife?*', '*Is there a God?*', '*What is reality?*', and so on. They seek answers to those questions in their personal consciousnesses and also in collective consciousnesses. Some even try the unconsciousness.

What is consciousness?

According to the *Encyclopedia Britannica*, the English philosopher John Locke understood consciousness as a psychological condition, the perception of what passes in man's own mind. What passes in the mind is about the mind itself, the body or bodies, and their environment(s). Consciousness is an awareness or perception of reality by a person. Its degree varies from an individual to another. In the human sphere, consciousness is inseparable from life. Indeed, *someone who is aware of nothing is not really living.*

During their growth process, people are conscious before they actually become conscious of their consciousness. When they are, they also notice that awareness changes according to time and space. The time and place in which birth takes place are some of the most determining factors that shape consciousness or the perception of reality. This includes correct perceptions and incorrect perceptions. The ideal that all long for is the state of 100% true perception and 0% false perception.

The major components of culture that have contributed and continue to contribute to the determination of that perception are philosophy, spirituality, religion, and science. *A person born in Saudi Arabia in 1996 is more likely to be a Muslim and perceive reality through that prism while a person born in the Kingdom of Abomey [in present day Benin Republic in West Africa] in 1807 is more likely to be an adept of Vodun.*

The culture of a person can enable him/ her to better perceive reality and accordingly have a more developed consciousness compared to another. Because it is difficult to find a culture that is completely bad, even the individual favored by the time and place of birth should be open to the positive elements about life that other cultures have to offer.

In matter of ideology or religious beliefs or spirituality, the phenomenon called crystallization manifests as it does on the physical plane. Water takes various shapes after freezing according to its container. To change the shape of the solid thus obtained into a more desirable one, heat must be applied to bring the ice back into liquid state. Then the water is put in the convenient container and crystallized again with in general a loss of heat. Long years of spirituality, religious practice, or philosophical and scientific under-standing, shape the psyche in a certain way and determine how it functions and influences fellow humans and nature.

When a person seeks better results or wants to be happier, he/she revises his/her philosophical, spiritual, religious, and scientific ideas and improves them. The elements for the improvement can come from within or be external like books, friends, teachers etc… Those possessing a great deal of humility and practical sense update their ideology or beliefs without feeling the pain of humiliation.

Humility is the absence of arrogance and is not humiliation, which is a loss of dignity. Receiving a teaching has nothing to do with a loss of dignity; rather, it has everything to do with growth and well-being. Authentic teaching is the empathic transmission of information. Among other qualities, perfect teachership requires that the informa-tion conveyer never look down on the receiver. In that case the gratefulness and excitement to be taught wonderful truths and awe-some wisdom during one's life time emerge as the results of teach-ing.

As time passes, adjustments may be required due to changes in human condition and environments. In the relationship patient-doctor, what one should wish for is that the first appreciates the services of the second. Of course the patient would have to trust the doctor first to authorize a checking and then confirm the difference between his/her state before and after care.

The physician can help the patient by giving enlightening informa-tion, comparing the results of the clinical examination, blood tests, scanner, and so forth. In this way, the care giver does not appear as a charlatan. The purpose of this example of patient-doctor relation-ship is to stress the necessity of the effectiveness or the positive transforming power of teaching.

Help me God!

Who really is the God whose help is asked by most of the presidents and vice-presidents of the United States of America as well as by many other rulers in the world when they take the oath of office? From President George Washington to President Barack Obama, forty three presidents out of forty four [97.72 %] have employed the formula 'So help me God.' Forty one of them have been identified by Daniel White[1] plus the presidents George W. Bush and Barack Obama.

So, why do these leaders entrusted with the confidence of the majority of their people call for the help of God when they are about to take on the highest functions of their countries? Why do most human beings consciously or unconsciously feel the need to appeal to that "power" at a moment or another of their lives? Of course, skepticism and atheism can easily develop when there is no answer [at least according to the expectations of the one facing challenges].

'So help me God' is used by legal systems and judges in the U.S. and is prescribed in oaths other than that of the president since 1789 in the judiciary act. The term 'God' is also present on the dollar bills and coins.

---

[1] Daniel Ernest White, "... so help me, God": the US presidents in perspective (New York, NY: Nova Science Publ, 1996), 1.

Science and secular philosophy; complementary to spirituality and religion

The cultures of the peoples who have lived and have crystallized their consciousness in the past can be known by studying history which relies a lot on archeology. Archeology in turn relies on dating techniques. The dating techniques are not perfect, however they are reliable enough to make the researcher trust the temporal and geographical coordinates provided by history. Archeology and history are complementary.

Official history informs that the most ancient advanced civilization is that of Sumer in present day Southern Iraq. Spirituality, religion, philosophy, and science since the Sumerian period have undergone many transformations in other civilizations and cultures until today's worldwide civilization.

In Sumer, spirituality and religion were more important than philosophy and science and included them. Priests and their gods were the organizers of the society. Today, despite the frequent separation of these branches of perception or knowledge of reality, 84 % of humanity is still considered religious and 16 % non-religious as showed by adherent.com.

The sacred texts of various civilizations and religions are useful as primary sources in the determination of the right knowledge about the nature of God and gods. As already stated in the first section of this introduction, useful information can be found in the writings of all civilizations and religions.

In his quest, Seeker has encountered some religious people so attached to one particular scripture that they do not search seriously enough for additional information in other texts. Some of these believers even think that reason is not important in the matter of spirituality or religion. Seeker cannot agree with that view point because he thinks there is a reason or several reasons at work, right or wrong, conscious or unconscious, behind every religious position a person decides to take. Therefore, philosophy should not be antithetical to religion or spirituality.

Pythagoras is said to have coined the word 'philosophy' defining it as the discipline that 'tries to find out'. When the esoteric scholar and Freemason, Manly P. Hall [1901-1990] reports this, he adds that the attitude of Pythagoras was more humble than that of the wise men that preceded him and called themselves *sages* or those who *know*[2].

When one considers the Bible, there seems to be a central line of patriarchs, prophets, and other followers of God which emerges. That line includes Adam, Abel, Seth, Enoch, Noah, Abraham, Isaac, Jacob, Moses, the major and minor prophets, and Jesus.

Abraham is often considered the central figure of his time that established a new covenant with God and became the father of the three great monotheistic religions of Judaism, Christianity, and Islam.

However, in the days of Abraham, according to scripture, there was a person highly revered for his spirituality called Melchizedek; the High Priest of God and King of Salem [later Jerusalem] to whom Abraham gave one tenth of what he gained at a war. He was Abraham's contemporary, not one of his elected descendants.

What was the source of the spirituality of that Melchizedek so well appreciated in the Bible? Why does the author of the Book of Hebrews [5: 6] call Jesus a High Priest according to the order of Melchizedek? In addition, people who believe in the Bible should seriously

---

[2] Manly Palmer Hall, *The Secret Teachings of All Ages: An Encyclopedic Outline of Masonic, Hermetic, Qabbalistic, and Rosicrucian Symbolical Philosophy* (New York: Jeremy P. Tarcher/Penguin, 2003), 192-93.

wonder what was the source of the spirituality of Balaam [Number 22-24], a non-Israelite, seer and diviner, able to exchange views with God, to receive the Spirit of God, to utter oracles, and who refused to disobey that God even for a house full of gold and silver?

From all this, again, it appears that a global and really significant understanding of God and gods should be based on the religious texts of all civilizations. Should it not? The secular literature, from oldest times to the present, whether primarily treating of science, technology, history, philosophy, or the critic even negative of religion and spirituality should all be integrated in the collection of texts on deities.

Considering the confusion, the fanaticism, the doubts, the skepticism, the negation, and fears that characterize societies of various époques including the present one, it is of utmost priority to revisit the spiritual and the secular lives of the civilizations of the past and the present in order to get a picture as broad as possible about divinities.

This volume would have been much more difficult to complete if philosophers, scientists, historians, religious people, and scholars, from various period had not spent a lot of time putting into written form their discoveries, inspirations, insights, and thoughts. For this, and despite the contradictions that can be found in their works, they all deserve great respect and homage.

While writing a book such as this one, the author should pay attention to language because the words used to describe experiences or ideas do not always mean the same things to the readers. To avoid useless polemic, words will be used in the way they are defined in dictionaries with the acknowledgment of multiple meanings when necessary.

Theology, comparative religion, interfaith dialogue, and peace

Theology is the systematic study of the existence, nature, and relationships of the Divine. This definition is very close to the definition of philosophy given by Cicero and reported by Manly Hall in his *Secret teachings of All Ages*. Theology is also an intellectual discipline that aims at setting in an orderly manner the content of a religious faith and of any spiritual organization as well as the ideas of an individual who does not belong to an organization but deals nevertheless with deities in general and God in particular. Theology is a rigorous dialogue with sacred scriptures and subsequent historical data, an intellectual inquiry associated with the mystical desire for an interior knowledge of God.

When *Pythagoras pursued a rational understanding of God*, man, and nature, he was doing more than philosophy, as understood today. Divinities took an important place in his ideas as in those of Plato, Socrates, and Aristotle. Even Immanuel Kant could not completely get rid of spirituality and religion.

Hence, theology does not focus on religion and spirituality alone, but on philosophy and science as well. Theology is a boulevard to access the general revelation from God hidden in nature and its phenomena. It is a discipline that helps place in its proper context any special revelation received from God in dreams and visions involving supernatural beings.

General revelation, the knowledge on the divine gained from nature, is very close to science and the theology based on it is close to secular philosophy. All the difficulty theology faces is with special revelation that particular individuals claim to have received. In general, people tend not to accept as credible the spiritual experiences in which they are not involved. Therefore, theology which is the discipline par excellence of spirituality and religion still needs to defend its credibility in front of secular philosophy and science.

Since theology is basically the study of God, the least a theologian could offer the world is a clarification about that God in order to contribute to cosmic harmony and joy eliminating the confusion, the doubts, the fanaticism, and skepticism mentioned earlier. In so doing, he/she should not avoid the discussion of the border between the knowable and the unknowable.

The theologian particularly needs to consider the view points and critics of the secular world [secularity being a state of separation from religion] as well as arguments from all fields. He/she has to even be prepared to end up as an atheist if such is the logical conclusion that the rigorous study leads to.

If on the contrary, it happens that the conclusion of that study is a clear confirmation of the existence of God and/or gods, then the theologian will have to go further and present his/her ideas in a way that could reconcile faiths and denominations thus providing a good tool not only for comparative religion, but also for interfaith dialogue and global peace.

In theology, the art of exegesis is crucial for a good understanding. When the Bible is used as primary material for instance, various commentaries on the Bible from different authors should be read as well as various versions of the Bible itself. Sometimes, the differences among the different translations are very significant. Then the theologian will have to relate to the "Higher Source" or God [at least postulate that that higher source exists], in his mind and heart to let the truth emerge.

Most of the time, the theologian in a practical way should deal with the reality he/she and others live; and the "truth" uncovered should not contradict that reality. Therefore, the experiences of the theologian as well as the quality of his/her connection with the "higher source" are capital. A famous spiritual guide, namely Jesus, once said that a children-like attitude is important for success to be at the end of the efforts. This supposes great curiosity, openness of mind, humility, honesty, enthusiasm, and love. But the sense of responsibility, the courage, the rational mind, the strength, and the endurance of an adult are required as well.

Some recent and significant publications on the issue of God and gods

In her book *From angels to aliens*, published in 2003, Lynn Clark explores the beliefs of teens in America who receive from the media many ideas concerning the supernatural, the paranormal, demons, hell, and the afterlife. Movies such as *Harry Potter* and *Buffy the Vampire Slayer* are conveyer of those ideas, she says. Clark points out that as consequence, a decline of adherence to formal religious bodies and an interest in alternative spiritualities as well as belief in "superstition" within that population occurred. A hope behind this work is the assessment of those ideas.

In 2006, Jeremy Campbell made public the book *The many faces of God* focused on the religious history, the philosophy, and science of the period from Isaac Newton [a man of the 1600s] to the present. For him, as leading scientists in the 17th century started to find answers for various mysteries of the natural world, they ignited an intellectual and cultural firestorm, replacing the will of God in public consciousness with physical laws.

Campbell mentions that in the hands of people like Galileo and Newton, science suddenly became the mediator between man and God, sweeping away divine messengers like angels, saints, demons, and idols. To him, philosophers were forced to suggest a more rational image of God from the unknowable force to the personal savior, kindly old man, and vengeful autocrat. Campbell also described the present world that has left doctrines and creeds disposable and has rendered theology obsolete.

Maintaining that religions harbor a secret fear that science may one day explain God away, Campbell brings his readers to notice that just as people have come to expect scientists to reveal exciting new explanations of the universe, so too must theologians reestablish their independence to reinvent the cosmos on their own terms.

Campbell has said many useful things in his book. However, this theological work will try to discover the cosmos, not reinvent it as he asks for. Therefore, emphasis will be placed on knowledge, reason, and experience rather than on beliefs and faith. Philosophy therefore will play an important role as it does in science. The goal is to invite people not to accept unreasonable, unproven, or not provable facts; but to ask for an honest consensus around what is reasonable, proven, or provable. The chapter on divinities and epistemology will offer details concerning the place to give faith and belief in the process of knowledge acquirement.

There is not and should not be a separation between science, religion, philosophy, and theology. Differences appeared especially around the historical time Campbell chose as the beginning of the period he inquired about. It is well known that many great men of antiquity such as Plato were scientists, religious, philosophers, and theologians. Newton that Campbell studied was a man of that kind.

From this angle, religion or spirituality should not be afraid that science explains many things about God, angels, and the universe because *the physical and the spiritual are opposed in no way. When physical science and spiritual science further develop filling the gap between them, the true dimension of science as embracing both the physical and the spiritual will become clear in many more minds.*

Paracelsus was a great scientist [physician and botanist] who also described a bunch of spirits. He lived before the time that Campbell studied. In his insightful book, Campbell did not find in any tradition or literature he bent over the evidence for the existence of angels. This book expects to furnish the evidences either that supernatural beings really exist or at least show strong indicators.

In the same year 2006, Michael Martin, professor emeritus of philosophy and Dr. Ricki Monnier, PhD in mathematical logic brought together, a collection of papers written by many distinguished scholars who presented a variety of arguments on how the existence of God is improbable. A part of chapter 15 will analyze these arguments and propose answers from a theistic standing.

Another interesting book on the subject of divinities, these recent years is *The Anonymous God* published in 2005. In its pages, Rev. Dr. David Adams affirms that in a recent past, when the term 'god' was used in public discourse in America, the vast majority of the population constructed that term to mean the God who revealed Himself in the Old Testament for Jews and Christians and additionally in the New Testament for the latter. For him, there have always been some who did not share this concept of god.

The god of American civil religion has no name, he is an anonymous God, Adams adds. In the ancient world, he says, gods had names related to the particular aspects of creation under their influences. Adams continues and tells that the common mythology of the ancient world spread westward and eastward from its Sumerian roots and encountered other gods. For him, the *Sumerian therefore Mesopotamian religious system was a true polytheistic one*. Another thing important to him is that within the framework provided by a monotheistic concept of god, one cannot add gods.

He affirms that the promotion of religious diversity has however created a new American pantheon in which all names by which men call gods are identified with a single spirit-being malleable enough to accommodate any and all religious conceptions. This for him is what creates the anonymous god; or the generic god according Rev. Dr. Joel P. Okamoto.

Okamoto states that the god who is invoked in the pledge of allegiance and who is asked to bless America is no god in particular. He has been related to the "Father" of Christians but this identification has always been implied. The god of civil religion in the mouth of Okamoto is a Unitarian god who resembles the divine reality of Deism. He is, by no means, a watchmaker God, but a God actively interested and involved in history.

Rev. Dr. Alvin Schmidt, another co-author of *The Anonymous God* adds that the Christian 'Father God' became deistic from about 1750 to the 1980s. The deistic movement developed in England during the 1600s and early 1700s and was a product of the Age of Enlightenment or the Age of Reason. According to Schmidt, the deistic conviction was spread in America by Freemasonry which had reorganized itself around that ideology.

To Schmidt, the focus shifted from the Trinity and Jesus Christ to one divine anonymous being. It shifted again beginning in the 1980s from deism to an increasingly polytheistic posture as a result of multiculturalism favored by the Virginia's Act for Religious Freedom of 1786. In this volume the deistic God will also be analyzed and polytheism assessed.

Eleven years before the publication of the *Anonymous God*, Karen Armstrong in *A history of God* had shown, how from the beginning of human history, there has been an alternation between monotheism and polytheism. Monotheism was dominant at the beginning and became such again with the rise of Judaism, Christianity, and Islam. However, *even in monotheism, the idea of God has not been uniform over the ages and has varied from Abraham to Mohammed, Armstrong also said.*

This volume proposes a scriptural presentation to incite readers to personally think about God and gods and get a self-made idea about the evolution of the divine image in human mind. This presentation goes beyond Judaism, Christianity, and Islam and tackles complex, advanced and sophisticated religious systems such as those of the Hindus, Gnostics, Theosophists, Hermeticists, Zoroastrians, Sikhs, esoteric schools, the New Age, and so forth.

Understanding like Armstrong that *religion has been more a matter of ritual rather than ideas or theology, that it has been a desire to respect tradition and be safe rather than to accept theological challenges and be inclined to change; this work also proposes to bring an end to the competition among the various ideas on God and let God be God as many have wished.* As several scholars had desired, an important place should be given to rationality and mystical experience.

This work ambitions to be a determining step in the reconstruction of philosophy and spiritual science that will make accessible to more and more people, the rational and empirical God, getting rid of illogical and not empirically grounded ideas while placing a few others in reserve for empirical confirmation. Reason and experience have been the foundation for the development of physical science; they should not be neglected in the reconstruction of philosophy and spiritual science.

Many in the religious sphere think that reason is only for physical affairs. But if the God they believe in has really created everything, then that God must be the Supreme Master of reason with a Reason that would help human reason grow and better comprehend phenomena including spiritual ones as the Apostle Paul had repeated in several of his letters.

There is a reason behind the phrase 'scientific discoveries'. Physicists, chemists, mathematicians, biologists etc… do not create the results of their research; they discover them, strictly speaking. Likewise, spiritual science reformulated should seek to *discover* spiritual reality, and divinities. This work seeks to be a neutral, non-biased, logical, scriptural, and empirical investigation leading to where the truth appears and not necessarily to where some people might be pleased to see it.

In physical scientific research, certain phenomena are rediscovered and others brought forth for the first time. X-rays existed millennia before Wilhelm Conrad Röntgen discovered them. In spiritual investigation as well, one comes across truths that others have already uncovered. It is possible to remove the dust from old ideas that have been wrongly neglected or definitely bring in new ideas.

It is possible that God [what God?] has always been there, variably accessible to humanity depending on the era. The notion of God is a lot more mysterious and more complex than X-rays that has remained unnoticed for thousands of years.

In its theological march, this work will try to find out which of deism, Trinitarian monotheism, polytheism or other isms appears the most justifiable and determine whether God is really anonymous or not. It will also propose a re-examination of the ancient gods in the present dominant monotheistic context.

The review of literature cannot end without making reference to *The Lost Symbol* of Dan Brown, published in 2009. Though a novel and consequently a work of fiction, the book should be considered seriously in this volume because its author is widely read and directly tackles two key theological concepts: divinities and the scripture. *The Lost Symbol* addresses major theological as well as anthropological issues and offers answers. Through it, Dan Brown proves he stands with several others at the apex of the contemporary theological and philosophical debate.

As he acknowledges, many ideas he expresses in the book are old ideas that are being confirmed by advanced scientific research conducted by the Institute of Noetic Sciences. In the present work, some of those ideas will be analyzed theologically and philosophically. Therefore, they will be remembered along the progression of this volume while important notions and concepts are addressed. It is important to unveil the true nature of all things as Brown expressed through the research of his character *Katherine Solomon.*

In a way or another, everybody should be informed about the topic of God and gods which is central not only to religious or spiritual people and to those who are confused and seek a clearer vision, but also to well rooted skeptics and atheists who have to often deal with religious and spiritual people in their activities.

Part I

MAJOR IDEAS ON GOD AND THE GODS

Chapter 1

Introduction to past or ancient civilizations

HISTORY being the account past events helps understand the

present and better plan the future. The oldest accounts about divinities vary according to the sources considered. For example the Bible brings its readers back before the flood to the first human ancestors from Adam to Noah and introduces them to monotheism. However, it also formally introduces polytheism from the patriarch Terah, the father of Abraham some nine generations after the flood. Abraham is commonly believed to have lived sometime after 2000 B.C.E.

The Bible does not say exactly when polytheism began. What is certain reading it is that Terah was a worshiper of several gods [Joshua 24: 2].

Outside the Bible; Sumerian mythology, Ancient Egyptian Mythology, and the Rig-Veda of Hinduism provide evidences of the existence of polytheism respectively long before 2900 B.C.E, before 3100 B.C.E and from 1700 B.C.E. To understand the existence and nature of God and the gods today, it is important to take a look at those ancient civilizations and others as well.

Definition of ancient and past civilizations

Two of the definitions of the term 'civilization' are helpful for discussion on the topic of God and gods. The first one is civilization as a stage of advanced human social development and organization. The second meaning is civilization as the culture and way of life of a particular place and time.

An ancient civilization is a civilization that has lived and died in the past in a certain place, or a civilization the culture of which has fundamentally changed in time even though there has been no discontinuity in the peopling of its territory.

In the matter of deities, the two meanings of the term civilization seen above are interesting and should be combined to allow a more exhaustive study. People do not need to have an advanced civilization before having a religious or spiritual system. On the other hand, advanced civilizations are interesting to study because they often have abundant [particularly written] records of their beliefs and practices.

Some advanced civilizations such as the Babylonian and Egyptian have had a pretty good level of technology. For example Mesopotamia is considered the birthplace of science and technology. Mathematics and astronomy are known to have been well advanced in Ancient Egypt.

Many remarkable figures of the Greek civilization, including the great mathematician and philosopher Pythagoras traveled to Egypt to obtain knowledge. This denotes of the significance of that civilization.

But, to believe Manly Hall, Pythagoras was also an initiate of the Babylonian and Chaldean mysteries and received the secret tradition of Moses from Rabbins. *That the two civilizations of Babylon and Egypt were at the same time fundamentally religious and technologically and scientifically advanced should incite to their meticulous study.*

God, god, gosh, and golly

The word 'God' is one of the most used in English language and its origin is very ancient. A good observer of society, particularly of the American society should notice that 'God' is more and more replaced by 'Gosh.' The expressions 'My gosh!' or 'Oh my gosh!' are among the most popular interjections. The phenomenon has been so remarkable that the word 'gosh' entered dictionaries.

Gosh is a euphemism for God; demonstrating that the reason behind the change is to avoid offending God, by using a neutral expression. The cause of that supersession is probably the belief of many in the Bible in which it is forbidden to take the name of God in vain [see Exodus 20: 7]. Another euphemistic superseding term is 'golly.'

With a capital 'G', 'God' is commonly used to speak of the ultimate source and power of the universe, subject of religious devotion, primal being or energy, Supreme Being, Creator, considered as the source of all moral authority, and ruler of the universe.

With small 'g', a god is any being conceived as supernatural and immortal or the idol of that being.

The third definition is 'god' as a deified human being or a deified thing because of their influence positive or negative, spiritual or not.

Terms such as 'deity' or 'divinity' are also employed for God or gods with a capital 'D' for God. Sometimes in sacred texts such as the *Pyramid Texts*, the Capital 'G' or 'D' is used to honor a god.

Myth, mythology, parable, and reality

A myth is a story involving supernatural persons, actions, and events. It embodies some popular ideas concerning natural or historical phenomena. Myths are vestiges of an old past.

A mythology is an exposition of myths associated with a particular culture or person. Mythology also designates the study of myths.

A parable is a comparison, an analogy, a similitude, a metaphor or an allegory. It is a short story that uses familiar situations to illustrate a religious, spiritual, or moral point. So, a parable can be a myth or be part of a myth.

Sometimes, some stories written in scripture particularly the Bible are called myths. Hence, a person like Rudolph Bultmann felt necessary to "demythologize" the scripture. However, it is not prudent to treat as unauthentic or unreal all accounts in which people said they have encountered spiritual beings because of the lack of the possibility to confirm or not those stories.

The attitude that seems wiser is to listen attentively to people's declarations about their spiritual experiences. Those experiences should be carefully compiled and analyzed to find out what look plausible according to the entire human knowledge. Unverifiable information should neither be used as truths nor be treated as lies. With the progresses of knowledge it is possible that those declarations find their logical, experiential, or experimental justifications or be confirmed as untrue.

Artifacts, timelines, and religious texts of ancient civilizations

The beliefs and practices that are said to have characterized ancient civilizations are grounded on materials evidences. People from all times and places have actually dealt with divinities whether those divinities were real or imagined. The archeological evidences are the artifacts found randomly by ordinary people of various lands in the course of everyday life, or purposively by archeologists who have followed certain archeological or historical clues and have organized methodic searches. A list of significant artifacts figures in appendix 1.

In history, archeological findings are interpreted. Meaning is given to the artifacts and ancient writings are translated. For example the statue of King Hammurabi in prayer is interpreted as a religious artifact and Ancient Egyptian hieroglyphs are known to have been deciphered by Jean-François Champollion.

In appendix 2 is presented the order of emergence of various civilizations according to four sources. A brief analysis of this timeline shows that historians agree on many key points in the history of civilizations. There are some differences in the dates given which could be explained, for example by the different perspectives of the historians. Some historians will give the dates of a civilization at its apex while others will consider the beginning of that civilization which can reach very far in the past. However those differences do not affect the general idea that one can get about the order of the development of civilizations.

Information on God and the gods have reached this époque thanks to sacred texts of ancient civilizations. Some do not figure in appendix 3 because they have disappeared due to war and conflicts that ended with the destruction sometimes of entire libraries. Other writings are not present there simply because the research did not find them. Finally, important magical texts such as the Picatrix, the Clavicules of Solomon, and the Voynich Manuscript are not mentioned in that appendix because the sources consulted have not put them in their lists.

The purpose behind the presentation of these three timelines is to point the readers, especially the least informed, in the direction of interesting paths for reading and research.

Chapter 2

Introduction to the pantheons and creation myths of ancient civilizations

MANY books, dictionaries, and encyclopedias on mythology
as well as many websites contain a detailed description of the gods
and goddesses of ancient civilizations. Here, just the name and the
title of those deities are presented to give an idea of them. That idea
will be reinforced by the creation myths of those ancient civilizations.

Sometimes a function is held by a god in a civilization but by a
goddess in another. For example the Goddess Ishtar and the God
Mars were patrons of warriors, respectively in Mesopotamia and in
the Roman Empire.

Other times two different gods have the same title like in the case
of Apollo and Helios. Both are sun gods but Apollo has several other
functions and Helios is said to be of Asiatic origin.

In some other cases the attributes of the gods vary in time becoming more important or less important like in Hindu and Mesopotamian mythologies. This variation can be attributed to political changes as well as the emergence of new thinkers.

When the detailed descriptions of these gods and goddesses is considered, many of them appear not to be exclusively good but a mix of good and bad. Some like Set of ancient Egypt play very negative roles. In all ancient civilizations and also in Old Religious Movements, there were deities from both sexes: males and females.

Each creation myth has several versions like the Bible due to different translations. Here figure some of the clearest ones. They are presented so that the readers could compare them with the creation story of the book of Genesis and identify common elements as well as dissimilarities. Then these commonalities and differences could be compared to those that Seeker has discovered and which are displayed here and there in this work.

Ancient Mesopotamian Civilization

Mesopotamia is the ancient region in southwestern Asia covering present day Iraq and also some parts of Turkey and Syria. Etymologically, 'Mesopotamia' means the regions between the two rivers which are the Tigris and the Euphrates. It has been the site of the people of Sumer, Akkad, Babylonia, and Assyria from 4500 B.C.E to 606 B.C.E.

The mythology of Mesopotamia, basically, has always been that of Sumer with slight modifications during the succeeding centuries. That mythology has been well preserved because of the existence of writings which first were cuneiform. Those writings were epics, hymns, incantations, lamentations, and proverbs.

Among the epics is the *Enuma Elish* or Babylonian creation myth. It was recovered by Henry Layard in 1849 [in fragmentary form] in the ruined Library of Ashurbanipal at Nineveh [Mosul, Iraq], and published by George Smith in 1876. The *Enuma Elish* exists in various copies from Babylonia and Assyria. The version from Ashurbanipal's library dates back to the 7th century B.C.E. The text written on 7 tablets was, according to historians, probably composed at Babylon in the Kassaite period to celebrate Babylon's victory [c. 1450 B.C.E] over the Sealand.

The name of the original author of the *Enuma Elish* is not known and the text does not say if the creation epic was written under the order or advise of a deity whosoever. What is available is a mythological story of creation that was widely if not unanimously believed in Mesopotamia and which was at the center of the religion of the first advanced civilization.

The deities:

Apsu: primeval god of fresh water

Marduk: most powerful of the gods

Enki/Ea: god of wisdom, art, and civilization

Enlil: god of wind

Inanna/Ishtar/Ereshkigal/Astarte: goddess of sexual love, fertility, warfare, and judgment

Utu/Shamash/Sama/Ahamash: sun god

Ninhursag/Ki: goddess of the earth

Nergal: sun god of noontime and summer solstice and god of the nether-world

Sin/Nanna: god of the moon

Tiamat: primeval monster goddess

Anshar: a sky god

Anu: another sky god

Nammu/Namma: goddess of the primeval sea

The creation myth of Mesopotamia [the Enuma Elish] as narrated by the CRI/Voice institute

In the beginning, the god Apsu, god of fresh water and thus of male fertility begat heaven and earth and the goddess of the sea. Tiamat, chaos, was their mother. *The waters of heaven and earth were mingled together. Then were created the gods in the midst of heaven*: Lahmu, Lahamu, Anshar, and Kishar who represented the boundary between earth and sky [the horizon]. To Anshar and Kishar was born Anu, god of the sky who in turn gave birth to Enki [or Ea], the god of wisdom.

The gods were too noisy and made Apsu and Tiamat uncomforta- ble. Counseled by Mummu, the minister of Apsu, Apsu and Tiamat decided to destroy the gods. But Enki happened to be aware of their plan. He killed Apsu and established with his wife Damkina his dwelling over his body. Marduk, most able and wisest of the gods was then engendered, created in the holly heart of Apsu, begotten by Enki and Damkina, his father and mother. He was called the Sun of the heavens. He was the god of spring and symbolized both by the light of the sun and the lightning in storm and rain. He was also the patron god of the city of Babylon.

Meanwhile Tiamat enraged at the murder of her husband Apsu vowed revenge. She created eleven monsters to help her carry out her vengeance. Tiamat took a new husband, Kingu, one of her sons, in place of the slain Apsu and put him in charge of her newly assem- bled army. Tiamat represented the forces of disorder and chaos in the world. In the cycle of seasons, Tiamat was winter and barren- ness.

To avenge the murder of her husband Tiamat prepared to unleash on the other gods the destructive forces that she has assembled. Enki learned of her plan and attempted to confront her. It is apparent that Enki failed to stop Tiamat. Then Anu attempted to challenge her but failed as well. The gods became afraid that no one will be able to stop Taimat's vengeful rampage.

At this point Marduk entered the conflict. He proposed to defeat Tiamat and her army in exchange of becoming the leader of the gods. His proposal was accepted. With the authority and power of the council, Marduk assembled his weapons, the four winds as well as the seven winds of destruction. He rode in his chariot of clouds with the weapons of the storm to Tiamat. After entangling her in a net, Marduk unleashed the Evil Wind to inflate Tiamat.

When she is incapacitated by the wind, Marduk kills her with an arrow through her heart and took captive the other gods and monsters who were her allies. He also captured her husband Kingu. After smashing Tiamat's head with a club, Marduk divided her corpse, using half to create the earth and the other half to create the sky complete with bars to keep the *chaotic waters* from escaping.

He constructed stations for the great gods, fixing their astral likenesses as the stars of the Zodiac. He determined the year and into sections he divided it; he set up three constellations for each of the twelve months. After defining the days of the year by means of heavenly figures, he founded the station of the pole star [Nebiru] to determine their bounds, that none might err or go astray. Alongside it, he set up the stations of Enlil and Enki. In Tiamat's belly he established the zenith.

The Moon he caused to shine, entrusting the night to him. He appointed him a creature of the night to signify the days and marked off every month without cease by means of his crown: 'At the month's very start, rising over the land, you shall have luminous horns to signify six days, on the seventh day reaching a half-crown. So shall the fifteen-day period be like one another-two halves for each month. When the sun overtakes you at the base of heaven, diminish your crown and retrogress in light. At the time of disappearance approach the course of the sun and on the thirtieth you shall again stand in opposition to the sun. I have appointed a sign, follow its path.'

After he had appointed the days to Shamash, he formed the clouds and filled them with water. He caused the rising of winds, the bringing of rain and cold. Putting Tiamat's head into position he formed thereon the mountains, opening the deep which was in flood, he caused to flow from her eyes the Euphrates and Tigris. He formed from her breasts the lofty mountains; therein he drilled springs for the wells to carry off the water.

When he had designed his rules and fashioned his ordinances, he founded the shrines and handed them over to Enki. The Tablet of Destinies which he had taken from Kingu he carried, he brought it as the first gift of greeting, he gave it to Anu. He made statues and set them up at the Gate of Apsu saying: 'Let it be a token that this may never be forgotten!'

When the gods saw this they were exceedingly glad. Lahmu, Lahamu, and all of his fathers crossed over to him, and Anshar, the king, made manifest his greeting; Anu, Enlil, and Enki presented to him gifts. With a gift Damkina, his mother, made him joyous, she sent offerings, his face brightened. To Usmi who brought her gift to a secret place he entrusted the chancellorship of Apsu and the stewardship of the shrines.

Being assembled, all the Igigi bowed down while everyone of the Anunnaki kissed his feet. They stood before him, bowed and said: 'He is the king!' After the gods, his fathers were satiated with his charms, Enki and Damkina opened their mouths to speak to the great gods, the Igigi: 'Formerly Marduk was merely our beloved son, now he is your king, proclaim his title!'

A second speech they made, they all spoke: 'His name shall be Lugaldimmerankia, trust in him!' When they had given the sovereignty to Marduk, they declared for him a formula of good fortune and success: 'Henceforth you will be the patron of our sanctuaries, what-ever you command we will do.'

Marduk opened his mouth to speak: 'Below I have hardened the ground for a building site, I will build a house. It will be my luxurious abode. I will found therein its temple; I will appoint its inner rooms. I will establish my sovereignty. When you come up from the Apsu for assembly, you will spend the night in it. It is there to receive all of you, when you descend from heaven for assembly. You will spend the night in it. It is there to receive all of you. I will call its name *Babylon which means the houses of the great gods*. I shall build it with the skill of craftsmen.'

When the gods, his fathers, heard this speech of his, they put the following question to Marduk, their firstborn: 'Over all that your hands have created, who will have your authority? Over the ground which your hands have created, who will have your power? Babylon, to which you have given a fine name, therein, establishing our abode forever!'

When Marduk heard the words of the gods, his heart prompted him to fashion artful works. Opening his mouth, he addressed Enki to impart the plan he had conceived in his heart: 'I will take blood and fashion bone. I will establish *a savage; 'man' shall be his name, truly, savage-man I will create. He shall be charged with the service of the gods* that they might be at ease! The ways of the gods I will artfully alter. Though alike revered, into two groups they shall be divided.'

Enki answered him, speaking a word to him, giving him another plan for the relief of the gods: 'Let but one of their brothers be handed over; he alone shall perish that mankind may be fashioned. Let the great gods be here in Assembly. Let the guilty be handed over that they may endure.' Marduk summoned the great gods to Assembly; presiding graciously, he issued instructions. To his utterance the gods paid heed.

The king addressed a word to the Anunnaki: 'If your former state-ment was true, now declare the truth on oath by me! Who was it that contrived the uprising, and made Tiamat rebel, and joined battle? Let him be handed over who contrived the uprising. His guilt I will make him bear. You shall dwell in peace!' The Igigi, the great gods, replied to him; to Lugaldimmerankia, counselor of the gods, their lord: 'It was Kingu who contrived the uprising, and made Tiamat rebel, and joined battle.'

They bound him, holding him before Enki. They imposed on him his punishment and severed his blood vessels. Out of his blood they fashioned mankind. He imposed on him the service and let free the gods. After Enki, the wise, had created mankind, he imposed upon them the service of the gods. That work was beyond comprehension; as artfully planned by Marduk, did Nudimmud create it.

Marduk, the king of the gods divided all the great gods [Anunnaki] above and below. Three hundred in the heavens he stationed as a guard. In like manner the ways of the earth he defined. In heaven and on earth six hundred thus he settled. After he had ordered all the instructions, to the Anunnaki of heaven and earth allotted their por-tions, the Anunnaki opened their mouths and said to Marduk, their lord: 'Now, O lord, you who have caused our deliverance, what shall be our homage to you? Let us build a shrine whose name shall be called Lo, a chamber for our nightly rest; let us repose in it! Let us build a throne, a recess for his abode! On the day that we arrive we shall repose in it.'

When Marduk heard this, he brightly glowed his features, like the day: 'Construct Babylon, whose building you have requested. Let its brickwork be fashioned. You shall name it The Sanctuary.' The Anunnaki applied the implement; for one whole year they molded bricks. When the second year arrived, they raised high the head of Esagila equaling Apsu [sky]. *Having built a stage-tower as high as Apsu [sky], they set up in it an abode for Marduk, Enlil, and Enki.* In their presence he was seated in grandeur. To the base of Esharra its horns look down.

After they had achieved the building of Esagila, all the Anunnaki erected their shrines. The gods, his fathers, at his banquet stated: 'This is Babylon, the place that is your home! Make merry in its precincts, occupy its broad places.' The great gods took their seats. They set up a festive drink, sat down to a banquet.

After they had made merry within it, in Esagila, the splendid, had performed their rites, the norms had been fixed and all their portents, all the gods apportioned the stations of heaven and earth. The fifty great gods took their seats. The seven gods of destiny set up the three hundred in heaven.

Enlil raised the bow, his weapon, and laid it before them. The gods, his fathers, saw the net he had made. When they beheld the bow, how skillful its shape, his fathers praised the work he had wrought.

Raising it, Anu spoke up in the Assembly of the gods, he kissed the bow: 'This is my daughter!' He named the names of the bow as follows: 'Longwood is the first, the second is Accurate; its third name is Bow-Star. In heaven I have made it shine.' He fixed its position with the gods its brothers.

After Anu had decreed the fate of the bow, and had placed the lofty royal throne before the gods, he placed it in the Assembly of the gods. When the great gods had assembled, they extolled the destiny of Marduk. They bowed down, and they pronounced among themselves a curse, swearing by water and oil to place life in jeopardy; when they had granted him the exercise of kingship of the gods; when they had given him dominion over the gods of heaven and underworld.

Anshar pronounced supreme his name, Asarluhi, saying: 'Let us do obeisance at the mention of his name. To his utterance let the gods give heed. Let his command be supreme above and below!

Most exalted be the Son, our avenger. Let his sovereignty be sur-
passing, having no rival. May he shepherd the black-headed ones,
his creatures. To the end of days, without forgetting, let them acclaim
his ways. May he establish for his fathers the great food-offerings.

Their support they shall furnish, shall tend their sanctuaries. May
he cause incense to be smelled . . . their spells, make a likeness on
earth of what he has wrought in heaven. May he order the black-
headed to revere him. May the subjects ever bear in mind to speak of
their god, and may they at his word pay heed to the goddess. May
food-offerings be borne for their gods and goddesses. Without fail let
them support their gods! Their lands let them improve, build their
shrines. Let the black-headed wait on their gods.

As for us, by however many names we pronounce, he is our god!
Let us then proclaim his fifty names: He whose ways are glorious,
whose deeds are likewise, Marduk, as Anu, his father, called him
from his birth; who provides grazing and drinking places, enriches
their stalls, who with the flood-storm, his weapon, vanquished the
detractors, and who the gods, his fathers, rescued from distress.
Truly, the Son of the Sun, most radiant of gods is he. In his brilliant
light may they walk forever!

The service of the gods he imposed that these may have ease.
Creation, destruction, deliverance, grace shall be by his command.
They shall look up to him! Marukka truly is the god, creator of all, who
gladdens the heart of the Annunaki, appeases the Igigi. Marutukku
truly is the refuge of his land, city, and people. Unto him shall the
people give praise forever. Barashakushu stood up and took hold of
its reins; wide is his heart, warm his sympathy. Lugaldimmerankia is
his name which we proclaimed in our Assembly.

His commands we have exalted above the gods, his fathers. Truly, he is lord of all the gods of heaven and underworld, the king at
whose discipline the gods above and below are in mourning. Nari-
Lugaldimmerankia is the name of him whom we have called the

monitor of the gods; who in heaven and on earth founds for us retreats in trouble, and who allots stations to the Igigi and Anunnaki.

At his name the gods shall tremble and quake in retreat. Asaruludu is that name of his which Anu, his father, proclaimed for him. He is truly the light of the gods, the mighty leader, who in fierce single combat saved our retreats in distress. Asaruludu, secondly, they have named Namtillaku, the god who maintains life, who restored the lost gods, as though his own creation; the lord who revives the dead gods by his pure incantation, who destroys the wayward foes.

Let us praise his prowess! Asaruludu, whose name was thirdly called Namru, the shining god who illumines our ways.'

Three of his names have Anshar, Lahmu, and Lahamu proclaimed; unto the gods, their sons, they did utter them: 'We have proclaimed three of his names. Like us, do you utter his names?' Joyfully the gods heeded their command, as in Ubshukinna they exchanged counsels: 'Of the heroic son, our avenger, of our supporter we will exalt the name!' They sat down in their Assembly to fashion destinies, all of them uttering his names in the sanctuary[3].

Ancient Egypt

There are at least two main explanations to the origin of ancient Egyptian spirituality, religion, and mythology.

To Christopher Ehret, a professor of African history, separate local deities of Egypt's pre dynastic Afrasan religion were co-opted into a new religious synthesis after 3500 B.C.E[4]. The Afrasan deities

---

[3]CRI/Voice.Institute.http://www.crivoice.org/enumaelish.html (accessed April 1, 2010).
[4]Christopher Ehret, *The Civilizations of Africa: A History to 1800* (Charlottesville: University Press of Virginia, 2002), 66 and 116.

became the gods in a newly polytheistic religion, he affirms. The religious unification of the country that paralleled its political unification gave the formerly independent small polities of Egypt an ideological stake in the new state. Because of the political unification that changed henotheism into polytheism, it was possible by the time of the third dynasty for a king to claim a status among the gods.

Ehret asserts that well before 10 000 B.C.E., Afrasans have introduced a new religion in pre dynastic Egypt with a language directly ancestral to ancient Egyptian.

According to other sources like Helena P. Blavatsky, degenerate descendants of the lost civilization of Atlantis, as affirmed by Plato, were those who had built the first pyramids in Ancient Egypt.

The deities:

Re or Ra: god of all creation

Shu: god of air

Tefnut: goddess of morning dew

Geb: god of earth

Nut: goddess of the sky

Isis: goddess of the home [ideal wife and mother], matron of nature and magic

Osiris: god of the afterlife, the netherworld, and the dead

Set: god of the desert, storms, and foreigners; considered in later myths as the god of darkness and chaos

Nephthys: goddess of mourning

Horus: god of life

Anubis: god of the dead

Hathor: goddess of love

Nekhebet: goddess of royal protection

Amun: soul of all phenomena

Apophis: serpent demon

Aten: sun disc, manifestation of Re

Atum: creator god, lord of all, personification of the primeval chaos

Maat: goddess of law, truth, and world order

Thoth: lord of the moon, lord of time, tongue of Re, god of judgment inventor of writing, science, and magic

Creation myth of Ancient Egypt
as told by Richard Wilkinson

In the beginning there were the Primeval Waters; without limit, with no surface, no up, no down, no side to side, endless, deep, dark, and invisible personified as Nun. There is a representation of Nun in one copy of the *Book of the Dead* from the new kingdom which shows him as a man rising from the waters to hold above his head the sacred boa of the sun-god. In the cosmogony of Hermopolis *depth, endlessness, darkness, and invisibility* were each given masculine and feminine forms: Nau and Naunet, Huh and Hauhet, Kuk and Kakuet, and *Amun* and Amaunet.

They were worshiped at Hermopolis as the eight genii with the heads of frogs and serpents. The name Knum [Eight Town] was given to the city of their worship. These genii were believed to have swum together and formed an egg in the darkness of Father Nun. From the egg burst forth the bird of light [or air according to other versions of the myth].

In another version from Thebes, the egg, origin of the world was laid by a goose, the Great Primeval Spirit called Ken-Ken Ur, the One whose voice broke the silence while the world was still flooded in silence [Book of the Dead Chapter 54]. The Greeks called the place

Hermopolis since they identify the chief diety of the place, the Ibis-headed Thoth with their god Hermes.

Thoth was regarded as the head over the eight genii. But it is possible that in earlier times he was a creator-god in his own right. By the dynastic period, he had become the inventor of the hieroglyphic system of writing, the original law giver, repository of all learning both sacred and profane, and master of enchantment [hika].

During the first intermediate period, the cosmology of Hermopolis became mingled with that of Heliopolis with the result that many original concepts were lost. The creator-god who held pride of place in the Heliopolitan cosmogony was Atum whose name possibly means the 'Complete One.'

The earliest information about this deity occurs in the Pyramid Texts. Later, Atum became associated with the sun-god Re [or Ra]. According to Heliopolitan account, Atum emerged out of Nun either in the form of a hill or on a hill. There was no fixed form for the Primeval Hill but an early formalizing of it into an eminence with sloping sides or ascending steps may have some bearing on the form of the pyramids.

While the priesthood of Heliopolis claimed that it was in Heliopolis that this event took place, other religious centers made the same claims. Thus, at Hermopolis in the midst of a rectangular space surrounded by a high wall, lay a pool of water known as 'The Lake of the two knives' symbolizing Nun. In the middle of the lake was an island, 'The Island of Flames' with a small hill, on which it was claimed the light first appeared. Memphis and Thebes also made that claim.

Atum's emerging was an act of self-volition. In Heliopolitan theology, he is known as Khopri 'The One who becomes' In the Chapter 85 of the Book of the Dead, Atum says of himself: 'I came into being of myself in the midst of the Primeval Waters in this my name of Khopri.'

The scarab or beetle was considered a manifestation of Atum due to the fact that its name was similar in sound to Khopri.

In the beginning, Atum was alone in the universe but he contained all things in himself. Though he spoke as male, he was really bisexual. Indeed in the *Coffin Texts*, he was called the *'Great He-She'*. In order to bring all things into being, he had to create them out of himself[5].

Ancient Greece

Little is certain about the first Greek settlers except that they brought with them Zeus, their sky-god, father of the gods and men, lord of the weather, and protector of the household. Greek religion incorporated elements from the religious beliefs of the aboriginal inhabitant of the Greek Peninsula as well as from Minoan civilization.

The general features of Greek religion and mythology can be traced back to the early feudal period known as the Mycenaean age [1568-1100 B.C.E.].

The principal deity in Minoan religion was a goddess associated with animals or snakes or the earth's fertility and with childbirth. Minoans may have believed in the after death. They buried their dead and offered them libations.

The Mycenaean divinities had distinct names and functions. The Homeric gods named in Mycenaean texts include Zeus, Artemis, Athena, Demeter, Paean, Hera, Hermes, and Dionysus. The Mycenaeans too buried their dead [the princes in magnificent tombs] with

---

[5]Richard H. Wilkinson, *The Complete Gods and Goddesses of Ancient Egypt* (New York: Thames & Hudson, 2003).

food and containers; evidence at least for belief in survival after death like in Ancient Egypt.

As mentioned in the introduction, all the four most famous Greek philosophers [Pythagoras, Socrates, Plato, and Aristotle] believed in the divine. Among them, *Pythagoras developed a monotheistic view which acknowledges a Supreme Mind distributed in all the parts of the universe which serves as its body.* Since Pythagoras was initiated in many religions including Ancient Egyptian Mysteries, one can conclude that he got his idea from Hermes Trismegistus who put forth exactly that same idea of God as it will be shown in chapters 4, 13, 14, and 15.

The deities:

Zeus: sky god and leader of the twelve great gods

Apollo: god of the sun, art, poets, prophecy, archery, and music

Hermes: god of boundaries, graves, shepherds, thieves, good fortune, inventor of fire, messenger of the gods

Athena: goddess of battle, snake goddess

Asklepios: god of medicine and healing

Kronos: archetypical fertility god

Metis: goddess of wisdom

Hera: wife of Zeus

Leto: goddess of graves, goddess of being unseen, parent with Zeus of Apollo and Artemis

Maia: earth goddess, goddess of the plains, minor consort of Zeus

Demeter: goddess of vegetation and death

Artemis: goddess of nature and of the initiation rituals of young girls, goddess of blood sacrifice and birth

Aphrodite: goddess of love, war, and victory

Eros: god of love, son of Aphrodite

Hephaistos: god of fire

Ouranos/Uranus: primordial god of heaven

Gaia: primordial essence of the earth, goddess of marriage and the taking of oaths

Helios: god of the sun

Ares: god of war and destruction

Hades: god of riches and the underworld

Poseidon: sea god

Dionysus: god of wine and sexuality

Creation myth of Ancient Greece as narrated by Wilkinson Philip and Neil Philip

In the beginning there was nothing but a swirling void called chaos. Eventually out of nothingness, a creator force emerged. Some say this force was Gaia, Mother Earth; some say it was a goddess called Eurynome, who took the form of a dove. Gaia or Eurynome laid a great egg, from which emerged Uranus the sky; Oureas, the mountains; Pontus, the sea, and many other parts of the cosmos. Gaia and Uranus made love and the earliest creatures to inhabit the Earth were born.

First, the Cyclopes, giant creatures that looked like people but had only one eye in the middle of their foreheads came. Uranus disliked the Cyclops and thought they might usurp his power, so he banished them to the underworld. Gaia and Uranus later produced six huge and powerful children who grew up to rule the Earth and became known as the Titans. The descendants of the Titans became some of the most important and enduring gods in classical culture: the gods of Mount Olympus.

Among the Titans was Cronos who became their leader. The Titans were giants of incredible strength. They settled down with female Titans [Titanesses] and began to rule the earth. Soon they began to have children, some of whom were destined to become the most powerful gods and goddesses. Eos the goddess of the dawn and Helios the sun god were the children of Hyperion. Cronos, king of the Titans had many children with his wife Rhea. The children of Cronos and Rhea became the gods of Mount Olympus also called the Olympians and they were to become as powerful a race as the Titans themselves.

The gods made two botched attempts to create people to inhabit the earth before the human race as we know it was created by the Titan Prometheus, acting on a request from the god Zeus. Prometheus then took on a guardian role helping humans on several occasions. This enraged the gods and the Titan spent many years suffering a terrible punishment after he made Zeus angry.

The first two attempts to create humans produced the peaceful Golden race, who had no children and died out and the Silver Race, who were banished to the Underworld by Zeus because they were evil. Then Prometheus fashioned the Bronze Race from clay, who thrived.

On one occasion, the people sacrificed one bull to Zeus. They could keep some of it and offer some to the god, but they could not agree on which parts. Prometheus helped them by dividing the meat into two: one portion was the good meat, wrapped in bull's hide; the other just bones covered in tasty looking fat.

Zeus chose the second and was so angry when he discovered the trick that he refused to give fire to humanity. But Prometheus stole it from Zeus and took it to Earth, showing everyone how to use it. Furious, Zeus punished him by chaining him to a rock where a great eagle pecked away at his liver. Zeus renewed the liver everyday causing endless torture until finally Prometheus was rescued by the hero Heracles.

The first rulers of the universe were the Titans, but they did not rule in harmony. The real trouble began when Cronos, the chief Titan began to have children with his wife Queen Rhea. Their offspring the gods and goddesses fought a long and bitter war against the Titans before finally achieving victory under their leader Zeus.

When Cronos began to have children, he was told by an oracle that one of his children would kill him. To prevent this, each time a baby was born; Cronos took the child and swallowed it. This happened five times, so when she gave birth for the sixth time, Rhea decided to deceive her husband. She hid her baby Zeus and wrapped a stone in swaddling clothes. Cronos took the stone and swallowed it and Rhea secretly sent Zeus to Crete where he was brought up by a faithful goat-nymph called Amalthea and nourished on honey supplied by Cretan bees.

Amalthea died as Zeus was nearing adulthood and he had her skin made into a magically strong shield. Zeus had learned about his parentage and how his father had treated his siblings, and now decided that he would return to Greece and take his revenge.

Back in Greece, Zeus met Metis, a cunning Titaness who told him that it was not too late to rescue his siblings. Metis gave Zeus a drug, which he in turn administered to Cronos causing him to vomit up his five other children: the gods Poseidon and Hades, and the goddesses Hestia, Demeter, and Hera. Then Zeus freed the Cyclopes who were sent to the Underworld by Uranus and kept there by Cronos. They also wanted to take their revenge on the Titans.

Under the leadership of Zeus, the gods and goddesses, along with the Cyclopes declared war on Cronos and the Titans. The struggle lasted ten years, and the hugely powerful Titans seemed invincible. But the Cyclopes were skilled craftsmen who produced some mighty weapon for the gods. They forged a thunderbolt for Zeus; a great trident for Poseidon, which could create earthquakes and storms; and a magical helmet for Hades that made him invisible when he put it on. By using these powerful weapons, the young gods eventually managed to defeat the Titans.

When the fight was over, the gods ruled the cosmos and decided to divide up power between them. Unable to think of any other way to determine who should rule which part of the universe, they decided to draw lots. Zeus became ruler of the sky, Poseidon was made god of the sea, and Hades king of the underworld. The defeated Titans were imprisoned in Tartarus, a deep region of the cosmos, deeper even than the underworld and peopled by dreadful monsters. One of the Titans, Atlas, was punished by being given the job of holding the heavens on his shoulders.

Gaia the mother of the Titans was furious when her children were imprisoned in Tartarus, so she started another war. She rallied together another group of her children, the giants and took them to war and the battle begun all over again.

Once more the Olympian gods were victorious, but then Zeus was forced to fight one last battle-with the monster Typhoon. The battle ended when Zeus cornered him in Sicily and hurled Mount Etna at the monster's head. The fire that erupts from Etna was sometimes said to come from the thunderbolt Zeus has used in this last fight. Zeus's struggle for power was now over and he reigned supreme over the universe[6].

Ancient Maya

According to the *Encyclopedia Americana* which is a good source of information on ancient civilizations, Ancient Maya developed in southern Mexico, Guatemala, Belize, El Salvador, and Honduras. It lasted nearly 2000 years from 400 years before the Common Era until the Spanish conquest in the 16th century.

---

[6]Philip Wilkinson and Neil Philip, *Mythology* (Eyewitness companions London: DK Pub, 2007), 36-39.

In the Maya society, religion was inseparable from secular activities. Worship included prayers, the burning of incense, mutilations [such as rasping the tongue with thorny vine or rope], and occasionally human sacrifice. The Maya calendar and the Maya religion were inseparable too: each unit each of time [day, month, and larger units] was represented by a god.

The deities:

Itzamna: god of all
Kinich Ahau: god of the Sun
Chac: god of rain
Yum Kaax: god of corn
Kukulkan: god of wind
Ek Chuah: god of war
Xaman Ek: god of the North Star
Ix Chel: goddess of childbirth
Ix Tab: goddess of suicide
Ah Puch: god of death
Manik: god of human sacrifice
Bolontiku: god of the lower world

Creation myth of ancient Mayans as told by criscenzo.com

Here is the story of the beginning, when there was not one bird, not one fish, not one mountain. Here is the sky, all alone. Here is the sea, all alone. There is nothing more, no sound, no movement; only the sky and the sea; only Heart-of-Sky, alone. And these are his names: Maker and Modeler, Kukulkan, and Hurricane. But there is no one to speak his names. There is no one to praise his glory. There is no one to nurture his greatness.

And so Heart-of-Sky *thinks*, 'Who is there to speak my name? Who is there to praise me? How shall I make it dawn?' Heart-of-Sky only says the word, 'Earth,' and the earth rises, like a mist from the sea. He only *thinks* of it, and there it is.

He thinks of mountains, and great mountains come. *He thinks* of trees, and trees grow on the land. And so Heart-of-Sky says, 'Our work is going well.'

Now Heart-of-Sky plans the creatures of the forest: birds, deer, jaguars, and snakes. And each is given his home. 'You the deer, sleep here along the rivers. You the birds, your nests are in the trees. Multiply and scatter,' he tells them.

Then Heart-of-Sky says to the animals: 'Speak, pray to us.' But the creatures can only squawk. The creatures only howl. They do not speak like humans. They do not praise Heart-of-Sky and so the animals are humbled. They will serve those who will worship Heart-of-Sky.

And Heart-of-Sky again, tries to make a giver of respect, and tries to make a giver of praise.

Here is the new creation, made of mud and earth. It doesn't look very good. It keeps crumbling and softening. It looks lopsided and twisted. It only speaks nonsense. It cannot multiply. So Heart-of-Sky lets it dissolve away.

Heart-of-Sky plans again. Our Grandfather and Our Grandmother are summoned. They are the wisest spirits. 'Determine if we should carve people from wood,' commands Heart-of-Sky.

They run their hands over the kernels of corn. They run their hands over the coral seeds. 'What can we make that will speak and pray?' asks Our Grandfather. 'What can we make that will nurture and provide?' asks Our Grandmother. They count the days, the lots of four, seeking an answer for Heart-of-Sky.

Now they give the answer: 'It is good to make your people with wood. They will speak your name. They will walk about and multiply.' 'So it is' replies Heart-of-Sky.

And as the words are spoken, it is done. The doll-people are made with faces carved from wood. But they have no blood, no sweat. They have nothing in their minds. They have no respect for Heart-of-Sky. They are just walking about, but they accomplish nothing.

'This is not what I had in mind,' says Heart-of-Sky. And so he decided to destroy these wooden people.

Hurricane makes a great rain. It rains all day and rains all night. There is a terrible flood and the earth is blackened. The creatures of the forest come into the homes of the doll-people.

'You have chased us from our homes so now we will take yours,' they growl. And their dogs and turkeys cry out, 'You have abused us so now we shall eat you!' Even their pots and grinding stones speak: 'We will burn you and pound on you just as you have done to us!'

The wooden people scatter into the forest. Their faces were crushed, and they were turned into monkeys. And this is why monkeys look like humans. They are what is left of what came before, an experiment in human design[7].

---

[7]Popol Vuh. http://www.criscenzo.com/jaguarsun/popolvuh.html (accessed April 3, 2010).

Chapter 3

Introduction to the present civilization

A global civilization

IT is not a secret that the world today is a global village, where people from two very distant countries can communicate as if they were living in the same neighborhood thanks to telecommunication media and fast transportation means.

This epoch is also characterized by a worldwide political organization under the form of the United Nations even though that organization is less strong than national political entities. From these perspectives, people of the present time belong to the same global civilization.

A religiously diverse civilization

From the religious standpoint, the world is not uniform. There are many religions with their God(s) and gods. Some are the heritage of very old times. Since those inherited religious movements have reached the current civilization, it appears preferable to include them in the present civilization rather than in ancient civilizations.

New and Old Religious Movements

It is the emergence of the New Religious Movements [NRMs] that renders necessary the creation of the category of Old Religious Movements [ORMs].

As David Bromley found out[8], scholarship has identified the main characteristics of the NRMs as: the importance of inclusiveness, the relationship to older religious traditions, the absence of common attributes apart from being new, their marginal position in society, the difficulty to hold the second generation, and changes in the social profile overtime to maintain existence and continue to attract new members.

On his part, John Saliba identified some attractive and negative features of the NRMs[9]. The attractive features are: great enthusiasm, stress on experience, and particular spiritual disciplines which help solve individual problems and improve physical and psychological health.

---

[8]David G. Bromley, *Teaching New Religious Movements* (Oxford: Oxford University Press, 2007), 30 and 32.
[9]John A. Saliba, *Understanding New Religious Movements* (Grand Rapids, Mich: W.B. Eerdmans, 1996), 11-20.

The negative characteristics are: the swearing of allegiance to an all-powerful tyrannical leader believed to be the Messiah, the discouragement of rational thought, often deceptive recruitment techniques, a weakening of the members' psychological make-up, the manipulation of guilt, the isolation from the outside world, an ethical system that adopts the principle that the end justifies the means, an aura of secrecy and mystery, frequently an aura of violence or potential violence, and so on.

The weakening of the psychological make-up is however relative. What is also observable is that the mental of the members can be boosted for a while or for their entire lives even if the boost is not grounded on reality. It is clear though that the members who come to a point where they identify lies at the core of their religions unavoidably pass through a dangerous period of psychological weakness as if the world was ending.

Two possible outcomes of this situation are the loss of faith in anything religious or the finding of a new spiritual path. However, it must be mentioned that a patient and unbiased analysis finds many of these negative features of the NRMs in Old Religious Movements as well.

Organizations often cited as NRMs are: the Brahma Kumaris, the Church of Scientology, the Church Universal and Triumphant, the Family Federation for World Peace and Unification formerly known as Unification Church, the Friends of the Western Buddhist Order, the International Society for Krishna Consciousness, the Osho [formerly Rajneesh], the Raëlian Movement, the Soka Gakkai International, and the Family [formerly Children of God][10].

---

[10]Geoge D. Chryssides and Margaret Wilkins, *A Reader in New Religious Movements* (London: Continuum, 2006) v.

David Bromely elaborated a more detailed list[11] adding the Jehovah Witnesses, the Theosophical Society, the Sufis, the Vedanta Societies, the Healing Tao, Tenrikyo, Wicca, the Celestial Church of Christ from Seeker's village, the Radha Soami Beas, the Nation of Islam, Hare Krishna, the Divine Light Mission, Madarom, ceremonial magic, the New Age movement, the Christian Science, Rosicrucianism, Speculative Freemasonry, Spiritualism etc....

Though esoteric movements deal with spiritual matters, they are not religious movements exactly as new and old religions. One can see this after consideration of the term 'esoteric' ['hidden to the public']. That is why they are put in a different category in this volume.

John Saliba has identified in the religious classification of Gordon Melton, eight categories that appropriately regroup NRMs. Those categories are: the Pentecostal family; the communal family; the Christian Science-Metaphysical family; the spiritualist, psychic, and New Age family; the Ancient Wisdom family; the Magic family; the Eastern and Middle Eastern families; and various New Unclassifiable Religious Groups, some being Christians[12].

In the designation of Old Religious Movements [ORMs], the term 'old' is preferred to 'ancient' to avoid a confusion with religions of ancient civilizations.

Esotericism

Esotericism is the belief in a doctrine which is the doctrine of an inner circle of advanced or privileged disciples, communicated or intelligible only to the initiated.

---

[11]Bromley, *Teaching New Religious Movements*, 30-33.
[12]Ibid., 20.

There are several esoteric movements but the conception about the divinities of only four of them, chosen as representatives, will be presented in chapter 6. Those four esoteric movements are: Rosicrucianism, Freemasonry, the Illuminati Order, and the Universal White Brotherhood.

Religious philosophy

Originally, philosophy as described by Pythagoras meant the love and the pursuit of wisdom in general without separation between secular wisdom and religious wisdom. However, the rise of agnosticism and atheism has rendered necessary the distinction between secular philosophy and religious philosophy. The non-partisan standing of the US constitution of 1787 in matter of religion and the adoption of secularism as law in France in 1905 have increased the gap between the two kinds of philosophy.

Another major event which contributed to that separation is the discredit of the Bible-based view of creation in front the theory of evolution during and after the Scopes Trial of 1925 in America. From that point, secular ideas progressively became the sole acknowledged foundation for teaching in schools though the Intelligent Design movement is trying to invert this inclination. Consequently, in today's global civilization, philosophy is generally understood as secular philosophy.

The *Encyclopedia of Religion* provides one of the best descriptions of religious philosophy in today's literature. Its first edition directed by Professor Mircea Eliade in 1987, presents the antique philosopher Plato and many modern philosophers as important religious philosophers.

Among the modern religious philosophers figure Immanuel Kant [1724-1804], the existentialists Gabriel Marcel [1889-1973] and

Jacques Maritain [1882-1973], and the religious thinkers Martin Heidegger [1889-1976] and Ludwig Wittgenstein [1889-1951]. The encyclopedia also ascribes an important value to the works of Anselm of Canterbury [1033-1109] and Thomas Aquinas [1225-1274].

Subjects that are dear to religious philosophers are the immortality of the soul, transmigration and the possibility of a future life or lives, the existence of the godlike, goodness, etc...

Still according to the same encyclopedia, philosophy of religion is the philosophical scrutiny of religion in which rational arguments are proposed and assessed in order to *justify or to criticize* religious beliefs. Because the philosophy of religion has its provenance in the West, theistic issues have dominated the discussion.

Agnosticism and atheism

The Encyclopedia Americana defines skepticism, in philosophy, as a critical attitude or methodology that questions the claims made by philosophers and others. It introduces agnosticism as a form of skepticism that maintains that the human mind lacks the information or rational capacity to make judgments about ultimate reality, and in particular about the existence or nature of God.

Most famous agnostics are David Hume [1711-1776], Thomas H. Huxley [1825-1895], and William K. Clifford [1845-1879]. Clifford who coined the word 'agnosticism' declared for example that '*It is wrong always, everywhere, and for anyone, to believe anything upon insufficient evidence*' and that '*Such belief, even if it should be true, is sinful.*'

Atheism is the denial of the existence of God and gods. Various reasons can be at the origin of the desire or the choice not to believe in God. Sometimes, the bad actions of some religious people are the cause while other atheists base their position solely on evidences, arguments, and philosophies that are contrary to those presented by theists.

On this ground, two sorts of atheism are distinguished: romantic atheism and rational atheism. However, most of the time, an atheist in a discussion would often present both kinds of arguments.

Major atheistic thinkers include Ludwig Feuerbach [1804-1872], Karl Marx [1818-1883], Friedrich Nietzsche [1844-1900], Sigmund Freud [1856-1939], and Jean Paul Sartre [1905-1980].

Chapter 4

Introduction to the pantheons and creation myths of old religions

Taoism

THE founders of the Chinese religion of Taoism were Lao Tzu [about 575-485 B.C.E] and Chuang Tzu [about 369-286 B.C.E.], says *The Encyclopedia Americana*. The *Tao Teching* and the *Chuang Tzu* are regarded as their respective texts. Their teachings deal with the central notion of the Tao.

Tao, meaning literally 'path' or 'road' has come to signify the basic principle that pervades man and the universe. Hence, the English word 'way' furnishes an apt translation for 'tao'. The Tao is eternal and absolute, infinite and immutable. It is nonbeing, that is, above all being, and therefore beyond description.

The female, the child, and water are the favorite metaphors employed in the *Tao Teching* emphasizing thereby the axiom of strength in weakness and honor in humility. The Tao is the original uncarved block, and the Te or the essence is the expression of Tao in individual men and things. This theory is similar to the Universal Mind and the Universal Body of Hermes Trismegistus, Pythagoras, etc...

The Tao teaches that the blessed ones might achieve an identification of the individual with the Tao in an experience of naturalistic mysticism. To Chuang Tzu, the world of daily life is a realm of relativity where differences and distinctions abound, but in the realm of the absolute or the Tao prevail unconditional freedom, *complete equality among all men,* things, and even indifference to life and death.

In the subsequent development of Taoism into a popular religion, the philosophical conquest of death was turned into a cult which preached the literal conquest of death, the achievement of physical longevity through deeds and rites, and the acceptance of a whole assortment of gods.

The deities:

Yuanshi Tianzun: The Perfect One, the Jade Pure, first supreme deity, creator, who resigned from his position

Lingbao Tianzun: The Highest Holy One, the High Pure, dominated the second phase of creation, in charge of energy and activity, devised the interaction of yin and yang

Shenbao Tianzun: The Greatest Holy One, the Supreme Pure. He represents mankind and dominated the third phase of the creation of the cosmos

Hongjun Laozu: The Great Ancestor, Master of the patriarchs, Personification of the vital principle in nature before the creation of the world

San Qing Daozu: The Three Pure Ones, supreme deities of the Taoist pantheon who rule the entire cosmos from the highest heavens, symbolic personification of the three life principles of breath, vital essence, and spirit

Jiu Tian Xuannu: goddess of marriage and fertility, the matron of matchmakers, molder of mankind out of primordial mud

Pangu: put order into chaos, separated the earth from the heavens, and became the progenitor of mankind

Jiang Ziya: commanding general of all ancestral forces, powerful protector of homes and shops

The Jade Emperor: Supreme Ruler of the Heavens and the underworld, protector of mankind, and successor of Yuanshi Tianzun at the position of supreme deity

Yang Jian: drives away demons and wards off demonic influences

Li Jing Tianwang: one of the Twenty Four Heavenly Generals, or Kings, a guardian of the Jade Emperor, destroyer of demons

Taiyin Xingjun: The Lady of the Yin [goddess of the Moon]

Creation Myth of Taoism as told by Tao Tao Liu Sanders

At the dawn of time the universe was a dark chaos, a black mass of nothingness. Heaven and earth were not separated, neither were night or day. The sun, the moon, and the galaxies were all quite unformed. Some people thought of that state as a large egg.

In this dark egg-like mass was born the first creature of the universe. He was called Pangu. Pangu grew in all enveloping darkness and slept a sleep lasting several thousands of years.

When he woke up at last, he had grown into a giant and, realizing he lived in chaos, he was determined to create order. He took a heavy axe in his hand and with a mighty blow split the egg apart. The lighter elements in the egg rose and floated upwards to become the sky; the heavier elements sank down to become the earth. With his hand he pushed the sky farther away because he was afraid they might close together again at the same time treading hard upon the earth to keep it well apart from the sky. For eons he remained in that position until the sky and the earth each in its own way solidified and there was no longer any danger of their closing together again to become the dark chaos.

Pangu felt that he could now lie down to take a rest. He was now so old in both body and spirit that his sleep grew deeper and deeper and he drifted slowly into death.

But Pangu did not return to the darkness from which he had come. As he died, his body changed to create the world as we know it: his breath turned into winds and clouds, his voice into thunder, his left eye into the sun, his right eye into the moon, his body and limbs into mountain ranges and his blood became flowing rivers.

Every part of his anatomy became part of nature. The hairs on his body turned into trees and flowers, the parasites living on his skin turned in animals and fishes, and his bones formed different kinds of precious stones and minerals. Later some believed that the mountains from Pangu's body acted as pillars to support the blue arch of the heavens. But there were yet no people.

The earth was inhabited in these early times by gods, giants, and other monstrous creatures. The most important of the gods was the mother goddess Nü Wa who was a creator and bringer of order. She was shaped like a human being in the upper part of her body, with a human face and human arms, but the lower part of her body was like a dragon's. She was also able to change shape and appear in different forms.

Nü Wa travelled around the world but though she found it rich and beautiful, it was also lonely and desolate. Nü Wa wished for the company of people who could love, feel and think as she did. One day, she came to the great Yellow River. From the river she scoped out handfuls of mud and shaped little dolls from them. She shaped the head and the arms like her own but instead of a dragon tail, she gave the dolls legs so that they could walk around up right.

She put a great deal of care into the making of these little images and was pleased with the result. Breathing life into them, she was delighted to see them spring up and dance around her shouting joyfully and calling her their mother. After she made a large number in this slow careful way, she decided to use her supernatural powers to achieve a quicker result.

She rolled a length of cane in the river mud and as she flicked the cane out onto dry land, small drops of mud fell off and were instantly transformed into men and women. Later some people say that she shaped with her own hand the fortunate and the well-endowed people of the world while those who were formed by the shaking of the length of cane were the poor and less fortunate people. She instituted marriage amongst human beings so that they could continue the human race without any further help from her.

Nü Wa had a companion who had the same shape as her called Fushi who was also a great benefactor of human kind. The greatest gift he bestowed upon people was fire. The humans had seen fire striking from heaven in the form of lightening, but it was Fushi who taught them how to harness it for their own use and showed them how to summon it by drilling one piece of dry wood upon another. They were able to hunt more effectively for all the wild animals feared the flames and only man could control them. Some stories say that Fushi was either the son or the brother of the thunder god himself and that was how he was able to pass on his great gift to mankind.

Fushi also taught people to make ropes and nets and also attended humans' spiritual needs teaching them music and the mystic art of divination. He was the first to draw the eight hexagrams, written symbols consisted of solid and broken lines, representing the eight elemental things of this world.

Each hexagram consisted of three short lines. Different arrangements of lines stood for heaven, earth, water, fire, mountain, thunder, wind, and river. The symbols used in combination had oracular meanings which were later interpreted through a manual of divination known as the Book of Changes [Yi Jing]. Some said that Fushi and Nü Wa were brother and sister, others that they were husband and wife.

According to some stories, long ago, the world was inundated by a mighty flood. The only people to escape were a young boy and a young girl called Fushi and Nü Wa who floated in safety in a large gourd. After the flood, they married and human race began again[13].

Hinduism

Hinduism is the oldest religion of India. Its first sacred texts, the Rig Veda, were written around 1500 B.C.E. according to most historians.

The deities:

The Trinity [Shiva-Vishnu-Brahma]

Shiva: the universal power of destruction, disintegration, and annihilation in which all existence ends and from which it rises again; supreme state of reality since beyond him there is only non-existence

---

[13]Tao Tao Liu Sanders.*Dragons, Gods & Spirits from Chinese Mythology* (World mythologies series. New York: Schocken Books, 1983) 13-17.

Vishnu: light and truth, centripetal tendency which holds the universe together, pervades all existence, hence is known as the Pervader, the inner cause, the power by which things exist, the universal intellect, the one who incarnates in Avatars: *'With the purpose of protecting the earth, priests, gods, saints, the scripture, righteousness, and prosperity; the lord takes a body'*

Brahma: the Immense Being, source of the manifest world, principle of space-time, Golden-Embryo, from which the universe was born before all the gods. The Cosmic Being, as the illusionist, is both the immanent cause, the substance of the universe, and its efficient cause, its builder. The part of the Cosmic Being connected with the universe is but a fragment of his totality.

Other deities
Prajapati: Lord of creatures. Primordial being, creator of the world, androgynous being who impregnated himself by fusing elements of mind and speech; guardian deity of the sexual organ in latter epic. Prajapati is also the name of the god Brahma in later Hinduism

Shakti: first appearance of energy, Kundalini. It takes the place of Brahma, the Cosmic-Embryo. In later mythology, the concept of Shakti comes to include both the notion of a concentrating, illuminating power that is Vishnu and active space-time principle that is Brahma to form the complement of the male, positive, ultimate knowledge that is Shiva

Agni: earthly or common fire, either visible or potential
Vayu: Lord-of-wind, mouth and breath of the gods, the cosmic life breath
Dyaus: The sky, father of all the gods

Surya: the sun, the solar spirit, the divinity that dwells in the solar sphere

Ushas: goddess of dawn

Nakshatra: the constellations

Soma: god of the moon

Indra: The ruler of heaven, king of the gods, made of the qualities of all the other gods, fire of space, the all-pervading electric energy which is the nature of cosmic as well as animal life. In the later mythology, Indra is considered an aspect of Shiva and is a minor deity when compared to the three main gods

Mitra: god of friendship

Varuna: The mysterious law of the gods; presides over the relationship of man with the gods, owner of the magic-power. He is the creator and sustainer of the world, having inherited the prehistoric function, of the Sky [Dyaus]. He established and maintains natural and moral laws, expression of the cosmic order. Varuna is omniscient. In the later mythology, Varuna came to be relegated to the position of god of death. Indra the ruler of the sphere of space took precedence over him, as the ruler of the sky. He is believed by many to have become Ahura Mazda in Iran

Daksha: god of Ritual Skill

Savitr: the vivifier, the magic power of words

Sarasvati: the Flowing-One, the divinity of knowledge, source of 'creation by the Word'. She is the goddess of eloquence, of wisdom, of learning; the patroness of arts and music. She revealed writing and language to man. She is the mother of poetry

Vac: the divinity of speech, vehicle of knowledge, mother of the Vedas [first Hindu sacred texts]

Lakshmi: goddess of fortune

Maha-Lakshmi: goddess of destiny or transcendent fortune

Parvati, Shakti, and Kali: the powers of procreation, development, and destruction, wives of Shiva

Ahladini-Shakti: the power-of-enjoyment

Kameshvari: goddess of lust

The creation myth of Hinduism as presented by Alain Daniélou

The Upanishads give a vivid picture of the personified Universal Being and the myth of creation.

In the beginning, verily, nothing existed. From non-Being, Being was produced. That Being changed itself into a Self, an Atman. Verily, this self was alone. There was no other winking thing. He thought: '*let me now create the worlds*'. With the self thus appear *thought* and *will* prior to all substance. He was afraid; therefore one who is alone is afraid. He thought: '*since there is nothing else than myself, of what am I afraid*?' Therefore, verily, his fear departed, for of what should he have been afraid? It is from a second that fear arises.

First there was the self, the Atman in the form of the Cosmic-man [purusha]. He looked and saw nothing but himself. He first said '*I am*' his name is '*I*'; so that even today a man first says, 'I am...' and then tells his name.

He desired: '*Would that I were many! Let me procreate myself!*' He warmed himself. Having warmed himself, he created this world, whatever there is here. Having created it, he entered it. Having entered it, he became both the perceptible and what is beyond, both the defined and the undefined, both the based and non-based, both knowledge and unknowing, both the true and the false. As the real, he became whatever there is here. That is what they call 'Real'. This existence desired, *'May I be many and procreate'*; and he created the Fire-that-is-Thought [tejas]. This Fire wished, *'May I be many and procreate'*; *and from it the causal-waters appeared.*

This water wished: *'May I be many and procreate'*; and it gave birth to food grains. Therefore when it rains, food grains multiply.

The lord-of-progeny [Praja-pati], verily, was longing for issue. He warmed himself. Having warmed himself, he produced a pair: water [semen, feminine] and breath [prana, masculine], *'These will pro-create for me many kinds of beings'.* The sun verily is this breath of life; the moon, indeed, is these waters. From the waters everything is made, both what is manifest and what is unmanifest. Therefore all manifestation is water. Verily he had no pleasures. Therefore one alone has no pleasures.

He desired a second. He became as large as a woman and a man in close embrace. He divided himself into two. There from arose a husband and a wife. Hence it is that everyone is but half a being. The vacant space is filled by a wife. He copulated with her. This is how men were created. From the self, verily, space [Akasha] arose, from space wind, from wind fire, from fire water, from water earth, from earth herbs, from herbs food, from food man.

He created these worlds: the causal waters, light, death, the earthly-waters. *The causal waters are beyond heaven,* the sky is their support; the world of light is the sphere of space; the world of death is *the earth, the earthly waters are below.*

He thought: *'Now here are worlds. Let me create world guar-dians'. From the waters, he drew forth and shaped a being.* He hatched it. When it has been hatched, its mouth was separated, egg like. From the mouth came forth speech and from speech fire. The nostrils were separated; from the nostril came forth the life breath, from breath the wind. The eyes were separated; from the eyes came forth sight; from sight the sun. The ears were separated; from the ears came forth hearing; from hearing the quarters of heaven.

The skin was separated; from the skin came forth the hairs; from the hairs the plants and trees. The heart was separated; from the heart came the mind, from the mind the moon. The navel was separated; from the navel came forth the outward breath [apana]; *from the outward breath sprang death* [mrtyu]. The virile member was separated; from this virile member came forth semen and from semen the earthly-water [ap].

First produced from the mind of Brahma, anxious to create, were the four classes of beings, which range from the gods to insentient things.

From his buttocks came forth the antigods [asura]. He cast away that body which became night.

In another body he experienced delight, thus from his mouth he created the gods. He then cast away that body which became the day.

In another body, he created the ancestors [pitr]. He then abandoned that body which became the twilight. Then in another body made of passion and darkness he created hungry monsters, demons, and genii. The hair of the creator gave birth to serpents. When he hatched the earth, the Fragrances [the celestial musicians] were born. He breathed in their words, hence they are known as Fragrances. Then he created birds and cattle: goat from his mouth, sheep from his breast, cows from his loins, and from his feet, horses, asses, camels, hares, deer, and mules.

Once the creator became separated into male and female, the female thought: *'How can he copulate with me when he has just created me out of himself? Come, let me hide.'* She became a cow. He became a bull and copulated with her. Thus cattle were born. She became a mare; he a stallion. She became a female ass, he a male ass; he copulated with her. Thence the hoofed animals were born.

She became a she-goat, he a goat; she a ewe, he a ram. Thus indeed he created all, whatever pairs they are, even down to the ants.

In the beginning, the world was peopled only with priests and sages. Brahma created further a superior form, the princely order and also those who are princes among the gods, the lord-of-heaven [Indra], the lord-of-the-waters [Varuna], the lord-of-offering [Soma], the lord-of-tears [Rudra], the lord of rain [Parjanya], the king-of-justice [Yama], the lord-of-death [Mrtyu], and I, the lord-of-space[Ishana].

There is nothing higher than a king, and at the royal sacrifice, the priest sits below the king. Upon the princely order alone is this honor conferred. The priestly order is the source of the princely order. Therefore although the king attains supremacy, he depends upon the priest as his own source. Whoever injures the priest destroys himself. He faces the worse as he injures one who is better.

He was to develop yet further. He created the craftsmen and the minor gods who are mentioned in groups, such as the spheres-of-existence, the divinities of life [Rudras], the sovereign principles, the universal principles, and the genii-of-the-winds. He created the lowest class, which is attached to the soil and in heaven, the Nourisher. Verily, this earth is the Nourisher for she nourishes everything that lives[14].

Deities and non- creationism in Jainism

Jainism is another old religion of India. Its time of birth is not exactly known. What most sources agree upon is that it became re-

---

[14]Alain Daniélou, *The Myths and Gods of India: The Classic Work on Hindu Polytheism from the Princeton Bollingen Series* (Rochester, Vt: Inner Traditions International, 1991), 243-248.

markable around the 6th century B.C.E. Like Hinduism, it acknowledges many gods; but they nature is very different.

Jains[15]believe that the universe and all its substances or entities
are eternal. It has no beginning or end with respect to time. Universe
runs on its own accord by its own cosmic laws. All the substances
change or modify their forms continuously. Nothing can be destroyed
or created in the universe. There is no need of someone to create or
manage the affairs of the universe. Hence Jainism does not believe in
God as a creator, survivor, and destroyer of the universe.

However, Jainism does believe in God, not as a creator, but as a
perfect *human* being. When a person destroys all her karmas, she
becomes a liberated soul. She lives in a perfect blissful state, in
Moksha, forever. The liberated soul possesses infinite knowledge,
infinite vision, infinite power, and infinite bliss. This living being is a
God in Jain religion. Every living being has a potential to become
God. Hence, Jains do not have one God, but Jain Gods are innumerable and their number is continuously increasing as more living
beings attain liberation.

Deities and non-creationism in Buddhism

Buddhism was founded approximately six centuries before the
Common Era in India. In its Mahayana form, it also has many gods.
But the Buddhist gods are not as powerful as those of Hinduism. A
man who lives a righteous life becomes superior to gods. Gautama
Buddha considered himself as the only one honored in heaven and
on earth [*Digha Nikaya* 2.15].

---

[15]JainUniversity.org. http://www.jainuniversity.org/jainism_god.aspx (accessed April 3, 2010).

Glenn Wallis pointed out in his article *The Buddha Counsels a Theist: A Reading of the Tevijjasutta* that Buddhists do not believe in a creator God or god; like Brahma of the Hindus. Indeed, no Buddhist scripture could be found presenting such an idea. Whenever the notion is evoked, it is immediately rejected.

Buddhist philosophy is non-Vedic. In Buddhism, gods are given a place but not in the way of other religions. Buddhism mentions the existence of gods and goddesses. But they are not considered as permanent. They too are born; face decay and death as human beings do according to their Kammas [Actions]. *Gods cannot decide the destiny of a person.* Buddhism does not teach of a creator but it teaches the presence of Brahmas who are superior to gods. Brahmas too are not eternal and face death and karmic force.

Some of the gods of Mahayana Buddhism are: Sakra [similar to Indra but his character is quite different], Visvakarma, and Mara. A human being who lives a virtuous life is far superior to gods. As regarding Buddhist practices, no place is given to gods.

Introducing the 2007 edition of the *Tibetan Book of the Dead*, the Dalai Lama portrays a dual state of human existence as the association of the gross body [physical] with the subtle body and mind. The subtle mind has the quality of awareness and the power of cognition. The subtle body or subtle wind is the energy of the subtle mind. The subtle mind and the subtle body are identified as the buddha nature or spiritual nature. Death is the point at which both physical and mental fields dissolve into inner radiance and where both consciousness and energy exist at their most subtle-non dual level, *as in deep sleep*: this is the Buddha-body or Reality.

These words of the Dalai Lama show that he believes in the existence of a supernatural world peopled by beings whose potential is great. The *Tibetan Book of the Dead includes one of the most detailed and compelling descriptions of the after-death state in world literature.*

Sikhism

Sikhs are the followers of the Sikh religion, particularly of Guru Govind Singh. The word *'sikh'* is derived from the Hindi and means *'disciple'*. The religion combines elements of Islam and Hinduism. Sikhism was founded during the 16th century by its first guru [teacher], Guru Nanak.

The deities

The following presentation of the Sikh conception of God and gods is based on the work of the Sikh Missionary Center in the State of Arizona and that of Dr. Kaur Rajinder[16] [1931-1989].

To Sikhs, there is only one God, Eternal Truth, Almighty Creator, Unfearful, without hate and enmity, Immortal Entity, Unborn, Self-Existent, Unseen, Infinite, Inaccessible, Inapprehensible, Pure, not subject to destiny, of no cast, without doubt, Formless, Markless, Creedless, Boundless, without distinguishing dress, without passion, without outline, Peerless, Changeless, with no enemy, no friend. He is far from all and near all. He cannot be described by anyone. He is the Spirit of Eternity, Self-Radiant.

God is concealed in every heart; his light is in every heart. He is contained in the ant as well as in the elephant. He becometh manifest by the True Word. He has no kinsman. He feeleth no lust and hath no wife or family.

---

[16]Kaur Rajinder, *God in Sikhism* (Amritsar: Sikh Itihas Research Board, Shiromani Gurdwara Parbandhak Committee, 1999) 32-36, 72-87, 97-107.

That God is to be worshiped. He created the whole world spontaneously and permeated the three worlds with His light. Without Him, this world is but illusion. Loving another than God, man loses Divine Knowledge; he becomes rotten in ego and eats poison. But if one loves His utterance, one obtains Nectar and mind and body in truth find joy. He alone permeates the whole world, He is not afar.

There is but One Lord. There is no other; Nanak remains merged in One Lord.

In the shelter of God's feet dwelleth Bhawani; Brahma and Vishnu have not found his limits. The *four faced Brahma* pointeth out that God is indescribable. He made millions of Indras and Bawans. He created and destroyed Brahmas and Shivas. He made endless demons, deities, serpents, Celestial singers, Yakshas, Excellent and beautiful. He knoweth the secret of every heart. He is not attached to any one love. He is contained in the light of all souls. He is of changeless purpose. He is the destroyer and creator of all. He is the remover of sickness, sorrow, and sin.

God having created animals made them subject to death.

The One God is in all ways, all forms, and all colors. He works through air, water, fire, and various shapes. The One soul wanders through the three worlds. If one realizes the One Lord, one is blessed with honor. *He who gathers Divine Wisdom and meditation abides in the state of Equipoise.* He who is blessed by His Grace, he attains Bliss. And he utters [the truth] through the Guru's Word. He who serveth the True Guru obtaineth the real boon, and is *delivered by repeating the Word.*

Truth is contained in pure vessels; few there are whose acts are pure. By seeking Thy protection saith Nanak; the soul blendeth with the Supreme Soul.

God is both Impersonal [Nirgun] and Personal [Sargun]. The Impersonal God becomes Personal and related when He reveals himself through His creation. Infinite can manifest into an unlimited

number of finites but *any finite form cannot be worshipped as God.*
He neither takes birth nor dies.

Answering the first of the three questions of the Muslim priest
Behlol in Baghdad, Guru Nanak said '*Before God, there was nothing
since when one counts, before one, there is nothing.*' To the second
question about where God lives, he replied that butter is present in
milk but cannot be seen and the same way, God is everywhere but
cannot be seen. The third question was about what God does and
Guru Nanak responded that God can put people sitting on thrones
down and those who are sitting down on thrones using the example
of Behlol's own throne.

God is the one and only one savior of humanity, but His devotees
[saints] are particularly near and dear to Him. The supernatural
miracles of God should be distinguished from the miracles of the
human beings which are performed by their magical powers. Miracles
performed by the Sidhas and Yogis were different from divine inter-
ventions. Supernatural and miraculous actions performed by his
Might are deemed as part of His doctrine for preservation of higher
values. It is a concept of Divine Justice overtaking evil deeds.

*God shows miracles to protect the righteous while other powers
shown by human beings with magic are against the Will of God and
are considered dangerous.* In every age, God created His devotees
and preserved their honor. He is not swayed by anyone. He does not
yield to any power. But he is ever pleased by the devotion of his
devotees. To those who know Him He giveth; to those who know Him
not He also giveth. He giveth to the earth; He giveth to the heavens.
O man, why waverest thou? The beautiful and Holy Lord will care for
thee. *He who with single heart meditateth on Him even for a moment
shall not fall into death's noose.*

The unity of Godhead may and does express itself in the multiplicity of existence; still there is the pre-existent unity, full, complete,
whole and unconditioned. God is 'Ek', One, 'Anek', many. The One

while manifesting Himself as the many does not lose His oneness but essentially and substantially or existentially remains One.

The Holy Sikh Scripture begins with the figure one, standing for the mathematical unity, prefixed to the monosyllable 'Om'. The sound 'Om' in the Hindu scriptures indicates the unity of the manifest God-head. This unity is the unity of all the created Trinities; like Brahma, Vishnu, and Mehesh; Sattva, Rajas, and Tamas; walking life, dream-life, and dreamless sleep. Though the term 'Om' used in the Sikh Scripture seems to be the same, by prefixing the figure one to it, its content becomes much different. 'Ek Onkar' in the Sikh Scripture does not mean that the Absolute is a unity of any trinity.

He is one in his Being, one in His Word or Logos, one in his order, one in His Will, and one in His existence. Beyond the unity of one is the unity of 'Sunn.' Sunn is 'nothing' not in the sense of no-thing but in sense of unutterable, inscrutable mystery, the Divine "darkness" which is God Himself. The unity of the Sunn may be termed as the unity of the infinite zero in the Western philosophical terminology. When zero expands, it comes to be known as, and becomes one. The unity of the Sunn is beyond human understanding, conception, and imagination. The highest unity that man is capable of conceiving is the mathematical unity of One.

God is the Supreme Reality and no second reality stands against Him on an equal footing imposing any limitation upon his being. He is one without a second. All created things have opposites by which they are conditioned and limited. To say that God is non-dual is only another way of saying that He is free absolutely.

God is free to be One, not bound to be One. The mystic sees God as 'all in all,' but to him *individual things are not lost, nor obliterated in the unity of Godhead, but transfigured, only seen as more perfectly and uniquely themselves, and not God.* The Guru believes in One Reality, the noumena behind all phenomena of multiplicity. The One

God expresses Himself as plurality and yet remains the unity just as an individual expresses himself in a variety of acts yet remains one.

God is the Unapproachable; if we somehow approach Him in our spiritual vision, He still appears to be Unapproachable and ever-Transcendent. God is the Perfect Person. Because He is Person, therefore He is unity in His Immanence, in His Transcendence. The Sikhs understand by God one who communicates with the individuals, by way of revelation and who himself is communicable by way of spiritual religious experience.

God is All Powerful Person, so that He possesses the ontological power of creating after the pattern and process of His own Being. *Only one who is supremely personal can be the Ground for the emergence of even the finite personality. If God is only an impersonal force, then the stream has risen higher than its Source, f*or we can at least be certain that personality appears in us.

In the Sikh Scripture, union with God is described under the imagery of marriage between two lovers. God is the dear Husband. He is the only Perfect Male. God alone is the male and all others are females. *God is the only Husband means that He is the only Ideal Person with whom Man wants to be one.* All creatures are created by God and have their being as if in God and their final goal is also in God.

God is related to man just as He is related to the rest of His creation. But apart from that, God has a special relationship with man because man represents God's own creative being more truly and more meaningfully than do other creatures. All other creatures, objects etc...exist to serve the end of spiritual illumination of man. Birth as a human being is the highest form of the Grace of God. Man is specially related to God as he reveals the being of God more than do other creatures.

God is in man as the *Word* or Name and *man has the capacity of activating His Name in himself. The Logos,* the Lord's Name [Nam] abides in every heart; it abides secretly as a spiritual power, spiritual nectar, spiritual knowledge, spiritual music, spiritual love, spiritual peace, and immortality. God also lives in the very body of the individual. God cannot be divided into parts therefore it cannot be said that a part of God is present in man; God, the Whole Total Actuality, is there in man. In other words, it can be said that God in His total Being reveals Himself in man as the soul [Atma] of man. If God is all, He is also in every individual.

Truth is high but still higher is truthful living. All that keeps us away from God is evil and all those activities which lead man toward God are good. Every activity that is done under the influence of 'Houmain' [I-ness] is evil. In order to become free from the bondage of passions and desires and to be free in the Being of God, *we have to overcome our I-ness* so that God may take possession of ourselves. God is also Absolute Truth.

The man who is in God and who has God in him, his activities in the world will demonstrate the true nature of his creator and of his Source. Those who realize God in their own selves, *they themselves become God. The God-conscious person herself is the Creator of the whole world. She is immortal and never dies. That person can grant life and salvation to others.* God reveals Himself in man as it is not the efforts of man but God's own Grace which is responsible for the change in man.

Jehovah descended and assumed the human in order to redeem and save mankind. He descended as divine truth which is the Word. He is the Father, the Lord, the Husband and the Guide of man. Those who know their own true self [Atman] know God.

God is in the world as His Name, and therefore it is only through this Name that He can be approached, worshipped, and contacted. Therefore every prophet and saint stresses the need of meditation on a Name of God that must also be continually used in the Holy offices of the Church, as in prayer, hymns, in all worship, and also in preaching and writing on ecclesiastical subjects. When He is solemnly invoked by this Name, He is present and hears; in these things, the Name of God is hallowed.

In the spiritual sense, the Name of God means all those things that the Church teaches from the Word, and by which the Lord is invoked and worshipped. All these things are the Name of God. Meditation on a Divine Name is only possible if the Name embodies a specific quality of God.

Here are some Names of God according to Sikhs: Prototype Person, Timeless Person, Unswerving Person, Unknowable Person, Inaccessible Person, Transcendent Person, The Lord, One Person, The Life of the Universe, the Creator, The Embodiment of Love, Supreme Person, Perfect Person, The Destiny of all, All-Powerful Person, True Person, the true Guru, The First and Best Person, Whose secret cannot be known, who eats nothing, Unfathomable, Who cannot be described, actionless, Unattached, Untainted, Beyond the Atman, Most beautiful, Without Name, Of no form, Unthinkable, Beyond the Tattvas, Depth Unfathomable, Being the three Gunas, Not-Alone, Beyond Aloneness, Incommunicable, Beyond qualities, Beyond the reach of Buddhi, Inconceivable, Without Purpose or Desire, Without activity, Nothingness, Divine Darkness, Filler of all space above and below and in the middle, Lord of Vegetable Kingdom, Ever-Present, Time of Time, Without Breaks, Beauty of Beauties, the Soul of all, the light of all, Master of every Heart, In all Robes or Garbs, In all Spaces, Full of all Powers, In all Deeds, All Pervading, Beauty of All, With Qualities, Lord of the three worlds, The First Beauty Form, Wondrous Beauty, Wonder Producer, Of Beautiful form or body, Heat-charming, The origin of all Music Harmony and Melody, Ever New, Supreme Beauty, Musical Form, Precious Stone, Beautiful, Note of Notes, Source of Refulgence and Power, Demon-Killer, Treasury of Mercy, Pain-Destroyer, Killer of the evil ones, Compassionate, The Hero with all Noble Qualities, Full of Grace, Without enmity, Holifier, Purifier, Preserver, Remover of Diseases, Sweet Tempered, Brave, Dauntless, All-Wise, Ocean of Bliss, Carrier across the Ocean of Becoming, of noble character, Tradesman, Businessman, Enjoyer, Abstainer, Possessor of wealth, Shepherd, Householder, Milkman, Yogi, Farmer, Tiller, Gardener, Noble King, The King of Kings, Soldier, Ruler, King, Without Fear, Swordsman, The Holder of the Sword, Unconquerable, The sword, The Best Hero, Warrior, Destroyer of armed forces, Destroyer of evil persons, Punisher of evil beings, Pride-Vanquisher, Lord of terrible actions, Sword of Swords, Steel of Steels, With Terrible wrath, Awe-inspiring, Terror Producing, All-steel, All-conquering, The Destroyer of the enemies, Relation, Brother, Husband, Master, Friend, Lover, Father, Love Itself, Most Beloved, Relative, Origin of all origins, Seed of Seeds, Brahma, Preserver and Destroyer of all, Life of the cosmos, Cause of the World, Destroyer of the world, Cause of the First Cause, Maker of Causes, Maker, Producer, Overhead, All Wise, Caretaker, Nourisher, Sustainer, Lord of the Breath, Giver, Shiva, Vishnu, *Does not belong to a particular country or place*, Indestructible, Unbreakable, Indivisible, Unpiercable, The Beginning, Unshakable, Free from birth and death, Without any beginning, Countless, Unweighable, Unestablishable, Beyond end, One, Changeless, The beginning of the Cycle of time, Not cognizable, Unascertainable, All-Form, Light, Always True, Eternal Truth, Consciousness and Bliss, True Name, Self-Created, Supreme Knowledge, Knowledge of Knowledge, Knower of all, Ever-conscious, Knower of the three worlds, Seer of the present, past, and future.

Creation story of Sikhism as presented by the Sikh Missionary Center in the US

For millions and millions of years before the creation of the world, there was utter darkness and God Himself was sitting alone in absolute trance. There was no earth and no sky. There was no day and no night, no sun and no moon. There was no air and no water. There was no man and no woman, no caste, no birth, and no death. There was no time. There was neither hell nor heaven. There existed no deeds and no religion, no Divine knowledge and no mediation. There was no contemplation, no penance, no self-contentment, nor fasting nor worship, no self-control. There existed no Vedas, no Smriti(es) [part of the Hindu religious texts] nor Shastras [treatises], nor the Puranas [Hindu religious and historical Texts], nor Semitic Texts. There was no Brahma, no Vishnu, and no Shiva. His limit no one knows.

'*It is through God that I have obtained this understanding*,' says Guru Nanak.

For countless of ages, there was nothing but utter darkness. Only existed the Almighty God's Infinite Will. There was neither creation, nor destruction nor transmigration. There was neither female nor male, neither pleasure nor pain. Nor any who could speak of duality. The Almighty Lord was in Absolute Bliss and valued himself His Own Glory, knowing only Himself His Unknowable Self.

When such was His Will, He created the world and without support sustained the firmament. He created Brahma, Vishnu, and Shiva and instilled in men the desire of attachment. Rare was the person whom He caused to hear His Word. He made His ordinance operative and watched over all. He created continents and solar systems.

Guru Nanak further explains that before the Creation, the Infinite and Boundless Lord sat in Absolute Trance for thirty six Yugas or ages [Yuga, a period of cosmic time, running into millions of years]. No one knows the lunar day, week day, season, and month when the world came into existence. The Almighty Creator who has created the world, He Himself alone knows the time, none else.

Pilgrimages, austerities, compassion, charity, all are approved if they bring even a grain of merit in God's eye. Whoever heartily hears believes and loves God's Name, obtains salvation by thoroughly bathing in the shrine within him. Without cultivating virtuous qualities, the Lord's devotional service cannot be performed. God is True, Beautiful and all joys abide within His Mind.

Zoroastrianism

Zoroastrianism existed in Persia [today's Iran] before the 6th century B.C.E. However, like Jainism in India, many believe it to be much older. According to John Hinnells[17], the knowledge of the mythology of Persia is derived from a variety of sources, the most important being the Zoroastrian Bible, the *Avesta*. Unfortunately, he says, only the part of the *Avesta* which is used in the ritual has survived, approximately one quarter of the original.

Although it was not written down until Sassanian times the contents are considerably older. Indeed within the general Zoroastrian structure of the *Avesta*, are reflected and preserved ancient pre-Zoroastrian myths.

Still for Hinnells, the most important part of this complex of material is the *Cathas*, the 17 hymns of Zoroaster. To him, the profundity of their teaching makes them rank among the most precious gems of the world's religious literature. The *Cathas* are embedded in the *Yasna*, a collection of prayers and invocations chanted during the Zoroastrian sacrifice of the same name.

Other sources for access to Persian mythology are the inscriptions of the Persian kings, the reports of classical and foreign authors, art, coins, reliefs, and archeology.

---

[17]John R. Hinnells, *Persian Mythology* (London: Hamlyn, 1973), 20-21.

The deities:

Ahura Mazda or Ohrmazd: the Wise Lord, the Supreme God in Zoroastrianism, protector of mankind

Angra Mainyu or Ahriman: his opponent that will finally be vanquished

The Amesha Spentas: seven sons and daughters of God

Vohu Manah: *good mind, personification of God's wisdom, first born of God, sits at his right hand*, acts almost as adviser, protector of animals who also deals with humans, keeps a daily record of men's thoughts, words, and deeds. Works in man and leads man to God

Aeshma [wrath], Az [wrong mindedness], Akah Manah [vile thoughts or discord]: opponents of Vohu Manah

Asha: *truth, most beautiful of the Immortals. Those who do not know Asha forfeit heaven*

Indra: spirit of apostasy, chief opponent of Asha

Kashathra Vairya: the desired kingdom, most abstract of the Immortals, personification of God's might, majesty, dominion and power, represents the kingdom of heaven, and on earth that kingdom which establishes God's will on earth by *helping the poor and the weak and by overcoming all evil.* Protector of metals

Saura: the Arch-demon of misgovernment, anarchy, and drunkenness. Opponent of Kashathra Vairya

Armaiti: devotion or fit-mindedness, daughter of Ahura Mazda, sits at his left hand, presides over the earth. She is said to give pasture to the cattle

Taromaiti [Presumption] and Pairimaiti [Crooked-Mindedness]: opponents of Armaiti

Haurvatat: integrity, feminine being, personification of what salvation means to the individual

Ameratat: immortality, literally deathlessness, is the other aspect of salvation

Haurvatat and Ameratat are associated with water and vegetation; their gifts are wealth and herds of cattle, so that they represent the ideals of vigor, the sources of life and growth

Hunger and Thirst: their opponents

Sraosha: obedience or discipline, warrior in armor, god that is present at every divine ceremony, embodies in men's prayers and hymns, conveys prayers to heaven, embodiment of the sacred word, victorious force in the constant battle against the destructive forces of evil

The Yazatas: the worshipful ones, less important than the seven Amesha Spentas. The main Yazatas are Vayu, Anahita, Haoma, Atar, Verethraghna, Rapithwin, and Mithra.

The creation myth of Zoroastrianism as presented by John Hinnells

Ohrmazd [or Ahura Mazda], dwelling on high and endless light, has no direct contact with the evil Ahriman [or Angra Mainyu] in his deepest darkness, for between the two lies the void. The power of each then is limited by the other and both are spatially limited by the void. Ohrmazd is eternal, but Ahriman is not for he will one day be destroyed.

At first, the two existed without coming into conflict. Although Ohrmazd in his omniscience knew of the Evil Spirit, Ahriman, ever ignorant and stupid was not aware of the Wise Lord's existence. As soon as he saw Ohrmazd and the light, his destructive nature prompted him to attack and to destroy. Ohrmazd offered him peace if he would only praise the Good Creation. But Ahriman, judging others by himself, *believed that an offer of peace could only be made from a position of weakness,* so he rejected the offer and sought to destroy that which he saw. Ohrmazd knew that if the battle were to last forever, Ahriman could, indeed, keep his threat, and suggested a fixed period for the battle.

Ahriman being slow-witted, agreed and thereby ensured his ultimate downfall. The point behind this idea seems to be that *if evil is allowed to operate quietly, steadily, and unobtrusively, it can disrupt and destroy, but once it is drawn out to the open, engaged in battle and shown for what it is, it cannot succeed.*

According to the orthodox tradition, history spans twelve thousand years. The first three thousand years is the period of original creation; the second three thousand pass according to the will of Ohmazd; the third three thousand is to be a period of the mixing of the wills of good and evil, and in the fourth period the Evil Spirit will be defeated. In the major Zoroastrian "heresy", *Zurvanism,* the twelve thousand years are divided very differently: the first nine thousand years being the period of the rule of evil and the final three thousand the time of the defeat of evil. It may be that this second form was the older tradition.

After fixing the period for battle, Ohmazd recited the sacred prayer of Zoroastrianism, the *Ahuna Var.* On hearing this kernel of the Good religion, the Evil Spirit realized his inability to defeat the forces of good and fell back into hell where he lay unconscious for three thousand years.

Knowing that Ahriman would never change his destructive character, Ohmazd began to create. *Out of his very essence of light he produced the spiritual, or menog, form of the creatures.* First he created the Immortals, then the Yazatas, and finally he begun the creation of the universe: first the sky, then water, earth, the tree, the animal, and last of all, man. All these creations are completely independent from Ahriman. They are not reliant on him at all for their happiness, for Ohrmazd, unlike Ahriman, does not contemplate anything he cannot achieve. The creatures belong entirely to God.

Ohrmazd is both mother and father to creation: as mother, he conceives the spiritual world and, it is said, as father he gives birth to it in material form.

Ahriman in his turn creates, or rather miscreates, his own offspring from his evil nature, giving rise to all that is vile-wolves, frogs, whirlwinds, sandstorms, leprosy and so on.

When first produced, the material creation was in an ideal state: the tree was without bark and thorn, the ox was white and shining like the moon, and the archetypal man [Gayomart] was shining like the sun.

After he had fallen unconscious into hell, the demons tried to arouse Ahriman with promises of how they would assault creation and inflict on it anguish and unhappiness, but all to no avail. Then the wicked Jahi, the personification of all female impurity came. She promised to afflict the holy man and the ox with so much suffering that life would not seem worth living. She also announced her intention of attacking the water, earth, the tree, fire, in fact the whole creation.

Thus revived, the Evil Spirit in gratitude granted her wish that men desire her. Then, with all the demons, Ahriman rose to attack the world. He broke through the sky which was afraid of him as a sheep of a wolf. Passing through the waters he entered the middle of the earth and assaulted the material creation. The earth became so dark that at noon it seemed like a dark night. Horrible creatures were released over the face of the earth and their pollution so thickly that not even as much as the point of needle was free from their contamination. The tree was poisoned and died.

Turning to the ox and Gayomart, Ahriman afflicted them with Greed, Needfulness, Disease, Hunger, Vice, and Lethargy. Before the Evil Spirit came to the ox, Ohrmazd gave her cannabis to ease her discomfort in the throes of death, but at last she died. Man, the chief ally of God and the arch-opponent of evil was then set upon by the might of a thousand death-producing demons, but even they could not kill him until his appointed time was come, for man's rule has been fixed for a period of thirty years.

Everything was being destroyed, smoke and darkness were mingled with the fire, and the whole creation was disfigured. For ninety days, the spiritual beings contested with the demons in the material world. Every archangel had an opposing arch-demon; every good thing was attacked by its counterpart: Falsehood against Truth, Spell of sorcery against *Holly Word*, Excess and Deficiency against Temperance, Idleness against diligence, Darkness against Light, and Unforgiveness against Mercy. Finally even man was killed.

The assault of Ahriman now seemed to be completely successful and the Good Creation to be totally ruined or destroyed. Disorderly motion, the production of evil, appeared to have won a victory over order and peace; and the work of the Wise Lord was an apparent failure.

Yet, despite all appearances, this was not the end of Good, for troubles were just beginning for Evil. Ahriman after his apparent victory sought to return to his natural home of darkness but found his way blocked by both the Spirit of the Sky, clad in armor like a warrior, and the fravashis of men [guardian spirits who send souls to the material world to fight evil and to whom those souls return from the morning of the fourth day after death].

As the whole of the material creation has a spiritual origin, man has his heavenly self, his fravashi. Whatever evil man may do on earth, his genuine heavenly self is unaffected, and it is only the earthly man, not the fravashi which will suffer for his sins in hell [although one text does state that even the fravashi can go to hell].

The host of just fravashis, elected of their own free will to assist Ohmazd in his battle and stood arrayed as valiant cavaliers with spears in hand, preventing Ahriman from escaping from the prison into which he had burst. Thus imprisoned in a hostile world, Ahriman discovered that life was beginning to flourish again. The rains were produced by Sirius; the waters washed the vile creatures into the holes in the ground, and the earth became productive.

As the ox died, fifty five species of corn and twelve species of medicinal herbs grew from it limbs and its seed passed to the moon where it was purified, giving rise to the different species of animals. Man too, as he died passed seed into the earth. Thus from his body, made of metal, the earth received the different kinds of metal, and from his sperm grew the human first couple, Mash ye and Mash yane.

Just as the sky, the waters [Sirius], the ox and man thus waged battle with the Destructive Spirit, so too, did the plants, the earth, the fire, and other components of creation. Life was triumphant. *Death the work of the Evil Spirit stood defeated,* for out of death came life, and life more abundant than before.

Never from the time of creation until the rehabilitation in purity has this earth been devoid of men, nor will it ever be. Though Ahriman may kill individuals, mankind as a whole ever increases, not only rendering his assaults failures, but even making them work against him[18].

Divinities and creation stories in Judaism, Christianity, and Islam

Divinities:

---

[18] John R. Hinnells, *Persian Mythology* (London: Hamlyn, 1973), 56-60.

In the Bible and the Qur'an

The fact that Judaism, Christianity, and Islam are divided each in many branches and in several cases with some differences of opinion on God(s) and gods, renders complicated the task of synthesis. Even within a branch there are sometimes several theologians whose opinions vary from one another. Since all of them agree on the Bible and the Qur'an, those scriptures will be analyzed instead of the different point of view of the denominations. However, the main views dear to those denominations will not be neglected.

There are so many important passages of the Bible and the Qur'an which explain about deities in Judaism, Christianity, and Islam that it would be inadequate to quote them all. The reader could almost always access their contents, since they are very popular books. However, it is important here to mention that polytheism is condemned both in the Bible and the Qur'an.

Additionally, the Qur'an disagrees with the concept of Trinity while many Christians think it is justified in the Bible. In this Bible, several metaphors are used and many readers have difficulty understanding them or have different understandings which are mainly responsible for schisms and the birth of so many denominations.

The key elements of division about the God of the Bible are "His" anthropomorphism, "His" Fatherhood and Motherhood, Jesus, the Trinity, the problem of evil, the other characteristic of God and the nature of angels. All these elements will be studied separately in entire chapters devoted to them.

In the Book of Enoch

In the Bible, Enoch is the 7th patriarch from Adam through Seth. Genesis 5: 24 says that he walked with God and disappeared because God took him. His name means the 'initiate,' the 'dedicated,' the 'consecrated,' and also 'teacher.' As paradoxical as it may appear, his deeds and sayings are not described under his name in the Old Testament or Hebrew Bible but some of them are cited, even if very few, here and there in the New Testament. Some of the passages concerned are the book of Jude particularly Jude 14-15 and Hebrews 11: 5. However the Old Testament passage in Genesis 6: 1-4 is also considered to come from Enoch.

The book ascribed to Enoch does not appear in the Bible except in the Ethiopian Orthodox Church. In it are described the visions shown to Enoch by some angels [Vol I, Chap I, verse 1]. Thanks to them, he was able to talk with the Holy Almighty Lord of this world, who would one day leave his heavenly residence for the summit of Mount Sinai and appear in his tabernacle [Verses 3 and 4].

Some angels led by Samyaza came down from heaven to have sexual relationship with the beautiful daughters of men who bore them children known as the wicked giants [chap 7]. These angels taught women, witchcraft, the properties of trees and roots, astronomy, and so forth. Each of those indulging angels taught a particular discipline including war. Enoch gave many of their names among which Azazel and Asael [Chap 8].

In the Bible [Leviticus 16: 7-10 and 20-22], Azazel appears as a shadowy figure to whom the God of the Ancient Testament says to send a goat charged with the sin of ancient Israelites. This biblical passage confirms Enoch Chapter 10 which relates Azazel to the desert. But unlike the Book of Enoch [chapters 8, 18, 12, and 53], Leviticus does not present Azazel as a fallen angel who has taught weapon making to humanity, has been bound by the angel Raphael, and thrown in the desert.

He also named some good angels such as Michael, Gabriel, Raphael, Suryal, and Uriel [chap 9]. In chapter 19, Uriel accuses demons of pushing men into errors to the extent of inciting them make sacrifices to demons like to God. In chapter 20, six angels described as watchers are named. Raguel and Sarakiel are added to Michael, Gabriel, Raphael, and Uriel [each with a specific role]. Phanuel appears in chapter 41 as the angel of penitence and hope.

Wisdom went forth to make her dwelling among the children of men and found no dwelling-place. Wisdom returned to her place, and took her seat among the angels. And unrighteousness went forth from her chambers and dwelt with them [chapter 42].

'And there I saw One who had a head of days, and His head was white like wool, and with Him was another being whose countenance had the appearance of a man' [Chapter 46].

Though the Book of Enoch confirms the Bible and even offer more details about some of it descriptions, it appears questionable at least in chapters 40, 46, and 53 which look a lot like the visions of Daniel and John in Revelation. In addition, Enoch 60: 1, at least in George H. Shodde's translation, states that Enoch live up to 500 years while the Bible only give him a 365 years life span.

The creation story

In Judaism and in Christianity

Since Christianity has made the Hebrew Bible its Old Testament, it has exactly the same creation story as Judaism. This story appears in Genesis 1 and 2 but additional and important information is offered in the Book of Job from the 38th chapter to the 41st chapter where God challenges Job.

In Islam

The creation story of Islam has a lot in common with that of Judaism and Christianity. The differences are about more details and precision given than about a contradiction. However in the Qur'an, the story is not as regrouped as in the Bible. It is rather scattered throughout the scripture, but some scholars have made useful synthesis. One of them[19] organized his synthesis nearly as followed:

Six Days: the creation was completed in six days (10:3).

Order: in four days the earth was completed. Then attention was given to the sky, which was still smoke. In two days seven heavens were created with the lower heaven adorned with lights (41:10-12). Everything on earth was created before Allah turned to the sky or heaven and fashioned seven levels of heavens (2:29, 41:10-12).

Flat Earth: the earth was leveled flat or spread out in the creation event (88:20, 15:19, 79:30). Allah will not let it cave in beneath mankind (67:16). Both the earth and the heavens would fall if it were not for the sustaining power of Allah. If they did fall, no one could hold them back (35:41, 16:45).

Mountains Set Down: mountains were set down on the earth like giant immovable weights or pegs in order to keep the flat earth from moving (15:19, 21:31, 31:10, and 88:19).

Man: man was created to be in distress (90:4). He was first created from clay. He then procreates as the essence of clay becomes a living germ and is put into the womb. The germ transforms into a clot of blood. The blood clot becomes a small mass, which is fashioned into bones. The bones are then covered with flesh. This is the amazing developmental process by which life is generated and regenerated (23:12-14).

---

[19]Creation and science.http://www.answering-islam.org/Authors/Fisher/Topical/ch07.htm (accessed April 3, 2010).

Woman: a mate for man was created so that he might find comfort as he rests with her and produces offspring (7:189). Men were made superior to women, which mean they exercise authority over females and must beat them if they are rebellious. This is why women depend on men for their support (4:34).

Stars Are Lamps: above the earth were constructed seven layers of heavens which are miraculously kept from falling. The lower level is decorated with lighted lamps (41:12, 67:5).

Zodiac Signs: the sky was decorated with the signs of the zodiac to make it beautiful (15:16).

Falling Stars Chase Genies: shooting stars are made for a special purpose. They are lamps that are thrown as fiery missiles at genies (jinns) or evil spirits who try to fly up toward the sky in order to spy on the activities of heaven (37:6-10, 67:5).

Satan: prior to the creation of humans, Satan was created out of smokeless fire. He was punished for refusing a command to bow before Adam, the man who was sculpted and brought to life from clay. When he was banished and degraded to the earth, Satan swore to mislead people. Adam and Eve were his first victims. He was one of the genies (15:28-39, 7:11-23, 18:50).

Evil Spirits: genies were made from fire that has no smoke (55:15).

Sun and Moon Orbit Earth: after the seven heavens were built over the earth, the sun was put into service (13:2-3). The sun swims its rounded course and comes to a resting-place (36:40, 18:86). The sun is not allowed to catch up with the moon and the moon is not allowed to overtake the sun as they run their prescribed orbits (36:37-40).

Adam and Eve: Adam and Eve were created in a garden paradise in heaven. All the angels but Satan obeyed Allah by bowing before Adam. Satan was forever degraded because of this disobedience. Satan, in turn, tempted Adam and Eve to eat from the tree that Allah had forbidden them to even approach. Because of this, Allah cast Adam and Eve out of the heavenly garden and placed them on the earth (7:11-25).

Birds: birds are a sign to encourage belief since there is no natural reason why they are suspended between the earth and the sky. It is only by Allah's miraculous power (16:79).

Throne: after the heavens were finished, Allah, who built them, went to sit down on his throne in heaven. Allah continues to hold the heavens and the earth so that they might not disappear (10:3).

Deities and creation in Gnosticism

Gnosticism is a spiritual school of various and complex thoughts. The diversity and complexity of these thoughts are so marked that it is difficult for the average mind to handle them. The vocabulary which is the sophisticated vocabulary of an ancient time does not render the task easy either for today's readers.

People with a strong interest in knowing, in details, about the Demiurge and the dualism of good and evil should read books such as *The Gnostic Religion: The Message of the Alien God & the Beginnings of Christianity* of Jonas Hans, *Beyond Gnosticism: Myth, Lifestyle, and Society in the School of Valentinus* of Ismo Dunderberg and *The Tree of Gnosis: Gnostic Mythology from Early Christianity to Modern Nihilism* of Ioan Culianu.

Dualism, succinctly, is the theory that the universe has been ruled from its origins by two conflicting powers, one good and one evil, both existing as equally ultimate first causes.

Most famous Gnostic thinkers were: Simon Magnus [1st century C.E.] and his disciple Menander, Basilides [died in 140 C.E.], Saturnius [2nd century], Cerinthus, Cerdon [2nd century], Marcion [85-160],

Valentinus [100 -160], Mani [216-276], Euthymius Zigabenus [12th century], Bonacursus [12th century], Salvo Burci, Moneta of Cremona, Balasinanza of Verona, and John of Lugio of Bergamo [born around 1180 C.E].

The most famous Gnostic schools were: the Syrian Cult, the Alexandrian Cult, the Valentinians, Manichaeanism, Bogomilism, Monarchians or moderate Cathars, Radical Cathars, and the Paulicians.

Absolutely clear lines between Gnosticism and Christianity did not exist until the later years of the 2nd century. Gnostics admit the existence of several supernatural beings. The teachings of the main Gnostic figures are so many and so different that it appears better to present just a sample of them.

Simon is said to have believed that two powers without beginning, the masculine Universal Mind and the female Great Thought, have united to create the universe.

Menander taught that the First Power is unknown to all and that the world was made by angels who emanated from the Ennoia, a female principle.

Carpocrates simply stated that the world was made by angels 'who are lower by far to the unbegotten Father'.

For Saturnius, the one unknown Father made the angels, archangels, powers, and dominions. However, the world and everything in it was made by seven particular angels and man too is a work of the angels. These angels are feeble artisans and rebellious.

Cerdon maintained that *the God whom Moses and the prophets preached is not the Father of Jesus Christ: the one is knowable, the other not; the one merely just, the other good.*

According to Marcion there are two antithetic gods. One is the craftsman [demiurge], the God of creation [or generation], the ruler of this eon, known and predicable; the other is the hidden God, unknown, unperceivable, unpredictable, the strange, the alien, the other, the different, and also the new. Known is the creator-God from his creation, in which his nature is revealed. *The known god is the just God; the unknown is the good God.*

Mani, the father of Manichaeism was one of the most important teachers of dualism which professes the primordial existence of good forces and evil forces.

To Euthymius Zigabenus, the Devil [Satanael or Samael or Sathanas] and Jesus [the archangel Michael] are brothers created by God. To him Sathanas was the elder brother and the Old Testament god, who made for himself a second heaven and a second earth, separated from the kingdom of God. Cosmas contradicted this data asserting that Jesus is the firstborn and the Devil is the younger.

The doctrine of the moderate Cathars is summarized by Bonacursus in his *Manifestio.* They believed the Devil to be the author of the human body, in which he imprisoned by force an angel of light. He made Eve, seduced her, and begat Cain. Abel in turn is the son of Adam and Eve and was killed by Cain. From his blood, the dog was born; this is why dogs are faithful to humans.

To these Gnostics, all things of the world, animated or not, have been created by the Devil. The daughters of Eve were made pregnant by the demons and gave birth to the race of Giants, who learned that the world had been created by an evil principle. This is why the Devil in his anger destroyed them with the deluge.

For moderate Cathars, Enoch belongs to the Devil and Patriarchs likewise. Moses followed the Devil's will and received his law. David was an assassin, and Elijah was abducted to heaven by the Devil himself. Yet the Holy Spirit spoke often through the mouths of the Prophets. John the Baptist belongs to the Devil. Mary's conception was immaculate, with no help from a man. Jesus had no physical body.

Still to moderate Cathars, the Devil himself is the Sun, Eve being the Moon, and the two of them commit adultery each month, like a man with a whore. All stars are demons.

Some radical Cathars believed in two gods, one entirely good, the other entirely evil, each of them creator of angels. Lucifer is the son of the Lord of Darkness. He transfigured himself into an angel of light to ascend to the heaven of the good God, where the angels interceded for him. God then adopted the stranger and made him into a steward of his kingdom.

God would live to regret it for Lucifer seduced his angels and pro-voked civil war in heaven. God was compelled to evict him, together with one third of the angels, those who took part in his rebellion. Angels are made of body, soul, and spirit. Their bodies and spirits remained in heaven. Only their souls fell and are imprisoned by Lucifer in human bodies. Consequently, humans have angelic souls but spirits from the Devil. Christ came down to save the angelic souls. The garments, crowns, and thrones of glory are awaiting their ancient owners in heaven. At the conclusion of numerous transmigrations from body to body, a sincerely repenting soul may recover its heaven-ly body and spirit.

John of Lugio, one of the radical Cathars, declared that this world was created by the Father of Devil who is Lucifer himself. The good God runs a parallel universe, invisible, and incorruptible. In God's parallel world there is marriage, fornication, and adultery; the men of that earth have married the daughters of the Devil and have thus generated the race of Giants. All this is the work of the Devil, who is stronger than God's creatures, and occurs without God's will or permission.

To the group of Gnostics called Paulicians, there is a god who is a heavenly father and who has no power in this world, but in the world to come; and there is another god, the world creator, who has power over the present world. Paulicians rejected the Old Testament accusing the prophets of being liars and thieves. They called Satan the creator God.

The Hermetic text of the Poimandres on God as reported by Manly Hall

Hermes, while wandering in a rocky and desolate place, gave himself over to *meditation and prayer.* Following the secret instructions of the Temple, he gradually freed his higher consciousness from the bondage of his bodily senses; and, thus released, his divine nature revealed to him the mysteries of the transcendental spheres.

He beheld a figure, terrible and awe-inspiring. It was the Great Dragon, with wings stretching across the sky and light streaming in all directions from its body [The Mysteries taught that the Universal Life was personified as a dragon].

The Great Dragon called Hermes by name, and asked him why he thus meditated upon the World Mystery. Terrified by the spectacle, Hermes prostrated himself before the Dragon, beseeching it to reveal its identity. The great creature answered that it was *Poimandres*, the *Mind of the Universe*, the Creative Intelligence, and the Absolute Emperor of all [Schure identifies Poimandres as the god Osiris.] Hermes then besought Poimandres to disclose the nature of the universe and the constitution of the gods. The Dragon acquiesced, bidding Trismegistus to hold its image in his mind.

Immediately, the form of Poimandres changed. Where it had stood there was a glorious and pulsating Radiance. This Light was the spiritual nature of the Great Dragon itself. Hermes was "raised" into the midst of this Divine Effulgence and the universe of material things faded from his consciousness.

Presently a great darkness descended and, expanding, swallowed up the Light. Everything was troubled. About Hermes, swirled a mysterious watery substance which gave forth a smoke like vapor. The air was filled with inarticulate moaning and sightings which seemed to come from the Light swallowed up in the darkness. *His mind told Hermes that the Light was the form of the spiritual universe and that the swirling darkness which had engulfed it represented material substance.*

Then out of the imprisoned Light a mysterious and Holy Word came forth and took its stand upon the smoking waters. *This Word, the Voice of the Light, rose out of the darkness as a great pillar, and the fire and the air followed after it*, but the earth and the water remained unmoved below.

Thus the waters of Light were divided from the *waters of darkness, and from the waters of Light were formed the worlds above and from the waters of darkness were formed the worlds below.* The earth and the water next mingled, becoming inseparable, and the Spiritual Word which is called *Reason* moved upon their surface, causing endless turmoil.

Then again was heard the voice of Poimandres, but His form was not revealed: '*I Thy God am the Light and the Mind which were before substance was divided from spirit and darkness from Light.* And **the Word which appeared as a pillar of flame out of the darkness is the Son of God, born of the mystery of the Mind**. The name of that Word is *Reason*. Reason is the offspring of Thought and *Reason shall divide the Light from the darkness and establish Truth in the midst of the waters.* Understand, O Hermes, and meditate deeply upon the mystery. That in which you see and hear is not of the earth, but is the Word of God incarnate. So it is said that Divine Light dwells in the midst of mortal darkness, and ignorance cannot divide them. The union of the Word and the Mind produces that mystery which is called *Life*. As the darkness without you is divided against itself, so the darkness within you is likewise divided. The Light and the fire which rise are the divine man, ascending in the path of the

Word, and that which fails to ascend is the mortal man, which may not partake of immortality. ***Learn deeply of the Mind and its mystery, for therein lies the secret of immortality.***'

The Dragon again revealed its form to Hermes and for a long time the two looked steadfastly one upon the other, eye to eye, so that Hermes trembled before the gaze of Poimandres. At the Word of the Dragon the heavens opened and the innumerable Light Powers were revealed, soaring through Cosmos on pinions of streaming fire.

Hermes beheld the *spirits of the stars, the celestials controlling the universe*, and all those Powers which shine with the radiance of the One Fire, the glory of the Sovereign Mind. Hermes realized that the sight which he beheld was revealed to him only because Poimandres had spoken a Word. The Word was Reason, and by the Reason of the Word invisible things were made manifest. Divine Mind, the Dragon, continued its discourse:

'Before the visible universe was formed its mold was cast. This mold was called the *Archetype*, and this Archetype was in the Supreme Mind long before the process of creation began. Beholding the Archetypes, the Supreme Mind became enamored with Its own thought; so, taking the Word as a mighty hammer, It gouged out caverns in primordial space and cast the form of the spheres in the Archetypal mold, at the same time sowing in the newly fashioned bodies the seeds of living things. *The darkness below, receiving the hammer of the Word, was fashioned into an orderly universe. The elements separated into strata and each brought forth living creatures.* The Supreme Being, the Mind, male and female, brought forth the Word; and the Word, suspended between Light and darkness, was delivered of another Mind called the *Workman*, the *Master-Builder*, or the *Maker of Things*. In this manner it was accomplished O Hermes: the Word moving like a breath through space called forth the *Fire* by the friction of its motion. Therefore, the Fire is called the *Son of Striving*. The Workman passed as a whirlwind through the universe, causing the substances to vibrate and glow with its friction, the Son of Striving thus formed *Seven Governors*, the Spirits of the Planets, whose orbits bounded the world; and the Seven Governors controlled the world by the mysterious power called *Destiny* given them by the Fiery Workman.

When the *Second Mind* [The Workman] had organized Chaos, the Word of God rose straightway out of its prison of substance, leaving the elements without Reason, and joined itself to the nature of the Fiery Workman. Then the Second Mind, together with the risen Word, established itself in the midst of the universe and whirled the wheels of the Celestial Powers. This shall continue from an infinite beginning to an infinite end, for the beginning and the ending are in the same place and state. Then the downward turned and unreasoning elements brought forth creatures without Reason. Substance could not bestow Reason, for Reason had ascended out of it. The air produced flying things and the waters those that swim. The earth conceived strange four-footed and creeping beasts, dragons, composite demons, and grotesque monsters. Then the Father, the Supreme Mind, being Light and Life, fashioned a glorious Universal Man in Its own image, not an earthy man but a heavenly Man dwelling in the Light of God. The *Supreme Mind* loved the Man It had fashioned and delivered to Him the control of the creations and workmanships. The Man, desiring to labor, took up His abode in the sphere of generation and observed the works of his brother, the Second Mind, which sat upon the *Ring of the Fire*. And having beheld the achievements of the Fiery Workman, He willed also to make things, and His Father gave permission. The Seven Governors, of whose powers He partook, rejoiced and each gave the Man a share of its own nature. The Man longed to pierce the circumference of the circles and understand the mystery of Him who sat upon the *Eternal Fire*. Having already all power, He stooped down and peeped through the seven Harmonies and, breaking through the strength of the circles, made Himself manifest to Nature stretched out below. The Man, looking into the depths, smiled, for He beheld a shadow upon the earth and a likeness mirrored in the waters, which shadow and likeness were a reflection of Himself. The Man fell in love with His own shadow and desired to descend into it. Coincident with the desire, the Intelligent Thing united itself with the unreasoning image or shape. Nature, beholding the descent, wrapped herself about the Man whom she loved, and the two were mingled. For this reason, earthy man is composite. Within him is the Sky Man, immortal and beautiful; without is Nature, mortal and destructible. Thus, suffering is the result of the Immortal Man's falling in love with His shadow and giving up Reality to dwell in the darkness of illusion; for, being immortal, man has the power of the Seven Governors, also the Life, the Light, and the Word. But being mortal, he is controlled by the Rings of the Governors, Fate or Destiny. Of the Immortal Man it should be said that He is hermaphrodite, or male and female, and eternally watchful. He neither slumbers nor sleeps, and is governed by a *Father also both male and female*, and ever watchful. Such is the mystery kept hidden to this day, for Nature, being mingled in marriage with the Sky Man, brought forth a wonder most wonderful, seven men, all bisexual, male and female, and upright of stature, each one exemplifying the natures of the Seven Governors. These O Hermes, are the seven races, species, *and wheels*. After this manner were the seven men generated. Earth was the female element and water the male element, and from the *fire and the æther* they received their spirits, and Nature produced bodies after the species and shapes of men. And man received the Life and Light of the Great Dragon, and of the Life was made his soul and of the Light his mind. And so, all these composite creatures containing immortality, but partaking of mortality, continued in this state for the duration of a period. They reproduced themselves out of themselves, for each was male and female. But at the end of the period the knot of Destiny was untied by the will of God and the bond of all things was loosened. Then, all living creatures, including man, which had been hermaphroditical, were separated, the males being set apart by themselves and the females likewise, according to the dictates of Reason. Then God spoke to the Holy Word within the soul of all things, saying: 'Increase in increasing and multiply in multitudes, all you, my creatures and workmanships. *Let him that is endued with mind know himself to be immortal* and that the cause of death is the love of the body; and let him learn all things that are, *for he who has recognized himself enters into the state of Good.* And when God had said this, Providence, with the aid of the Seven Governors and Harmony, brought the sexes together, making the mixtures and establishing the generations, and all things were multiplied according to their kind. He who through the error of attachment loves his body, abides wandering in darkness, sensible and suffering the things of death, but he who realizes that the body is but the tomb of his soul, rises to immortality.'

Then Hermes desired to know why men should be deprived of immortality for the sin of ignorance alone. The Great Dragon answered:

'To the ignorant, the body is supreme and they are incapable of realizing the immortality that is within them. Knowing only the body which is subject to death, they believe in death because they worship *that substance which is the cause and reality of death.*'

Then Hermes asked how the righteous and wise pass to God, to which Poimandres replied: 'Because the Father of all things consists of *Life and Light, whereof man is made. If, therefore, a man shall learn and understand the nature of Life and Light, then he shall pass into the eternity of Life and Light.*'

Hermes next inquired about the road by which the wise attained to Life eternal and Poimandres continued:

'Let the man endued with a Mind mark, consider, and learn of himself, and with the power of his mind divide himself from his not-self and become a servant of Reality.'

Hermes asked if all men did not have minds, and the Great Dragon replied:

'Take heed of what you say, for *I am the Mind, the Eternal Teacher. I am the Father of the Word, the Redeemer of all men, and in the nature of the wise the Word takes flesh. By means of the Word, the world is saved. I, Thought* [Thoth], *the Father of the Word, the Mind, come only unto men that are holy and good, pure and merciful, and that live piously and religiously, and my presence is an inspiration and a help to them, for when I come they immediately know all things and adore the Universal Father.* Before such wise and philosophic ones die, they learn to renounce their senses, knowing that these are the enemies of their immortal souls. I will not permit the evil senses to control the bodies of those who love me, nor will I allow evil emotions and evil thoughts to enter them. I become as a porter or doorkeeper, and shut out evil, protecting the wise from their own lower nature. But to the wicked, the envious, and the covetous, I come not; for such cannot understand the mysteries of *Mind*; therefore, I am unwelcome. I leave them to the avenging demon that they are making in their own souls, for each evil day increases itself and torments man more sharply, and each evil deed adds to the evil deeds that are gone before until finally evil destroys itself. The punishment of desire is the agony of unfulfillment.'

Hermes bowed his head in thankfulness to the Great Dragon who had taught him so much, and begged to hear more concerning the ultimate future of the human soul. So, Poimandres resumed:

'*At death, the material body of man is returned to the elements from which it came, and the invisible divine man ascends to the source from whence he came, namely the Eighth Sphere.* The evil passes to the dwelling place of the demon, and the senses, feelings, desires, and body passions return to their source, namely the Seven Governors, whose natures in the lower man destroy but in the invisible spiritual man give life. After the lower nature has returned to the brutishness, the higher struggles again to regain its spiritual estate. It ascends the seven Rings upon which sit the Seven Governors and returns to each their lower powers in this manner: upon the first ring sits the Moon, and to it is returned the ability to increase and diminish; upon the second ring sits Mercury, and to it are returned machinations, deceit, and craftiness; upon the third ring sits Venus, and to it are returned the lusts and passions; upon the fourth ring sits the Sun, and to this Lord are returned ambitions; upon the fifth ring sits Mars, and to it are returned rashness and profane boldness; upon the sixth ring sits Jupiter, and to it are returned the sense of accumulation and riches; and upon the seventh ring sits Saturn, at the Gate of Chaos, and to it are returned falsehood and evil plotting. Then, being naked of all the accumulations of the seven Rings, the soul comes to the *Eighth Sphere, namely, the ring of the fixed stars*. Here, freed of all illusion, it dwells in the Light and sings praises to the Father in a voice which only the pure of spirit may understand. Behold, O Hermes, there is a great mystery in the Eighth Sphere, for the Milky Way is the seed-ground of souls, and from it they drop into the Rings, and to the Milky Way they return again from the wheels of Saturn. But some cannot climb the seven-ringed ladder of the Rings. So they wander in darkness below and are swept into eternity with the illusion of sense and earthiness. *The path to immortality is hard, and only a few find it.* The rest awaits the Great Day when the wheels of the universe shall be stopped and the immortal sparks shall escape from the sheaths of substance. Woe unto those who wait, for they must return again, unconscious and unknowing, to the seed-ground of stars, and await a new beginning. Those who are saved by the light of the mystery which I have revealed unto you, O Hermes, and which I now bid you to establish among men, shall return again to the Father who dwelleth in the White Light, and shall deliver themselves up to the Light and shall be absorbed into the Light, and in the Light they shall become Powers in God. This is the Way of *Good* and it is revealed only to them that have wisdom. Blessed art thou, O Son of Light, to whom of all men, I, Poimandres, the Light of the World, have revealed myself. I order you to go forth, to become as a guide to those who wander in darkness, that all men within whom dwells the spirit of *My Mind* [The Universal Mind] may be saved by My Mind in you, which shall call forth My Mind in them. Establish My Mysteries and they shall not fail from the earth, for I am the Mind of the Mysteries and until Mind fails [which is never] my Mysteries cannot fail.'

With these parting words, Poimandres, radiant with celestial light, vanished, mingling with the powers of the heavens. Raising his eyes unto the heavens, Hermes blessed the Father of All Things and consecrated his life to the service of the Great Light.

Thus preached Hermes: '*O people of the earth, men born and made of the elements, but with the spirit of the Divine Man within you, rise from your sleep of ignorance! Be sober and thoughtful. Realize that your home is not in the earth but in the Light. Why have you delivered yourselves over unto death, having power to partake of immortality? Repent, and change your minds. Depart from the dark light and forsake corruption forever. Prepare yourselves to climb through the Seven Rings and to blend your souls with the eternal Light.*'

Some who heard mocked and scoffed and went their way, delivering themselves to the Second Death from which there is no salvation. But others, casting themselves before the feet of Hermes, besought him to teach them the Way of Life. He lifted them gently, receiving no approbation for himself, and staff in hand, went forth teaching and guiding mankind, and showing them how they might be saved. In the worlds of men, Hermes sowed the seeds of wisdom and nourished the seeds with the *Immortal Waters*.

And at last came the evening of his life, and as the brightness of the light of earth was beginning to go down, Hermes commanded his disciples to preserve his doctrines inviolate throughout all ages. The *Vision of Poimandres* he committed to writing that all men desiring immortality might therein find the way.

In concluding his exposition of the *Vision*, Hermes wrote: 'The sleep of the body is the sober watchfulness of the Mind and the shutting of my eyes reveals the true Light. My silence is filled with budding life and hope, and is full of good. My words are the blossoms of fruit of the tree of my soul. For this is the faithful account of what I received from my true Mind, that is Poimandres, the Great Dragon, the Lord of the Word, through whom I became inspired by God with the Truth. Since that day my Mind has been ever with me and in my own soul it hath given birth to the Word: *the Word is Reason, and Reason hath redeemed me*. For which cause, with all my soul and all my strength, I give praise and blessing unto God the Father, the Life and the Light, and the Eternal Good.

Holy is God, the Father of all things, the One who is before the First Beginning.

Holy is God, whose will is performed and accomplished by His own Powers which He hath given birth to out of Himself.

Holy is God, who has determined that He shall be known, and who is known by His own to whom He reveals Himself.

Holy art Thou, who by Thy *Word [Reason] hast established all things.*

Holy art Thou, of whom all Nature is the image.

Holy art Thou, whom the inferior nature has not formed.

Holy art Thou, who art stronger than all powers.

Holy art Thou, who art greater than all Excellency.

Holy art Thou, who art better than all praise.

Accept these *reasonable sacrifices* from a pure soul and a heart stretched out unto Thee.

O Thou Unspeakable, Unutterable, to be praised with silence!

I beseech Thee to look mercifully upon me, that I may not err from the knowledge of Thee and that I may enlighten those that are in ignorance, my brothers and Thy sons.

Therefore I believe Thee and bear witness unto Thee, and depart in peace and in trustfulness into Thy Light and Life.

Blessed art Thou, O Father! The man Thou hast fashioned would be sanctified with Thee as Thou hast given him power to sanctify others with Thy Word and Thy Truth.'

The *Vision of Hermes*, like nearly all of the Hermetic writings, is an allegorical exposition of great philosophic and mystic truths, and its hidden meaning may be comprehended only by those who have been "raised" into the presence of the True Mind[20].

Shintoism

Shintoism is an old religion born in Japan. Its fundamental scriptures are the Kojiki [712 C.E.] and the Nihongi [720 C.E.]: the records of the myths and lore previously transmitted orally. In ancient Japan, there were local and seasonal festivals, and shrines in honor of innumerable deities and supernatural forces, with legends of creation and descent of the gods to populate the land. Shinto has little theology and no congregational worship.

The deities

---

[20]Hall, The Secret Teachings of All Ages, 97-106.

Izanagi: first god of earth who created the world. Father of Amate-rasu, Tsuki-Yome, and Susano

Izanami: wife of Izanagi, and first goddess of the earth

Kagu-Zuchi: the fire god, also known as Ho-Masubi [or causer of fire]; the last child of Izanagi and Izanami. His birth killed his mother. It was important to propitiate Ho-Masubi during the Japanese windy season when wooden houses and buildings were prone to be destroyed by fire.

Amaterasu: sun goddess and ruler of heaven

Tsuki-Yome: Amaterasu's brother and god of the moon

Susano: wicked storm god and brother of Tsuki-Yome and Amate-rasu

Wakahiru-me: younger sister of Amaterasu, probably a goddess of the rising sun

Kusa-nada-hime: the 'Rice Paddy Princess' and wife of the evil Susano

O-kuni-Nushi: god of medicine and sorcery, son of Susano

Ame-no-Oshido-Mimi: Son of Amaterasu that she sent to control the earth, but he refused to go because it was too full of disturbances

Ninigi: grandson of Amaterasu finally sent to reign over earth

Kono-Hana-Sukuya-Hime: daughter of a mountain god and wife of Ninigi

Takami-Musubi: one of Amaterasu's chief assistants

Amo-No-Uzume: solar deity, thought to be goddess of the dawn

Inari: rice god and god of prosperity

The creation myth of Shintoism
as presented by Grange Books

In the beginning, there was nothing but a shapeless egg of swirling gases. Slowly, the lighter areas rose up to form the heavens, and the darker, denser material sank to form the earth. Three gods created themselves and hid in heaven. Land masses floated about on the surface of the earth until eventually something appeared drifting between heaven and earth. It looked like the first shoot of a new reed and two gods were born from it, who also hid. Seven more gods were born in this way, the last two being Izanagi and Izanami.

Izanagi and Izanami were commanded by the heavenly deities 'to complete and solidify the drifting land,' in other words to form the Japanese Islands.

Standing on the 'Floating Bridge of Heaven,' they wondered whether there was anything below them, and so dipped the heavenly Jeweled Spear into the sea below to find out. They stirred the brine with churning sound and when they lifted up the spear again, the dripping brine from the spear piled up and became the Island of Onokoro. Descending from the heavens, Izanagi and Izanami decided to make their home there and stuck the spear into the ground to form the Heavenly Pillar.

Discovering that their bodies were differently formed, Izanagi asked his spouse Izanami if she was agreeable to giving birth to the land in order to produce more islands. When she agreed, they devised a marriage ritual: they walked around the Heavenly Pillar in opposite directions. When they met, Izanami said 'How lovely! I have met a handsome man!' and then they made love.

Instead of producing an island, however, she gave birth to a deformed leech-child, which they cast adrift on the sea in a reed boat. They returned to heaven to consult the gods who told them that their mistake lay in the marriage ritual: Izanami should not have spoken first when they met around the pillar, as it is not a woman's place to initiate a conversation.

In order to have children, they repeated the ritual, but this time, Izanagi spoke first. On their return to earth, they tried again and were successful. Over time, Izanami bore all the islands of Japan. They produced gods to beautify the islands, and also made gods of wind, trees, rivers and mountains; completing the creation of Japan. The last god produced by Izanami was the fire god, whose birth scorched her genitals so badly that she died.

However as she died, she continued to produce more gods from her vomit, urine, and excreta. Izanagi was so angry that he cut off the fire god's head, but drops of his blood fell on the earth, producing still more deities. Scholars of the late Edo period [18th century-early 19th century C.E] regarded the pillar simply as a phallic symbol. It clearly resembles the European maypole, which is believed to capture the vital powers latent in a tree, and is also linked with the ancient Japanese belief that processions round tall trees are needed to summon down the deities who live in the heavens or high mountains.

After giving birth to numerous islands and other features of nature [waterfalls, mountains, trees, herbs, and the wind], Izanami died of a terrible fever. Izanagi followed her to Yomi, the land of the dead but was too late: she had already eaten at the hearth of Yomi, which meant that to return to the land of the living was impossible. She asked Izanagi to wait for her patiently as she discussed with the gods whether she could return, but he could not.

Impatiently, he threw down the comb he was wearing and set light to it and then he entered the hall. What he saw was dreadful: Maggots were squirming and roaring in Izanami's corpse. In her head was Great-Thunder, in her breast was Fire-Thunder, in her genitals was Crack-Thunder, in her right hand was Earth-Thunder, in her left foot was Sounding-Thunder, in her right foot was Reclining-Thunder. Altogether there were eight thunder deities.

Izanagi was frightened by the sight of Izanami, and he turned and fled. Shamed by his actions, Izanami sent the hags of Yomi to pursue him, but he evaded them using magic tricks. When he arrived at the border between the land of the living and the underworld he attacked his pursuers with three peaches he had found nearby. They all retreated as fast as they could. Then Izanagi said to all the peaches 'Just as you have saved me, when any of the races of mortal men fall into pain and suffer in anguish, then you will save them also.'

Finally, Izanami herself came in pursuit of Izanagi. He pulled a huge boulder across the pass from Yomi to the land of the living, and Izanagi and Izanami stood facing each other on either side of the boulder. Izanami then said: 'O my beloved husband, if you do thus, I will strangle to death 1,000 of the populace of your country.' To this Izanagi replied: 'O my beloved spouse, if you do this I will each day build 1,500 parturition huts' meaning that this number of people would be born. She told him that he must accept her death, and Izanagi promised not to visit her again. Then they formally declared their marriage at an end. Their separation or 'divorce' is the beginning of mortality.

On his return to the land of the living, Izanagi rid himself of the sullying effects of his descent into the underworld by undergoing purification. He arrived at the plain by the river-mouth, where he took off his clothes and the articles worn on his body. As each item flung on the ground, a deity came into existence.

And as Izanagi entered the water to wash himself, yet more gods were created. Finally, the most important gods in the Japanese pantheon were created when he washed his face. When he wiped his left eye, Amaterasu, the sun goddess was born; the moon god Tsuki-Yome emerged from his right eye; and the storm god Susano from his nose.

Izanagi decided to divide the world between his three children, instructing Amaterasu to rule heaven, Tsuki-Yome to rule the night, and Susano to rule the seas. Susano however said he would rather go to the underworld with his dead mother, so Izanagi banished him, and then withdrew from the world to live in high heaven.

Of the many stories recounted about Amaterasu, the tale of her withdrawal of labour is much known. The most beautiful of Izanagi and Izanami's children, Amaterasu climbed the pillar connecting earth and heaven to rule the sky. Before he was banished to Yomi, her brother Susano announced that he wanted to say goodbye to his sister first.

He was jealous of his sister's beauty and seniority and, wary of her brother's intentions, Amaterasu armed herself with a bow and arrow before meeting him. Susano however charmed her by suggesting that they produce children together as a mark of good faith. Amaterasu agreed and asked for his sword. She snapped it into three pieces, and while crunching each bit in her mouth, created the goddesses with her breath.

Susano asked for Amaterasu's five necklaces, which he chewed up to produce five gods. An instant custody battle ensued, as Amaterasu claimed them as her children since they were created from her jewelry. Her brother, however thought he had tricked the sun goddess, and he celebrated by breaking down the walls of the rice fields, blocking irrigation channels and defecting in the temple where the harvest festival was to be held. His appalling behavior laid the seeds of their enmity.

One day, while Amaterasu was weaving clothes to the gods, Susano threw a flayed horse through the roof of the weaving hall, terrifying one of her attendants so much that she pricked her finger and died. Amaterasu herself was so scared that she hid in a cave, blocking the entrance with a huge boulder.

Without the sun goddess, the world was plunged into darkness and chaos. The paddy fields lay fallow, the gods misbehaved, and an assembly of 800 deities met to discuss how to lure Amaterasu out of the cave. They followed a plan introduced by Omobikane, 'the thought-combining deity' who suggested that they should make her curious outside her dark cave. They decorated a tree with offerings and jewels, lit fires and drummed and danced, taunting her with the beauty of another goddess. They put a magical mirror outside the cave, collected roosters to crow outside it, and persuaded the goddess of the dawn, Amo No Uzume to dance on it. Completely carried away, she started to take off her clothes, much to the amusement of the other gods, who called her the "Terrible female of Heaven".

As they have hoped, Amaterasu peered out to see what was going on. The gods replied that they were celebrating as they had found her successor, an even better goddess than she. Emerging from the cave, Amaterasu saw her reflection in the magic mirror and the 'hand-strength male deity,' Tajikawa, pulled her out of the cave, blocking it to prevent her return. Nature was restored to life and since then the world has experienced the normal cycle of day and night. The mirror was entrusted to the mythical first emperor of Japan as proof of his divine power.

The 800 gods punished Susano by fining him, cutting off his beard and moustache, tearing out his fingernails and toenails, and expelling him from heaven.

Japan was said to have been created by the will of the sun goddess Amaterasu and the stark emblem of the Japanese flag shows the people's evident pride in their origin. Amaterasu is supposed to be the direct ancestor of the Japanese imperial family and a mirror, the Yata Hagami, forms part of the imperial regalia. Pictures of her emergence from the cave show her holding a sword which she passed on to her grandson Prince Ninigi and which is another part of the royal regalia. The obedience that was owed to the emperor is still echoed in the veneration of the sun goddess.

Japan is a mountainous country with over 60 active volcanoes, and is prone to earthquakes. In Tokyo it is not unusual to feel shocks every day or so. It is not surprising therefore; that the Japanese revere mountain gods and almost every mountain has its own deity worshipped by the local people[21].

Sub-Saharan Africa: Fon and Yoruba cultures of West Africa

The deities:

Fon culture of Benin/Dahomey

Mawu-Lisa: Mawu-Lisa is a diety with two faces. The first is that of a woman, Mawu, whose eyes are the moon; the second is that of a man, Lisa, whose eyes are the sun. Mawu rules the night and Lisa rules the day.

Aido-Hwedo: the rainbow serpent is the servant of Mawu who helped her create the world. Like Mawu-Lisa, Aido-Hwedo is a twinned male-female form; one half lives in the sky and the other in the sea. On the latter half depends the safety of the world.

Da-Zodji: god of the Earth
So: god of thunder
Agbe: god of the sea
Gu: god of iron and war
Legba: malevolent god and god of divination [fa].

---

[21] *Japanese Gods and Myths*, Ancient cultures. Hoo, nr (Rochester, Kent: Grange Books, 1998), 18-30.

Gbadu: Legba's dual-sexed sister who has sixteen eyes and lives at the top of a palm tree, watching over the whole world. An earthly Fa diviner also learns Mawu's will by throwing palm kernels to open Gbadu's eyes[22].

Sakpata: god of smallpox.

Yoruba culture of Nigeria and Dahomey/Benin

The Yoruba is a West-African tribe found in countries such as Nigeria, Benin Republic, Togo, Ghana, Ivory Cost, Liberia, and Sierra Leone. There is also a significant number of Yoruba people in Brazil, Cuba, the USA, and so on.

Attributes of the Supreme God

Olodumare, Olorun, the Supreme God is real, unique, and incomparable. This God is one, the only God of the whole universe, creator, king, omnipotent, all wise, all knowing, all seeing, eternal, immortal, and transcendent. This God judges, is immortal, and holy.

Olodumare is the origin and ground of all that is; the starting point, the frame of reference for all other things. The Yoruba never rank Olorun who is Elder [the creator] with the divinities of the creatures. They know that he is over and above all Divinities and men. In Yoruba concept, the Supreme God is close to his creation.

Some names of God are: Molder, Creator of souls, Giver of breath, God of destinies, Giver of rain, one who brings round seasons, giver of sunshine, the limitless, the irresistible, the wise one, the

---

[22]Wilkinson, Philip, and Neil Philip, *Mythology*, 240-241.

Great Mother, Greatest Friend, God full of pity, God of comfort, the high upon, the high chief of heaven, the inexplicable, Eledaa, Alaaye, Olojo oni, Oyigiyigi, Oba Aiku.

Gods are the ministers of God. The Supreme Being brought into being a number of divinities and spirits to act as his functionaries in his theocratic government of the world. These divinities are of different categories but they all serve the will of the Supreme Being.

The intermediary gods

Gods or Orishas are object of worship and get religious, ceremonious, or loyal devotion. They are seen as being in intermediate position between humans and Olodumare. There are various opinions on the number of the gods: 200, 201, 400, 401, 460, 600, 601, 1700, and even more according to the various sources.

The roles played by the gods in relation to human beings are many, and those roles vary from god to god.

Some Yoruba gods

Ogun: god of iron and war
Shango: god of thunder and justice.
Orumila: goddess of divination and fate.

The creation myth of the Fon culture of Dahomey/Benin as reported by Wilkinson Philip and Neil Philip

When Mawu was making the world, Aido-Hwedo, the rainbow serpent was her servant. It is said that he came into existence with the first man and woman, Adanhu and Yewa. Aido-Hwedo carried Mawu in his mouth whenever she wanted to go, which is why Earth curves and winds: it was carved from the sinuous movements of the serpent. Wherever they rested, there are mountains, which are the excrement of Aido-Hwedo. It is for this reason that great riches [metals] can be found within the mountains today.

When Mawu had finished her work of creation, she saw that she had made too many things: too many trees, too many mountains, too much of everything. The Earth could not bear the weight. So she told Aido-Hwedo to coil himself into a circle beneath the Earth, to support it. Aido-Hwedo did not like heat, so Mawu made the cold sea as a home for him. When the earth chafes him, Aido-Hwedo shifts and causes earthquakes. He eats iron bars forged for him by red monkeys that live beneath the sea, and when the iron runs out, Aido-Hwedo will begin to starve. He will convulse, and the Earth with all its burdens will tip into the sea.

Mawu-Lisa, the male-female creator god became pregnant and gave birth to seven children including Da Zodji, god of the Earth; So, god of thunder; Agbe, god of the sea; and Gu, god of iron and war. The god's female half, Mawu, then populated the Earth and sent her male half, Lisa, with Gu down on it to teach people how to live. Mawu then made the animals and found that one of them also needed a lesson in good behavior.

After Mawu had created people, she started to create all the animals. She told them she would name them when she had completed her task, but first they must help her work the clay from which she was molding more creatures. The animals all began to knead the clay, softening it in readiness for Mawu's creative hands. Mawu happened to notice the monkey she has made, and said: 'As you have five fingers on each hand, if you work well I will put you among men, not among animals.'

Monkey was thrilled at the prospect. He went around to all other animals in turn the lion, the elephant, the hyena, and all the rest, boasting that he was so much better than they were. 'Tomorrow, I will not be among you animals, I'll be a man' said monkey, utterly pleased with himself. Monkey was so busy showing off to the other animals that he did not do any work at all. When Mawu came back, she saw Monkey clapping his hands and singing: Tomorrow I will be a man.' Mawu was so angry she kicked him and said to the foolish creature: 'You will always be Monkey, and you will never walk erect.'

Chapter 5

Understanding of divinities in some New Religious Movements

Swedenborgianism

T HE Swedenborgian understanding of divinities and the super-

natural appears mainly in the writings of Emanuel Swedenborg [1688-1772]*Heaven and Hell*.

To Swedenborg, first and foremost, *we need to know who the God of heaven is, since everything else depends on this.*

According to his mystical experience, there is no other God than Jesus Christ and the Lord appears in a divine *angelic form, which is a human form*, to people who acknowledge and trust in a visible Divine Being; but not to people who acknowledge and trust in an invisible formless Divine Being. He finds a confirmation of this form in the way the Divine appeared to Abraham, Lot, Joshua, Gideon, Manoah and his wife, and others. However, Swedenborg says nothing about God the Father that Jesus himself talked about.

Even though they saw God as a person, they still worshiped him as the God of the universe, calling him *'God of heaven and earth'* and *'Jehovah' he* adds. For Swedenborg, in John 8:56, the Lord himself teaches that it was he whom Abraham had seen.

Heaven's sun is the Lord; light there is the divine truth and warmth; the divine good that radiates from the Lord as the sun. The reason the Lord in heaven appears as the sun, continues Swedenborg, is that he is the divine love from which all spiritual things come into being and, through the agency of our world's sun, all natural things as well. That love is what shines like a sun.

All angels are from the human race. They want Swedenborg to testify on their behalf that in all heaven there is not a single angel who was created as such in the beginning, nor is there in all hell a devil who was created as an angel of light and cast out.

Since heaven comes from the human race, which means that there are angels of both sexes there, since by creation itself woman is for man and man for woman, each for the other, and since this love is inborn in both sexes, it follows that there are marriages in the heavens just as there are on earth. However, the marriages in the heavens are very different from earthly ones. Here too, Swedenborg contradicts his Lord Jesus who said that there is no marriage in Heaven [Matthew 22: 30 and Mark 12: 25] unless it is said that those words of the gospels are not from Jesus but fabricated.

Theosophy, Helena Blavatsky, and the Temple of the People

The main theosophical understandings on deities are found in The *Secret Doctrine* and *Isis Unveiled* written by Helena Blavatsky [1831-1891].

In the first book, the core ideas are as followed:

(1) The Secret Doctrine teaches no *Atheism,* except in the Hindu sense of the word *nastika,* or the rejection of *idols, including every anthropomorphic god*

(2) It admits a Logos or a *collective 'Creator'* of the Universe; a *Demiurge* inthe sense implied when one speaks of an 'Architect' as the 'Creator' of an edifice, whereas that Architect has never touched one stone of it, but, while furnishing the plan, left all the manual labor to the masons. The plan was furnished by the *Ideation of the Universe*, and the constructive labor was left to the Hosts of intelligent Powers and Forces. But that *Demiurge* is no Personal deity meaning an imperfect *extra-cosmic god*.

(4) Matter is *Eternal.* It is the *Upadhi* [the physical basis] for the *One infinite Universal Mind* to build thereon its ideations

Theosophy considers a group of angelic beings that serve together as vehicle to the Universal Mind as the creators of the universe. However, since those angelic powers and forces were obeying the injunction of the Universal Mind, *it is better to state that the Architect [or Ideation of the Universe or Universal Mind] is the Real Creator.*

In the section *Demon est Deus inverseus* of the *Secret Doctrine*, Blavatsky and Theosophists declare that Satan never assumed an anthropomorphic and individualized shape, until the creation by man, of a 'one *living* personal god.'

For them, evil is but an antagonizing blind force in nature; only the shadow of light, without which light could have no existence, even in our perceptions. *If evil disappeared, good would disappear along with it from Earth. Demon est Deus inversus* is a very old adage. There would be *no* life *possible without* Death, *nor regeneration and reconstruction without destruction.*

The great Serpent of the Garden of Eden and the 'Lord God' are identical. Jehovah turns into the fiery serpents to bite those he is displeased with; and Jehovah forms the brazen serpent that heals them. In human nature, evil denotes only the polarity of matter and Spirit.

Blavatsky sees the biblical story of the war in heaven in the ancient Greek war between Olympian gods and Titans. She thinks the origin of the fall goes farther in past to India were there are accounts of three heavenly wars.

The Temple of the People, a theosophical group, considers that a hierarchy of beings in combination represent the Godhead. It states in the lesson 64 of its first volume of teaching that Jesus is a man that achieved a high spirituality through several reincarnations. *The Holy Spirit is Prana, a life force, a form of electric energy or fire.*

There is no beginning to creation; neither will there be an end says the Temple in the chapter on the fall of angels [vol II]. Great spiritual masters become angels of God.

Humanity requires a *Master* Spirit, a Spirit Who has conquered *all* matter; and because of the very laws governing the manifestation of spiritual substance, it is almost impossible for a perfect Master to appear in material conditions. In the case of Jesus, there was a series of incarnations from the beginning of time for He was in truth the first born among many brethren. *This does not imply that mankind is to fall down and worship Jesus. That entity must be a help instead of a hindrance to grasp the reality that there is this possibility of perfection for all men.*

Rudolph Steiner and anthroposophy

Rudolph Steiner [1861-1925] in his book *Knowledge of the Higher Worlds*, gives several pieces of advice as to the kind of patient training one must undergo in order to experience the supernatural. In his spiritual science, he joins Hermes who said he had gone through a long process of purification and sanctification before he could have his mystical experiences. Steiner described many phenomena some of which can be confirmed by Seeker as true.

All these preparations continues Steiner, lead to two important supernatural experiences: the meeting of the lesser and the Greater Guardians of the Threshold.

The Unification Movement

The Unification Movement was founded by Sun Myung Moon [1920- ...]. To this movement, and as written in its main scripture, the *Divine Principle*, God is the Subject in whom the dual characteristics of original internal nature and original external form are in harmony. At the same time, God is the harmonious union of masculinity and femininity, which manifest the qualities of original internal nature and original external form, respectively. In relation to the universe, God is the subject partner having the qualities of internal nature and masculinity [*Divine Principle*, Chapter 1, section 1, 1.1].

God, the Creator of all things, is the absolute reality, eternal, self-existent, and transcendent of time and space. The fundamental energy of God's being is also eternal, self-existent, and absolute. It is the origin of all energies and forces that allow created beings to exist. This fundamental energy is the universal prime energy [Section 2, 2.1].

The Divine Principle considers that the account of the creation of the universe recorded in the Bible thousands of years ago nearly coincides with the findings of modern scientific research and therefore it must be a revelation from God [Section 5: 5.1].

Like all beings, angels were created by God. God created them prior to any other creation. When God in the Bible spoke in the plural saying: '*Let us make man in our image, after our likeness,*' He was not referring to Himself as the Holy Trinity, as many theologians have interpreted the passage. Rather, He was speaking to the angels, whom He had created before human beings.

Because God created us as His children and gave us dominion over all creation, we are meant to rule over the angels as well. It is written in the Bible that we have the authority to judge the angels. Many who communicate with the spirit world have witnessed hosts of angels escorting the saints in Paradise. These observations illustrate the fact that angels have the mission to minister to human beings [Chapter 2: section 2, 2.1].

God created the angelic world and assigned Lucifer to the position of archangel. Lucifer was the channel of God's love to the angelic world. However, after God created human beings as His children, He loved them many times more than He had ever loved Lucifer, whom He had created as His servant. Yet when Lucifer saw that God loved Adam and Eve more than him, he felt as if there had been a decrease in the love he received from God. This was why he seduced Eve, and this was the motivation of the spiritual fall [Chapter 2, Section 2, 2.2].

Jesus is the tree of life portrayed in the Bible. Adam, had he realized the ideal of perfection symbolized by the tree of life in the Garden of Eden, he and Jesus who is symbolized by the tree of life in the Book of Revelation would be identical in the sense of having realized the goal of creation. As such, they would have equal value [Chapter 7, Section 2, 2.1].

To give rebirth to fallen people, Jesus came as the second Adam, the True Father of humankind, with the mission symbolized by the tree of life. This being the case, should not there also have come the True Mother of humankind, the second Eve with the mission symbolized by the tree of the knowledge of good and evil? The one who has come as the True Mother to give rebirth to fallen people is the Holy Spirit [Chapter 7: Section 4, 4.1.2].

Chapter 6

Understanding of divinities in some Esoteric Movements

Ancient and Mystic Order Rosae Crusae

I N the *Positio Fraternitatis Rosae Crucis* published in 2005, Rosicrucians of the AMORC declared that their conception of spirituality is based upon the conviction that God exists as an Absolute Intelligence that created the universe and everything therein and also on the assurance that each human being emanates from God.

To them, the fact that the existence of God cannot be proven does not justify the declaration that God does not exist. Truth may have many faces, they add. To remember only one in the name of rationality is an insult to reason, they continue. And to ask: *'Is science itself rational, when it believes in chance?'* On its part, the AMORC agrees with Albert Einstein's comment about chance when he described it as: *'The Path that God takes when [God] wants to remain anonymous.'*

In the *Positio*, one reads that people are no longer satisfied to re-main on the periphery of a system of beliefs, even though a particular religion is said to be revealed. Those *people now want to place themselves in the center of a system of thought arising from their own experiences.* In this respect, the acceptance of religious dogmas is no longer automatic. Believers have acquired a certain critical sense regarding religious questions, and the basis of their convictions corresponds increasingly to a self-validation.

Humanity's presence on Earth is not the result of mere happens-tance; rather, it is the consequence of an intention originating from a Universal Intelligence commonly called 'God.' Although God is incomprehensible and unintelligible because of Transcendency, this is not true of the laws through which God manifests within Creation. *We have the power, if not the responsibility, to study these laws and to apply them for our material and spiritual welfare.*

To Rosicrucians, since the universe includes approximately one hundred billion galaxies, and each galaxy has about one hundred billion stars, there probably exist millions of solar systems compara-ble to ours. Consequently, to think that only earth is inhabited seems to be an absurdity and constitutes a form of egocentrism.

For the AMORC, among the forms of life populating other worlds, some are probably more evolved than those existing on Earth; others may be less so. Yet they are all a part of the same Divine Plan and participate in Cosmic Evolution. Contact with aliens will happen someday, but Rosicrucians do not spend their entire time waiting for that. They have other businesses to take care of they assure in the *Positio Fraternitatis.*

Position statement of Freemasonry as presented on fultonfriendship.org/religion

The following position statement has been prepared by the Masonic Service Association of North America and has been endorsed by the Grand Lodge of New Jersey[23].

The Supreme Being: masons believe that there is one God that people employ many different ways to seek, and to express what they know of God. Masonry primarily uses the appellation, *'Grand Architect of the Universe'* and other non-sectarian titles, to address the Deity. In this way, persons of different faiths may join together in prayer, concentrating on God, rather than differences among themselves. Masonry believes in religious freedom and that the relationship between the individual and God is personal, private, and sacred.

Position of the Illuminati Order as written on illuminati-order.org/positions

God: Existence of God as creative, organizer, and maintainer of the Universe

Spirit: Formed for God initially straightforward. 'It sleeps in the mineral, it dreams in the vegetable, it wakes up in the animal, it lives in the man, and it shines in the angels.'

---

[23]Freemasonry and religion.http://www.fultonfriendship.org/religion1.htm (accessed April 3, 2010).

The Universal White Brotherhood

On its website, the Universal White Brotherhood in America [FBU-USA] states the following:

"The Master [Omraam Mikhael Aivanhov] tells that according to Ancient Wisdom, Melchizedek, King of Righteousness and High Priest of the Divine World, initiated Abraham into the knowledge of God and his Heavenly Kingdom. These ancient teachings became a spiritual tradition now known as Kabbalah. In order to comprehend, and navigate what the journey of the soul is all about, we need a road map. This road map is called The Tree of Life.

It is impossible to have a true understanding of this map or blueprint without the guidance of a Spiritual Master. It is also impossible to understand without being prepared. Through the numerous conferences given by Omraam Mikhael Aivanhov, people become educated, and prepared to evolve spiritually, and to begin to study Kabbalah. All of these lessons are available through the collections of books and tapes that were transcribed from oral lectures given by the Master.

The FBU declares that it teaches a better understanding of the relationship between God, Archangels, Angels, Nature, and Humanity. 'True magic, divine magic, consists in putting all one's powers, all one's knowledge, at the service of the Kingdom of God on Earth.'

Chapter 7

God as seen by atheists: summing up 'The Improbability of God'

T HE book '*The Improbability of God*' as stated in the introduc-

tory chapter is a compilation of writings against the existence of God made in 2006 by Pr. Michael Martin and Dr. Ricki Monnier. It presents a rich and updated variety of arguments against the existence of God that should not be neglected in an attempt in this époque to prove the existence of divinities and speak of their nature. The arguments against the existence of God are the following.

Cosmological arguments

In general, *the cosmological argument is the argument used by the believers in God which states that the existence of the universe is a strong evidence for that of God because the only adequate expla-*

nation of the universe is that it was created by God. The following are the counter arguments of atheists.

    1. The scientific case against a God who created the Universe (By Victor Stenger)

    Since there is no empirical evidence, no memory in the universe of a supernatural creation that violates the universal natural laws of physic, a miracle; we can conclude that a God who is highly intelligent and powerful supernatural creator does not exist. Furthermore:

    a. the existence of matter in the universe did not require the violation of the energy conservation [E= mc2]. Therefore there has been no creator

    b. the universe began with no structure, no organization, it was a state of chaos. The order we now observe could not have been the result of any initial design built into the universe at the so-called creation. The universe preserves no record of what went on before the big bang. The creator left no imprint

    c. the universe has no beginning because even the big bang is not said to be the beginning. It is possible that there have been a prior universe. Some suggest that our current universe could have appeared from a pre-existing one, for example by the process of quantum tunneling or so-called quantum fluctuations. Since there is no beginning, there is no creator

    2. The first cause and the big bang argument for God are not correct (Theodore Schich Jr.)

a.   To say that everything except God has a cause other than itself as Thomas Aquinas did is not true because first, it would then be better to say that the universe directly considered does not have a cause rather than looking for God. ***Hence the universe is God***. Second, it is not only an eventual god who does not have a cause; modern physics has shown that certain things are uncaused. In perfect vacuum, occasionally but according to Heisenberg uncertainty principles, an electron, positron, and photon emerge spontaneously. When this happens, the three particles exist for a brief time, and then annihilate each other leaving no trace behind [energy conservation is violated]. Additionally, there is no such a thing as an all-powerful, all-knowing, and all-good God as Aquinas thought. If God were all powerful, he would be able to create more than the one universe we know. There is no evidence in the universe for an all knowing God. If the universe was created by an all-powerful, all-knowing, and all-good God, it would be perfect and more hospitable to humans who would not need to improve it.

b.   To prove that the universe which began with time has a cause, Ross creates another time dimension for God, but the general theory of relativity does not speak of such a time dimension and Ross did not succeed in proving its existence. In the two-dimensional time of Ross, the notion of precession or succession makes no sense. From the fact that the universe has a beginning in a higher time dimension, it does not follow that it has a cause [in the ordinary sense].

c.   There are good reasons for believing that the universe does not have a cause. Edward Tyron and others have suggested the universe is a result of a vacuum fluctuation.

d.   The theory of Lee Smolin that we live in a continually growing community of universes, each born from an explosion following the collapse of a star to a black hole, is better than that of Ross. It shows that the universe needs not an external cause and also that as a whole it does not necessarily come from a previous "big crunch" when a previous expansion phase has stopped and the universe contracted. Several "little crunches," the formation of black holes and their singularities is a conceivable explanation.

3. Non-theistic explanation of the big bang (Quentin Smith)

a. Since God wanted a universe of animated creatures, since the earliest state of the universe [the singularity involving life-hostile conditions] is inanimate, and since the earliest state of the universe is not ensured to lead to an animate universe, therefore God does not exist.

b. The idea that God has no more reason to create an animate universe than an inanimate one is inconsistent with the kind of person *we normally conceive* God to be. If God intends to create a universe that contains living beings at some stage in history, there is no reason for him to begin the universe with an inherently unpredictable singularity. It would be a sign of incompetent planning. The rational thing to do is to create some state that by its own lawful nature leads to a life-producing universe. It is illogical that God would have created something whose natural evolution would lead with high probability only to inanimate states. There are countless logically possible initial states that lead by a natural law like evolution to animate states; and if God had created the universe he would have selected one of these states. Given that the state posited by the Big Bang cosmology is not one of these states, it follows that Big Bang cosmology is inconsistent with the hypothesis of divine creation. To ascribe a rational behavior to God, one is not justified by omitting the singularity and its unpredictability from the classical Big Bang cosmology. The fact that God is omniscient does not entail that he knows, logically prior to creation that the Big Bang singularity would evolve into an animate universe. According to the theory called the Wave Function of the Universe, the universe has 95 % probability to naturally and mathematically come into existence without the intervention of any supernatural forces. If God created the universe, the probability would be 100 %.

Teleological arguments against the existence of God

The teleological argument ['teleos' meaning 'end' or 'purpose'] for the existence of God states that the *order observable in the universe is oriented toward a purpose rather than no purpose and that an end was set by the creator God.* This is the argument from design. Nicholas Everitt, Victor J. Stenger, and Richard Dawkins express their disagreement with this argument as followed.

1. The argument from scale (Nicholas Everitt)

a. If the God of *classical theism* existed, with the purposes traditionally ascribed to him, then he would create a universe on a human scale, i.e., one that is not unimaginably old, and in which human beings form an unimaginably tiny part, temporally and spatially.
b. The world does not display a human scale. So:
c. there is evidence against the hypothesis that the God of *classical theism* exists with the purposes traditionally ascribed to him.

2. The anthropic coincidences: a natural explanation (Victor J. Stenger)
Many theistic scientists say that they see strong hints of purpose in the way the physical constants of nature seem to be exquisitely fine-tuned for the evolution and maintenance of life including intelligent life. One gross and fatal assumption is that only one kind of life, ours, is possible in every configuration of possible universes.

The best evidence that we do not make our own universe is the fact that the universe is not what most of us want it to be. A wide variation of the constants of physics has been shown to lead to universes that are long-lived enough for life to evolve and exhibit 'anthropic' coincidences, though human life would certainly not exist in such universes. The most powerful laws of physics, the conservation laws, are evidence against design rather than for it.

3. The improbability of God (Richard Dawkins)

Why do people believe in God? Dawkins asks. And to answer: for most, the reason is still some version of the ancient Argument from Design. We look around us at the beauty and intricacy of the world, at the aerodynamic sweep of a swallow's wing, at the delicacy of flowers and of the butterflies that fertilize them. We reflect on the electronic complexity and optical perfection of our own eyes that do the looking. If we have any imagination, these things dive us to a sense of awe and reverence. Moreover, we cannot fail to be struck by the obvious resemblance of living organs to the carefully planned designs of human engineers.

This is wrong or at least superfluous says Dawkins. The order and apparent purposefulness of the living world has come about through an entirely different process. A process that works without the need for a designer and one that is a consequence of basically very simple laws of physics. This is the process of evolution by natural selection, discovered by Charles Darwin and, independently, by Alfred Russel Wallace.

What does all objects that look as if they must have had a designer have in common? The answer is statistical improbability. If we find a transparent pebble washed into the shape of a crude lens by the sea, we do not conclude that it must have been designed by an optician: the unaided laws of physics are capable of achieving this result.

But if we find an elaborate compound lens, carefully corrected against spherical and chromatic aberration, coated against glare, and with 'Carl Zeiss' engraved on the rim, we know that could not have happened by chance. We can conclude that living bodies are billions of times too complicated, *too statistically improbable, to have come into existence by sheer chance*. How then did they come into being? The answer is that *a whole series of tiny chance steps*, *each one small enough to be a believable product of its predecessor, occurred one after the other in sequence*. These small steps are caused by genetic mutations and random changes.

Most of these changes lead to death, a minority of them turn out to be slight improvements leading to increased survival and reproduction. By this process of natural selection, those *random changes that turn out to be beneficial* eventually spread through the species and become the norm. The stage is now set for the next small step in the evolutionary process.

Evolution is then capable of doing the job that, once upon a time, seemed to be the prerogative of God. The evidence that evolution happened dwells in the millions of fossils found in exactly the places, at exactly the depths that we should expect if evolution has happened. The fact that the genetic code is the same in all living creatures overwhelmingly suggests that all are descended from one single ancestor that lived more than 3,000 million years ago. The evidence for evolution is so compelling that *the only way to save the creation theory is to assume that God deliberately planted enormous quantities of evidence to make it look as if evolution had happened*.

The argument from Design then has been destroyed as a reason for believing in God. *People have contradictory conceptions of God*. There is no doubting the power of such convictions to those that have them, but this is no reason for the rest of people to believe them.

There is a temptation to argue that, although God may not be needed to explain the evolution of complex order *once the universe with its fundamental laws of physics had begun, we do need a God to explain the origin of all things. This idea does not leave God with very much to do*: just set off the Big Bang, then sit back and wait for everything to happen like the *lazy God* portrayed by Peter Atkins in his book *The Creation*.

Inductive evil arguments against the existence of God

1. If God exists, then God possesses certain attributes
2. Based on the weight of the evidence relative to the widespread and horrendous evil in the world, God does not possess all these attributes
3. Therefore, God does not exist

Some of the advocates of these arguments are Quentin Smith, William L. Rowe, Michael Martin, and Thomas Metcalf.

Non-belief arguments against the existence of God

1. If God exists, then God possesses certain attributes
2. Based on the weight of the evidence relative to the widespread life or the reasonable non-belief in the world, God does not possess all these attributes
3. Therefore, God does not exist

The major proponents of this theory are Theordore M. Drange, Victor Cosculluela, Walter Sinnott-Armstrong, and J. L. Schellenberg.

Chapter 8

Evolutionary Religion

The Theory

RELIGION is a set of common beliefs and practices generally

held by a group of people, often codified as prayer, ritual, and religious law while evolution is a process of development. Consequently evolutionary religion is the development of those beliefs and practices. But this explanation of evolutionary religion is not sufficient.

To better understand what evolutionary religion is, it is important to remember Charles Darwin and his theory of the evolution of species through natural selection. That theory has already been tackled in the preceding chapter from a different angle, the wish of atheists to find in it the proof of the non-existence of God. In the present chapter, accent will be put, not on the cause of the evolution of species, but on the particular applications of that theory to ideas and actions of religious nature, in their structure or make-up.

According to Darwin, within a given population, only the individuals who develop the ability of resistance to hard environmental changes survive. This leads to find equivalences in both Darwinian evolution and evolutionary religion.

The correspondents of the species of natural selection in evolutionary religion are human societies; the hard environmental changes of the first theory are wars between rival societies in the second; and the ability that enables individuals of an animal population to survive [genotypic and phenotypic adaptations] corresponds to new beliefs and practices.

As genotypic and phenotypic adaptations do, the new beliefs and practices enable a particular group of human beings to survive in situations in which it could have perished otherwise.

It is well known that a human being has a soul that is invisible to the physical eye. Emotions from the soul can be particularly powerful. Generally, human beings act according to the nature of their inner self. If that inner self is weak, then the person is a looser also on the material plan; but if the soul is strong, it makes the body accomplish great things.

Religion is recognized to have the power to strengthen the soul. So the nature of the religion of a people determines its mental and physical power. Consequently when facing big challenges such as survival in case of war; the evolution of beliefs and practices can give a significant advantage to one society over another.

This is evolutionary religion. A group of people even in small number can achieve victory over a bigger army if it uses well the power of religion. The evolution of a religion also gives other advantages besides survival. Among them are:

- Group cohesion
- Loyalty or support
- Leadership and order in society
- Reinforcement of law
- Common history

- Preservation of a common language

The concept of evolutionary religion according to its proponents explains the rise of monotheism for example. At a moment of history, precisely during the 14th century B.C.E, all religions were polytheistic. The dominant cultures in the world at that time were the ancient Egyptian civilization under Amenophis IV and the neighboring but enemy Kingdom of the Hittites.

In order to win the war against the Hittites, Nefertiti, wife of the king of Egypt asked her husband to use a secret weapon which is the belief in one God. She was able to see in monotheism the potential for the survival and greatness of Egypt and convinced Amenophis IV. The name of the unique god that Amenophis IV proposed was Aten. He changed his own name into Akhenaten meaning 'the servant of Aten.' First Akhenaten stated that Aten was the most powerful God [henotheism], but later on, he made Aten the only one God [monotheism] and built a city and a temple in his honor. For him, *Aten is invisible but has the sun as symbol* so that through their relationship with the sun, worshipers can benefit from Aten.

Before presenting some of the proponents of the theory of evolutionary religion, it is important to add that war is not the only factor able to induce a revision of the system of religious thoughts and practices. Besides war which is a more or less urgent situation, there is also philosophical or theological thinking also known as meditation and sometimes contemplation. Important traces of this activity have been left by several prominent historical figures.

Among these figures are Hermes Trismegistus, Moses, Buddha, Pythagoras, Aristotle, Jesus, Augustine, Thomas Aquinas, Mohammad, and many Hindus, esoteric, and New Religious Movements people. The elements that often nourish meditation are social tragedies such as diseases and suffering and injustices such as imprisonment and mistreatments of all kinds. In other cases, meditation is sustained by deep joyful experiences.

Seeker, deep within, has the desire to pass into history as someone who has brought from God, clear spiritual ideas and practices which are also deep, efficient, adapted to his time, and able to help future generations stay without shaking on the road of good and happiness for all; avoiding the hell of evil and egoism. His wish is that his work of today always be in agreement with the Divine that reveals itself in his generation as well as with the enormous progresses that the next generations will bring, still thanks to that same Divine, in all areas of existence.

Some advocates of the theory

Some scholars believe that the origin of ancient Israel's monotheism dwells in the work of Akhenaten. One of the first to mention this was Sigmund Freud, the founder of psychoanalysis[24]. Sigmund Freud claimed that Moses was an Egyptian, a servant and great preacher of Akhenaten who prolonged monotheism with the Jews.

Some believe that the people who left Egypt did not have only one national identity, a reason why they wandered in the wilderness. They were called the Hyksos composed of a mixture of different people including some Egyptians. This variety of national origin to some scholars could be the reason why there are many names for God in the Hebrew Bible; each tribe preserving its name: Adonai, Yahweh, Elohim, and so forth.

---

[24]Sigmund Freud and Katherine Jones, *Moses and Monotheism* (New York: Knopf, 1939).

One influential advocate of the theory of religious evolution is Jonathan Kirsch. In his book *God Against the Gods: The History of the War Between Monotheism and Polytheism*, he affirms that in contrary to the lower orders of animal life, there is something deep rooted in human nature that pushes humanity to conceive of a higher power to worship.

There are, according to Kirsch, evidences that first human species, the Neanderthals, as well as Homo sapiens [rational men], are also "homo religiosus" [religious men]. However, to him, nothing in human nature suggests that religiousness should only focus on monotheism. In the contrary, from its beginning until now the polytheistic form of religion has continued to exist despite the attacks of monotheism characterized by ferocity, fanaticism, and heart-shaking cruelty.

Kirsch accuses the essence monotheism to have a dark side and to be responsible of the cruel conflicts and violence in the world since 3000 years. He cites as example recent events such as the events of September 11th in America, the dynamiting of ancient Buddhist statues in Afghanistan by the Talibans, the stoning of adulterous women in Nigeria, the terrorist acts performed by Palestinians in Israel, and so forth.

Kirsch draws the attention of the reader toward the Bible which contains proofs of the violent nature of monotheism. He stresses how Yahweh, the mythic God of Hebrews, decreed holy wars to massacre entire tribes and how historical events such as the liberation fight of the Maccabees and the Zealots in the Name of God illustrate the dark side of Monotheism.

In kirsch's understanding also, monotheism actually began in Egypt with King Akhenaten in the 14th century B.C.E. and was borrowed later by the Jews. In this, he is aligned with Sigmund Freud. Monotheism contains according to him the seed of violence and intolerance that becomes fruitful only when it is supported by the power of the state like at the times of Akhenaten, King Josiah of ancient Israel, and more importantly at the time of the Roman Emperor Constantine who established the first totalitarian state in history.

Kirsch also states that if the successor of Constantine, Emperor Julian had lived for a long time, his attempt to abolish monotheism and reestablish polytheism in its glory in the Roman Empire could have been successful and the world today would live better without the cruelty of monotheism. He indicates that even today, many TV evangelists and celebrities such as Jerry Falwell and some Hollywood movies portray polytheism as abomination while pagans themselves find it a noble form of religion.

The belief that there is only one true God gave birth to rigorism which when turned inward may inspire a true believer to punish himself. Turned outward, it may inspire the same man to punish others who fail to embrace the religious beliefs that he or she finds so compelling. Zeal in rigorism can turn into terrorism. This is illustrated in the Bible where the first use of the word 'zeal' is to describe the murder of an Israelites and his Midianite lover by another Israelite.

Justin L. Barrett agrees with Kirsch that the belief in God is natural because it depends on mental tools possessed by all human beings. But to Barrett, the way the human mind is structured and develops renders the belief in the existence of a supreme God with qualities such as omniscience, omnipotence, and immortality highly attractive.

Part II

WHAT DIVINITIES FOR A UNIVERSAL PHILOSOPHY, SCIENCE, AND SPIRITUALITY?

Chapter 9

Significance of the various schools of ideas for the subject of God and gods

Particularity of Mesopotamian mythology

Comparison with the Bible

APART from being officially the cradle of civilization and having a written description of its spirituality that emphasizes gods,
Mesopotamia through Sumer and the *Enuma Elish* is significant for
the subject of divinities because it has a lot in common with the
creation story of the Book of Genesis.

Its significance also lies in one major difference with the biblical
story: in the Babylonian creation myth, man is created from the blood
of a god by a college of gods led by Marduk while in the Bible God
made man from clay and breathed into his nostrils after declaring '*Let
us make mankind in our own image, in our likeness*' [Genesis 1: 26].

The other difference is that according to Genesis, human kind is destined to dominate earth and this was very good in the eyes of the creator. In contrary to the *Enuma Elish*, there is no mention that men were created to serve the gods. Even the idea of worship widely present in the Bible as a whole cannot be seen in the *creation story* of Genesis.

That idea began to appear only with Cain and Abel [Genesis 4: 3-5] who belonged to the second generation of humans of the Bible. Before them Adam and Eve their parents had just to respect the commandment not to eat of the fruit of the Tree-of-the-Knowledge-of-Good-and-Evil [Genesis 2: 16-17].

If there are major differences between the Mesopotamian mythology and the Bible, there are some interesting common points as well. A first resemblance worth noticing is the role played by water in the creation of heaven and earth [see the first paragraph of the *Enuma Elish* and Genesis 1: 2 and 6-10].

The Mesopotamian civilization preceded that of Ancient Israel. Abraham according to Genesis came from Mesopotamia, particularly from Haran [Genesis 12: 4]. All his ancestors, from Adam to his father Terah through patriarchs like Seth, Enoch, Methuselah, and Noah; have lived in Mesopotamia.

Genesis 11: 31 states that Terah, the father of Abraham, left his son Nahor, and his family in Ur. He took his other son Abraham married to his half-sister and moved out of Ur. He also took Lot the child of his third son Haran who has died in Ur. Milcah, Lot's sister and daughter of Haran was married to her uncle Nahor and may have remained in Ur with her husband.

Terah, the father of Abraham was heading toward the land of Canaan when he left Ur but he stopped and settled in Haran, still in Mesopotamia. Haran is indeed closer to Canaan as is the region of Assyria comparing to Ur which was part of Sumer and Babylonia.

This is not only geographically accurate but also theologically thought provoking.

It is indeed strange that Terah, without any mentioned Divine intervention, packed his baggage, left Ur, and decided to go to Canaan while Abraham pursued and fulfilled the dream of his father, this time under the injunction of God.

The Bible attests that Abraham's father, Terah, was an idol worshiper [Joshua 24: 2] as historical account says Mesopotamians were. So Abraham at a time was also probably an idol worshiper. Whether Genesis is a real story or a mythological construction, one thing remains troubling. What was the reason why Terah, an idol worshiper, was so in tune with the will of God who is supposed to be in opposition with polytheism, idolatry, and gods?

Was Terah unconsciously following God or was he following the plan of the gods in order to take control of a strategic land for the future of mankind? Why Canaan then? Did God stroke the enemy by taking the son of one of its champion Terah, thus bending the balance of the conflict with the gods in His favor or Terah despite his condition of idol worshiper was part of God's plan in general? Was Terah's attitude a pure nomadic instinct?

When at the call of God Abraham [now head of a larger group than his nuclear family] left Haran for Canaan after the death of his father; he left nobody in Haran [Genesis 12: 4-5].

Later in his life, Abraham, as the Bible says, insisted that his favorite son Isaac gets married with a woman from his family left in his country, his homeland Mesopotamia [Genesis 24: 1-10], in Ur where his bother Nahor has remained. He did not want Isaac to marry one of the Canaanite women. He still considered himself a stranger in the land, but it is not certain at all if that was the reason to his reluctance. Isaac also did not like Canaanite women to be married to his progeny and sent his blessed son Jacob to Padam Aram in Syria [Genesis 28: 5].

How did the patriarchs relate to God? In the first chapters of Genesis, it is written that God spoke to Adam, Eve, Cain, and Abel who responded to Him, that Enoch walked with Him, and that He spoke to Noah who also walked with Him [Genesis 6:9].

God spoke to Abraham in a vision [Genesis 15: 1] and appeared to him many times. In Genesis 18 He appeared to Abraham as a man accompanied with two other men who according to Genesis 19: 1 were actually angels. Therefore, one is right to affirm that God appeared to Abraham *as* an angel. That God is an angel and therefore a god, probably more powerful than the other gods is a quick conclusion that will not yet be made, even though it confirms Mesopotamian understanding of divinities.

This could mean that Enoch and Noah walked with "God", not only symbolically but also literally, at least spiritually or through a direct and conscious interaction of spiritual bodies. Jacob saw many of God's angels in a dream ascending and descending on a ladder and God was standing above it [Genesis 28: 12-13]. This continues to suggest that God is a powerful god. Jacob wrestled with a man [Genesis 32: 24] but the man told him that in fact he has wrestled with God and men and won [Genesis 32: 28]. Jacob and many of his descendants believed the man who wrestled with him was God Himself [Genesis 32: 30-32].

This section has raised many questions but only those related to the existence and nature of deities will be addressed as fully as possible from the scriptural, theological, and logical standpoints.

With the Mesopotamian history, culture, and religion's help, the hope is that the obscure and troublesome passages of the Bible concerning the nature of gods, and especially the nature of God, become clearer.

It is also very important to signal the heavy presence of astrology and astrotheology in the Mesopotamian creation myth.

Sumerian mythology in movies and cartoons

Sumerian mythology is present in the film industry but not as abundantly as other mythologies such as the Greek one certainly because the works of scholars such as Zecharia Setchin that made it better known are recent. The movie and the cartoon *Conan the Adventurer* show how gods, sorcerers, spells, and temples permeated all the aspects of Sumerian culture.

Significance of Ancient Egyptian mythology

Ancient Egyptians and the quest for immortality

The first things that come in the mind when one thinks of Egypt is probably the pyramids which are unique in the world because of their old age, their impressive size, and the technology required to build them which the scientists of this époque have various opinion on. However, researchers such as John Anthony West are pointing out that beyond the material and scientific aspects of the pyramids, it is the spiritual information they contain that are important and should draw the curiosity of today's human beings.

Even the official history of ancient Egypt has shown how much religion and spirituality were central to ancient Egyptians including their rulers who called themselves "gods and High Priests of the other gods".

In the documentary *Magical Egypt* accessible on Youtube in which West presents many of his findings, René Schwaller de Lubicz is said to have demonstrated that there was in Egypt a "Sacred Science", the original unified source of mysticism, occultism, esotericism, and magical disciplines that exist today as well as the unified source for such diverse contemporary sciences as chemistry, physical sciences, philosophy, medicine, geometry, astronomy, architecture, music, and mathematics.

Like ancient Egyptians, almost every human being has the desire of eternity. In many cultures, the quest for the Elixir for eternal youth exists. Ancient Egyptians wanted to achieve that goal through the life in the hereafter and used their earthly lives to prepare for the entrance to that realm at their death. The function of many pyramids as temples, tombs, and place of secret teaching and initiation is very illustrative of that. The mummification of bodies, the many spiritual and religious inscriptions on the walls of tombs and the treasures buried in them are also key elements that inform on how the ancient people of Egypt, particularly the pharaohs intended to gain immortality.

Some international relations of Ancient Egypt

Another interesting aspect of the civilization of Ancient Egypt is its relationship with Ancient Israel as recorded in the Bible. That relationship has been sometimes very antagonistic as shown by the Exodus and sometime peaceful and even familial as shown by the marriage of King Solomon in the beginning of his reign to the daughter of the pharaoh of Egypt [1 Kings 3: 1], a pagan and polytheistic country.

Solomon at that time still had the favor of his God. That the wisest of the kings of Israel and even of the entire world at his time [2 Chronicles 9: 22], during the peak of his relationship with his God married and made queen a woman of an important and polytheistic foreign nation, while preparing to build the "house" of the Lord, should make any spiritual seeker meditate deeply. The sojourns of Abraham, Joseph, and Jacob in Egypt are all significant not only because they show an acquaintance between those patriarchs and Egypt but also because they served as a bridge between the Mesopotamian and Egyptian civilizations.

The pharaoh Akhenaten, his monotheistic cult of Aten, and the comeback of the Cult of Amon-Re are more elements that render the study of ancient Egyptian civilization fascinating.

That renowned conquerors and rulers such as Alexander the Great and Napoleon Bonaparte took ancient Egypt in high esteem is worth consideration. As Dan Brown in *The Lost Symbol* and several other authors have mentioned, *ancient Egyptian symbols are present in many public and private places in the USA and Europe*. There has also been a transfer of knowledge, of wisdom, of philosophy from Egypt to Greece through figures such as Thales, Pythagoras, and Plato.

Ancient Egypt in the movie industry, music and modern symbolism

Many movies such as *King Scorpio*, the *Mummy*, and *Star Gate SG1* are significantly contributing to the popularization of ancient Egyptian civilization and mythology. In the movie *Star GateSG1*, the mythology of ancient Egypt, its gods, its spiritual centers such as Abydos, and pyramids, are presented in a way that any theologian officially trained or self-appointed should carefully analyze.

In *Star GateSG1*, ancient Egyptian gods are introduced as extra-terrestrial beings with advanced knowledge. This tends to confirm the belief that Mesopotamian gods, the Annunaki and Igigi, were of extraterrestrial origin. The Rosicrucians of the AMORC also believe as expressed in their *Positio Fraternitatis*, that we are not alone in the physical universe.

The gods portrayed in *Star Gate SG1* [the first season] are larva or snake-like parasites that aggressively take control of human bodies and use them as hosts while giving those bodies superhuman powers. The movie presents them as one of the various galactic and intergalactic life forms. It even shows planets on which communities of humans deported from earth are established.

The minds, hearts, and consciousnesses of children are also trained to know about the Egyptian civilization through cartoons describing the ancient gods such as Thoth and Seth, and mythological places like Ombos. In the anime *Fullmetal Alchemist*, various forms of esoteric teachings are introduced among which alchemy with some ancient Egyptian symbols such as the pyramid and the stars.

On the symbols of many organizations, the pyramid is present as well as on the dollar bills. It is amazing that the phrase '*In God we trust*' and the pyramid, one of the most important symbols of the ancient Egyptian polytheistic civilization co-exist on the dollar bills, like Solomon and the daughter of Pharaoh.

Some might feel not at ease with this kind of fact; however the assessment of monotheism and polytheism, as in chapter 17, should be conducted in order to begin perceiving the reasons behind those associations. Pyramids are also present in the music industry; the video clip of the song *Holler* of the Spice Girls is a good illustration.

Mystic commonalities of ancient Egypt, Hinduism, and the Bible

The representation of the serpent on the forehead of ancient Egyptian gods and rulers as visible in the pyramids and temples matches the red marks on the forehead of Hindu gods, priests, and devotees. This also matches the teaching of yoga concerning the 2nd chakra or third eye.

The correspondence between the Egyptian tradition and the Indian yogic teachings are obvious when one considers the works of René Schwaller de Lubicz on the temple of Man, the temple of Karnak at Luxor dedicated to Amon, the invisible, the animator of form, and the breath of life across the waters. That temple was the house of Amon. It is striking that Paul also taught that man is the temple of God [1 Corinthians 3: 16], the temple of the Holy Spirit [1 Corinthians 6: 19], and that Jesus thought of himself as a temple [John 2: 19].

"Amen," another form for "Amon," is used in important declarations in the Old Testament [1 kings 1: 36, Nehemia 5: 13] and is taught by Jesus himself in the New Testament as a concluding word for prayer [Matthew 6: 13]. Dan Brown in *The Lost Symbol* correctly points out that the form "Amin" is used for the same purpose in Islam.

That Amon was the breath of life in Ancient Egypt and that God breathed into the nostrils of Adam in Genesis 2: 7 show another connection between ancient Egyptian religious mysteries, Judaism, Christianity, and Islam. As it will be shown in the chapter devoted to the Holy Spirit, the breath is also the invisible, the life giving spirit. So the notion of Holy Spirit appears also connected to Egypt and India.

Influence of Greek culture

Under Alexander, the Greeks, destroyer of the powerful Persian and Median Empire, conquered Egypt in 322 B.C.E. and established a vast empire. Hence Greek culture particularly its language has been exported rendering possible more exchanges between different peoples.

Greece served as the base for Western civilization in two ways. First, as it is repeatedly said, by inventing democracy and showing its attractiveness to other nations. Second, Greek thinkers of antiquity addressed the fundamental questions of the universe and transcribed their reflections which became widely spread. Various schools of philosophy flourished and offered alternative social models to those offered by the religious mind before their time. Today, in most academic schools of the world, whether public or private, on all continents, teachings on the beginning of philosophy are always traced back to ancient Greece.

Not only did Greeks make important philosophical contributions in the history of humanity as a whole, their scientists also followed the same path. That is why the names of many Greeks are found in the fundamental teachings of science: Herodotus in history; Archimedes, Euclid, Pythagoras, and Thales in mathematics; Hippocrates and Parmenides in medicine; Aristotle, considered the father of science, Ptolemy, Hypparchus, and Heracleides in astronomy; and so on.

Additionally to science and philosophy, ancient Greece also influences modern civilization through its art of enjoyment. It is not a secret that the Olympic Games held every four years, after a rude competition between world nations to host it, have their origins in ancient Greece. Thousands of athletes in the world center their lives on those games and when the time comes, hundreds of millions of people around the world manage to watch them.

When the Roman Empire became the world's political power, ancient Greece remained the cultural power. Such affirmation can be supported by the fact that Koine Greek was the original language of the New Testament; before a Latin version of the Bible [the *Vulgate* of St Jerome] appeared several centuries later. It should also be remembered that Christianity spread to the world beginning with many Greek cities where Paul traveled. The New Testament and particularly the book of Acts is full of the names of Greek cities.

A quick look at Hollywood reveals that many historical movies are based on the civilization of ancient Greece. Some of them are: *Troy, Spartacus, 300, the Clash of the Titans, Hercules in New York* etc...

Significance of Ancient Maya

Astronomy, human sacrifice, and ritual suicide

Mayan astronomy is renowned for its high precision. Some researchers such as the writer Erich Von Däniken believe in the possibility of Mayan contact with aliens in the past. A third particularity worth mentioning is the open practice of human sacrifice under the godship of Manik and the existence of a goddess of suicide, Ix Tab. This shows that the "copyright" of the idea of ritual suicide does not belong to Jim Jones or other people of his kind.

Like men, like gods

Mayans represented their gods at their image as did ancient Sumerians, Egyptians, Greeks, Hindu, Chinese, Japanese, and Africans. Many reasons could be advanced to explain this fact. Isolation or national pride could explain that the gods bear the image of their people rather than that of the "enemy".

It looks like gods in ancient times were at the image of their worshipers and not the contrary. Atheists could find here a great argument. However theists could defend themselves with two arguments. The first is that gods or angels are humans as Swedenborg affirmed and as the Sumerian story of creation of man from the blood of a god suggests.

The other argument is that spirits have the power to choose the form in which their followers will best relate to them. This is the kind of idea developed in the movie *Stargate SG1* when the Asgard, a technologically advanced alien race counting the god Thor of Germanic mythology in its ranks, chooses to appear to several human societies under the form of humans instead of showing their true morphology. Ancient Egyptians believed that the Ba [soul], which gods and humans possess, can take various forms.

On the ideological level, what mattered to the people mattered to the gods. For example corn was central in Mayan society and good or bad crops determined life or death. Therefore the pantheon contains a god of corn, the young and friendly Yum Kaax. There was no god of rice, but a god of war and a goddess of suicide. Atheists can still argue that those people created their gods, but again, theists can return the ball saying that the relationship with gods was based on mutual interests and that there is no need for a god of rice when it is corn that grows well in a given place.

Chinese Ki compared to Hindu Shakti, kundalini, and psychic body

China has contributed in several ways to the richness of the spirituality and philosophy of the present global civilization. Taoism, Confucianism, and Moism alone could suffice to make a solid case. The doctrine of the Tao; that of the five elements; the *I Ching* or book of Changes; and the celestial rulers are realities that one can neglect only to appear as adept of spiritual or religious laziness. China through acupuncture helps man in the understanding of the invisible realm. The psychic body of Yoga is equivalent to the ancient Egyptian 'Ka' while the kundalini, the energy of Shakti the Hindu goddess, becomes known as the vital force or Ki.

In the movie industry of China, many movies, whether epics or horrors came out based on Chinese mythology.

Philosophy and mysticism in Indian religions: vast, deep, high, and changing

In the mind of the post-modern person, India and its religions may at first be linked to Yoga and the development of the astral or psychic body with its chakras. Nowadays, there are yoga centers or meditation centers or schools on all continents. Through them, Hinduism and Buddhism have been largely popularized to the extent that some of their techniques are part of many academic activities as well as practiced even in many businesses. "To be zen" or "to stay zen" are phrases often used.

Through Theosophy and the New Age movement, the popularity of these two religions has reached high peaks. The teachings from India have greatly influenced Theosophy which is itself a masterpiece in the universe of spiritual thought.

What is not much obvious is the depth and the richness of Hindu philosophy. Some may accuse Hinduism to be confusing. However it is hard to imagine a different situation since the teachings are from a remote past and have changed as different philosophers and religious teachers appeared.

The student of religion and philosophy, when tackling India must be prepared to sit down for a while if he/ she wants to do a serious work. If it can be concluded that Hinduism like the ancient Egyptian Mysteries is a powerful religion from the psychic and magical standpoint, it can also easily be said, without fear of being wrong, that the pioneers of Hinduism have left a work of great intellectual nature. The book of Alain Daniélou, *The Myths and Gods of India* is a testimony of that quality.

The ideas on creation and the roles of the word or logos, the waters, the abyss, light and fire, and so forth contained in the Bibleare also present everywhere in Hindu teachings as well as the incarnation of God in avatars. Like in the other mythologies, the creation by the gods is explained, but in Hinduism, this is sometimes done in a way that religions said to be monotheistic can understand. An example can be found in the creation myth where Prajapati, the primordial deity expresses his wish to create the world guardians.

If sex is important in the Egyptian and the Greek mythologies, it pervades Hindu teachings where almost everything in life can be explained in term of sex. Hindus do not just give an important symbolic place to sex; they actually celebrate sexuality in Tantrism. If the Greek system has Aphrodite and Eros to deal with the libido of worshipers, Hindus do not only have deities for love and sex, but they have a whole system and philosophy around these two topics.

Kamasutra is a word very familiar around the planet today and its origins are in Hinduism. People might be surprised if they learned that the various sexual positions of Kamasutra originated from the god Shiva and his wife Parvati. Another concept developed in Hinduism, before the Christian era is that of the "Trinity."

Several aspects of the Hindu mythology and the Egyptian Mysteries are scientific in nature. For example, Hindus describe their sun god Surya saying: '*Made of fire that consumes its own substance, the sun is identified with cosmic sacrifice*'. The idea that comes into the mind is hydrogen consumption within the sun. It is incredible that this fact was known to people of ancient India hundreds of years before Jesus.

Sikhism speaks of God as a male figure and a husband. This notion corresponds to the description of the Hindu god Shiva and matches Paul's conceptions on Jesus and the Church. *One important merit of Jainism is to encourage humans to strive to become gods and goddesses.*

Zoroastrianism and the Bible

The significance of Zoroastrianism remarkably appears through its connections with the Bible. History tells that Persia under Cyrus and Darius freed ancient Israel from its Babylonian exile and impacted the Jewish culture. The Book of Daniel is a proof of that influence. Indeed, its content is close to Zoroastrian teachings.

The idea of archangels opposed to archdemons taught in Zoroastrianism appears in the Bible for the first time in the Book of Daniel [10: 20-21]. The mention of the name of Persia in that passage is a confession of its author that Persian thought is at work. The same thing can be said about the Book of Revelation the Messiah of which has many common points with the Zoroastrian gods Vohu Mana and Sraocha.

The portrait of Jesus in the Gospels has a lot to do with these two gods. Sraocha and Jesus are the embodiments of obedience to the Supreme God. Both are saviors, both are mediators between men and God, both will lead the final and cosmic war that will defeat the Devil, and so on. Also, like Vohu Mana, Jesus is called the Word [or Wisdom] of God that sits at His right. Even the birth of Jesus was marked with the seal of Zoroastrianism in the persons of the masters, the magi or wise men who visited him guided by astrology.

Another Zoroastrian idea found in the New Testament is the defeat of death as stated in the creation myth of Zoroastrianism and by Paul in 1 Corinthians 15: 55. Other passages in the Old Testament like Isaiah 25: 8, Hosea 13: 14, and Hebrews 2: 14 also express that idea.

An additional parallel between the Bible and Zoroastrianism is the concept of the Old of the Days expressed in Daniel 7: 13 and Revelation 4 on the one hand and the description of Ahura Mazda, the Zoroastrian supreme God, on the other hand. The concept of the seven main spirits of God is present in both Zoroastrianism and in the Revelation of John. Astronomy and astrology appears to be important in Zoroastrianism as it was in ancient Egypt, Mesopotamia, India, and Mesoamerica.

The story of the wise men should be a lesson of religious tolerance, not just because they honored Jesus, but because they were acknowledged by God who manifested Himself to them in their dreams. It could be argued that it was because of Jesus, but the fact is that Herod for example did not receive that kind of favor from God. Those wise men must have had something valuable in the sight of God, something conferred to them by Zoroastrianism.

Judaism, Christianity, and Islam

Mystical and humanistic conquests

Judaism is crucial for spirituality, not only because it allowed the rise of Christianity and Islam, the religions of more than two billion people, but also because it made possible the existence of Kabbalah. Kabbalah does not look like an easy science. According to most spiritual researchers, it can even be very dangerous. The minimum of 40 years is often required from those who wish to begin its study. Indeed death and madness are two plausible outcomes for the unprepared if the student is not simply deceived by the spiritual powers invoked.

Christianity has offered many saints and mystics to the world. It has been the center of intense debate about deities for almost 2 millennia now. It has "offered" Jesus to the world with his high understanding of love and service to others. *Jesus, like Hermes Trismegistus, Ancient Israel, Buddhists, Jains, and certainly other spiritual teachers, put an emphasis on the fact that godship is the glorious destiny of mankind [John 10: 34, Psalms 82: 6].*

Islam has brought organization and development to many lands. It has given Sufism to the world, another opportunity to dialogue with reality at the subtle level.

Thanks to Judaism, many myths containing important lessons to guide people in life have been compiled in the Hebrew Bible or Old Testament. Because of that, billions and billions of people throughout history have been able to ease their pains when fellow humans misunderstood them, and they were able to find a new hope.

The necessary march toward the eradication of violence and dogma

It is nevertheless important to acknowledge the bloody struggles between and within the so called three great monotheistic traditions and between them and other faiths or ideologies. *The conflict between Israel and Palestine today is not just political; it has deep religious roots. The misunderstanding and fight between Jews and Muslims are rooted in a non-agreement about God, His Nature, and His Will.*

The clarification proposed in this book is different on several levels in comparison to Jewish and Muslim views. But if this view appears just and contains the philosophical strength to enable a lasting peace between Israel and the Muslim world, then it would have proven worth expressing. For that peace to happen, both parties would have to be open-minded and consider the possibility of change as stressed in the introduction [thinking and consciousness].

In the so called three great monotheistic religions, many people ask themselves tons of questions without answer. Maybe the answers exist and necessitate a global consideration of scripture or sincere and humble research of the good elements in other cultures or civilizations in order to emerge.

Anybody who is familiar with the Bible and the Qur'an and who has read the numerous histories, mythologies, and philosophies of the world sees that the Bible and the Qur'an are the receptacle of many sacred stories of humanity and that something is also missing in them. Therefore for the answers to come, people must be ready to look for God in those two books in a new way, but to even look outside them.

Far is the intention to say that everything is perfect or better outside the Bible and the Qur'an. The exhortation for the seeker of divinities is to simply consider all the evidences for God and gods and work on them with the most sublime part of the soul. May the less intelligent become more intelligent! May the less loving give more love! May the weak become strong and may the unwise become wiser!

Gnosticism: a love for wisdom and mysticism and the development of dualism

One thing that can be ascribed to Gnosticism is its love for divine wisdom, for religious philosophy, and its encouragement for the detection of divinities through personal experience. Gnosticism gives an idea of the value of Hermeticism and Neo-Platonism, two systems of spiritual thought worth exploring.

Gnostics have let a heritage made of almost all kinds of ideas about divinities. A person may disagree with them, but if he/she succeeds in going over the obstacle of their complicated terminology, the result would be a risky but extraordinary journey into the realm of wisdom.

Several theories of the ancient Gnostics, especially those concerning scientific subjects, have been substantiated by modern research said Manly Hall. Gnosticism is the spiritual current besides Zoroastrianism that fundamentally shaped dualism with a wide range of internal schools, thinkers, and arguments. Sometimes theirs ideas may appear as real eye opener. For example their rejection of the Old Testament God may appear foolish, but beneath, there is a lesson to the one who opens enough the ears and the eyes.

Significance of the other theistic movements, agnosticism, and atheism

Divination is one of the strengths of Shintoism and African traditional religions. Their voice should be heard for a full exploration of the divine potential. Emmanuel Swedenborg has offered a unique out of body experience that increases the field of analyze of the spiritual researcher. Despite some points one may rightly disagree with in his messages, their potential for leading to a good spiritual life is rarely equaled. *Heaven and Hell* is just one of his messages. Several others can highly be recommended if the risk of philosophical wandering is avoided.

With Theosophy and the Temple of the People, spiritual philosophy has considerably expanded. Of course the book *Knowledge of the Higher Worlds* of Rudolph Steiner should be read by any serious seeker. The New Age is following the traces of Theosophy and is trying to achieve a better result. Its acceptance of good ideas wherever they come from is very honorable.

Esoteric movements seem to know many things about deities; but their teachings are secret. Both agnosticism and atheism have posed fundamental questions to theism. Their secular character does not make their sophos or wisdom meaningless. By challenging theology, spirituality, and religion, secularity should have the effect of improving them. There are two types of sciences: the physical and the spiritual. Both belong to sacred science as René Schwaller de Lubicz recognized or to science to make it simpler.

Chapter 10

Epistemology and divinities

EPISTEMOLOGY is the branch of philosophy that studies the nature of knowledge, its presuppositions and foundations, its extent and validity. There is individual knowledge and there is collective knowledge. How then does a person come to the certainty of the existence or not of deities and how does the human society as a whole reach the same result? Such is the fundamental question to which this chapter proposes an answer.

Religion, science, spirituality, and philosophy are the ways by which the existence or not of deities can be proved. The degree of validity of each method is different. A combination of all of them makes a more solid case.

Religion as a mean of knowing deities

Religion has been and remains the most common way of knowing deities. As a *set of beliefs and practices*, it imparts certain teachings, most of the time of dogmatic nature to the seeker. The latter is expected to almost unquestionably follow the path walked by others [founders, saints, leaders, and so forth].

The trouble with religion is that it remains a *system of beliefs and practices* for the majority of people. Very few have the opportunity to live bliss, mystic experiences, and psychic perceptions that give the assurance of the knowledge of the subtle world. Many religious people oppose faith to knowledge stating that faith is what is required in religion while knowledge is in rapport with science. They declare that the attempts to explain religion and most importantly God are vain, unwise, and should not be tried.

The result is the absence of significant religious progress, the existence of conflicts within and among religions, and so on. One of the sad things in religion is that people give up a great extent of their rights and will, and find themselves manipulated by other humans, superior in no way.

Stephen Pepper in *God in Contemporary Thought: A Philosophical Perspective* states that a large number of persons in "civilized" countries have set themselves outside the membership of classic religions in large part due to the dogmatic attitude of religion which demands implicit faith and unquestionable belief in rituals and creeds and offers a security that is not genuine[25].

Religion has been one of the most terrible form of exploitation of man by man that almost erased the work of sincere, humble, wise,

---

[25]Sebastian A. Matczak, God in Contemporary Thought: A Philosophical Perspective: a Collective Study (Philosophical questions series, 10. New York: Learned Publications, 1977), 985.

and compassionate people in that field of life. The damages caused by some religious persons are so many that several people originally inclined toward the supernatural end up the heart filled with pain and bitterness. Sometimes, they become ferocious adversaries of religion.

Religion seeks unity with the divine. However this unity should not necessarily come through blind faith. No matter how blessed or happy an individual is by having such a faith, it remains undeniable that knowledge and reason are better. *A decision based on knowledge, reason, and understanding always gives more confidence than blind faith*. Actually there is a kind of faith associated to knowledge and reason. That kind of faith is called real assurance, or unshakable confidence. *Someone who knows cannot be converted, it is someone who believes who can be*.

All this is to say that *religion should be a science of the things divine rather than a set of beliefs and practices*. Then maybe the word 'religion' could recover its value.

Belief can come forth only when spiritual science is blocked. One can sense a spiritual truth, believe, and work to prove it as physical scientists do. Indeed these scientists also have their beliefs. What one should never do is to prevent others from sleeping because of beliefs. Even rational knowledge requires prudence in its transmission.

It is well known that science or knowledge is power. Spiritual science contains even greater power. Originally, as it has been demonstrated, religion was about physical things as well as the spiritual ones. But as every power, in a wrong hand, a bad person, it destroyed and did not build. Therefore theurgy, magic, alchemy, divination, and many other disciplines have become negative things that are forbidden in several passages of the Old Testament such as Deuteronomy 18: 9-12 and Leviticus 19: 31.

A thoughtful reading of the Bible leads to the acceptance of the fact that Moses, Jesus, seers such as Balaam, Daniel, and Paul used exactly the same power pertaining to the spiritual or psychic disciplines just cited. The difference dwells in how and why they used it. The God of the Old Testament forbade certain practices, but He taught most of them to his people. Exodus 28: 30 shows that that God gave instruments of divination, the Urim and the Thummin, to the High Priest of Israel. All in all, the purpose of God in the Old Testament was to make sure people use power correctly.

Why is the God of the Old Testament so against other gods and forbids their cults? It is because those gods such as the one known as Baal taught an evil way of using the power. Child sacrifice is one of the most important reasons of the opposition of God in the Old Testament to the gods [Leviticus 18: 21, Deuteronomy 18: 10, 2 Kings 23: 10].

It is affirmed in religious and spiritual scriptures that many fallen angels have taught spiritual disciplines to women and men. The problem, still according to scripture is that they were disobeying the God of the Old Testament. Power is neutral and given by the Supreme God who created spiritual and physical beings. When those beings choose to misuse it, this is evil. The conclusion is that one must not be afraid to engage in spiritual science as many did under the inspiration of the God of the Old Testament. The difficulty dwells in finding a good teacher and using knowledge in a constructive manner.

There is a famous saying that power and money corrupt. To dominate them instead of being their slaves, one needs to be of strong theoretical and practical morality. *In 1 John 4: 1, it is asked to test spirits, not only false human prophets, but also their manipulators, the fallen angels. According to this verse there are people who worship angels.*

Testing spirits can only be done thanks to a kind of knowledge or science. No one drinks a cup of water by simply believing it is clean and safe, but because such attitude is based on the proofs of good color, good smell, the absence of visible scrap etc... This kind of judgment, knowledge or, discernment is needed for spiritual actions as well, as Paul acknowledges in 1 Corinthians 2: 12-15.

History shows that there have been more failures than successes in the spiritual quest. That is another reason why slowly, spiritual science has been rejected and religion has become a set of beliefs with all the consequences briefly described above.

In short religion as it is now cannot help much to know divinities including the Supreme God because knowledge is different from belief. Success stories can only be rare and when they happen, it will be difficult to convince outsiders of their validity.

Religion finds its real place, meaning, and purpose after systematic and rigorous spiritual research has ascribed a positive and verifiable value to what needs to be practiced. *Religion would then be defined as the science of human spiritual development and union with the divine, particularly the Supreme God.*

It is useful that spiritual research and religion be two separate disciplines because real spiritual development and union with the divine should be based on a knowledge provided by research and not on a belief that can be proved wrong tomorrow. Many religious people including preachers have had the experience of strongly defending a belief at a moment and have a different understanding later with important negative consequences for those who have followed their previous thought. That is why belief and religion in its most spread form are not reliable enough for the divine to be truly known.

The science of physical things or physicality as a way to know the divine

The debate can quickly be closed here by saying that physicality known as "science" is in opposition to spirituality and therefore there is no way it can help a person know God or gods. This would be a huge mistake. That attitude will correspond to an ignorance of reality.

Karen Kelly in *The Secret of 'The Secret'* presented the reticence of professor Barry Sanders to establish correlations between quantum physics and mysticism or between quantum energy and spiritual energy or ki [chi]. Sanders affirms that the laws of quantum physics have nothing to do with mystic energy. His point of view is understandable when one tries to be in his shoes. But someone like Seeker who experiences mystic energy is not that categorical and prefers that more scientific research in both spiritual and physical areas brings a better informed answer.

Karen Kelly also quoted Fred Alan Wolf who said there are seekers who have no idea of what science is. She explains quantum quackery as characterizing academics who are not scientists, but are mainly in the humanities, using quantum mechanics theories that they do not understand as scholarly sounding proof of any claim they care to make about anything and everything under the sun.

It ought to be remembered that there are seekers and academics in humanities who know what science or physicality is. Seeker for example though a theologian is also doctor of medicine. He could have embraced any scientific discipline of his choice but chose medicine. The first years at medical school deepen students' knowledge in various branches of physics including biophysics and different sort of chemistry including biochemistry.

It would be difficult to say that medicine which combines several scientific disciplines is not scientific. On the contrary, it uses "science" to understand the nature and function of human body and mind, to prevent their dysfunction, and to help restore their balance when it is lost. Seeker may not be a pure physicist but could be granted the ability to read and comprehend basic quantum physic when it comes to the structure and function of human beings at least.

Modern educational system gives a lot of credit to the knowledge gained in official institutions, but from ancient times until today many gained knowledge through self-education, studying books, and analyzing their experiences. This is to say that if indeed it is possible that there exist some people who speak about things they do not understand, many have done their homework in the contrary.

In the matter of quantum physics and mysticism or spirituality, complex laws are not what are first required. Understanding that matter is energy as Einstein determined and knowing that the smallest particles are blocks of energy is a key. Speaking of nano-anatomy or fento-anatomy could be a way of description. Seeker thinks many scholars of humanities can comprehend the level of quantum physics necessary to make their claims which could be true or false at the end if their analysis is not completely rigorous.

A teacher, dear to the Temple of the People, affirmed that the understanding of the mystery of the universe will come through a multidisciplinary study. He encouraged students to study as many disciplines as possible and make the necessary connections. Seeker understood and is trying to follow that advice. It is therefore a good thing when scholars in humanities are interested in quantum mechanics.

The hope is to see more and more people who were primarily "scientists" investigate theological questions as well and to witness the disappearance of the ostracism toward those who make such an attempt. A group of such scientists gathered by the Nour Foundation at the United Nation for a conference in fall 2008 acknowledged that situation of exclusion and sometimes of persecution as did Harvey Irwin in *An Introduction to parapsychology*[26].

---

[26]Harvey J.Irwin, *An Introduction to Parapsychology* (Jefferson, N.C. [u.a.]: McFarland, 1999), 71.

With the ground thus prepared, the following presentation, which is not an attempt to distort physics but to comprehend the universe from various angles, can be made.

There is physical substance and there is spiritual substance. There are several definitions for the word 'spirit'. Others will be used in due time. The one that is interesting here is 'spirit' described in religion or spirituality as the substance of the spiritual world, of which the inner person of man or woman is made.

In fact matter is unique but with different forms and degrees as one can notice in the teachings of the Temple of the People. There is physical matter and there is spiritual matter. Matter can also be divided into visible and invisible. When it is visible to the human eye, it is called solid, liquid, and in some instances gas. Invisible matter corresponds to matter that cannot be seen with the naked physical eyes. It comprises certain forms of gas, microbes, and the different kind of particles and waves. The smallest forms of matter that science has evidences for are electrons, protons, and neutrons, and beyond them quarks and the photons of lights.

Invisible matter includes both spiritual matter and physical matter that the physical eye cannot perceive without the help of instruments. Hence, *the notion of invisibility varies with the progress of the science of physical things or physicality. Elements that formerly belong to the invisible realm come to pass into the visible realm through the mediation of instruments. Accordingly, it appears that invisibility is relative a notion and that it is not exactly synonymous to spirituality.* In fact elements previously considered spiritual have already passed into physical science as anybody who studies a little the Dogon spirituality will recognize.

One day, Seeker was sitting under a tree at a public place of New York City reading a book. Then a man came to pass. As he reached the level of Seeker, his cell phone rang. He picked the phone up and started talking. This little event which has nothing extraordinary for

most human beings of the 21st century, triggered in Seeker a medita-
tive experience which gave him the opportunity to remember that
many beings and phenomena are not perceived by the naked eye.

He remembered that a videophone relies on the movement of
sound and light waves and sometimes radio and TV waves from an
interlocutor to another, in order to perform its function. He also
remembered that the brain too emits waves; four of which are known
to physicality: beta, alpha, theta, and delta. The theta waves are
associated by some with the coming of good ideas and by others to
meditation. The beta waves are associated with thinking.

Telepathy is defined as the transfer of information as thoughts
and feelings between individuals by means other than the five physical senses. *Seeker wondered if the beta and/or theta waves or any
other brain waves could not be the support of telepathy as sound and
light waves serve as support for verbal and visual information. Telepathy could then be a spiritual function, different from that performed
by the five physical senses but with connection (s) to them.*

Many ideas, dreams, and vision which are treated as hallucinations or delusions and as imagination and unreal things are nonethe-
less *real* components of the universe carried and conveyed by waves
of some kind. Images that appear on the 'mental screen' could be
original from the seer or the dreamer or projected in his or her soul by
an exterior source.

To understand the phenomenon, one might consider one picture
or video record that is authentic and one that is fabricated. In both
cases, the final product, the vision, is real but results on one hand
from a "natural" process and on the other hand either from a distor-
tion of the "natural", or a pure imagination, or a mix of distortions and
external ideas. This understanding explains the different sort of
dreams people have.

The origin or source of the distorted or purely created *idea, vision,
or dream* could be beings living in the mental or spiritual spheres

whether good or evil. The source could also be physical, for example a wizard. This kind of explanation may be dismissed being considered as a story that can only be found in science fiction movies such as *Harry Potter*. But a scientific explanation of thought transmission requires speaking of an emitter and a receiver.

If there is a receiver [the seer, the ideologist, or the dreamer]; and if the wave phenomenon on the thought level is more than a hypothesis, then the possibility of the existence of a source or emitter as described in the "stories" does not belong solely to the realm of imagination and fiction.

Since spiritual and physical substances are on the same scale, there must be at least a degree of matter or substance that is the bridge that connects both and mediate interactions from one side to the other. Solid state, liquid state, and gaseous state are the common degrees of physical matter. It is not impossible that spiritual matter also has several degrees that can explain, at least partially and under the reserve of experiential confirmation, the different heavens or spiritual planes in various theologies, ontologies and cosmogonies.

Some religions and spiritual schools teach that there is no fundamental difference between physical substance and the spiritual one. Physical substance is matter highly concentrated or in a low vibratory state while spiritual substance or spirit is diluted matter in low concentration or high vibratory state.

The spiritual substance or spirit can be contained in the physical substance in the way gas can be contained in a liquid. Aerated water and oxygenated blood are two illustrative examples. So, physical scientists have a ground to understand why spirituality and religion teach that a human physical body contains a spiritual one shaped in a similar way. Sometimes, a seven-fold, even a forty nine-fold constitution of matter is offered with the possibility of more forms. Schools such as the Temple of the People consider matter as energy, electricity, or fire.

From these perspectives there is or should be no border between "science" and religion or between physicality and spirituality. This sets the ontological bed [the theory about the nature of being] for a proper epistemology [way of knowledge] of deities.

It has been said quite rightly that physical science was once united with spiritual science and that many of its disciplines emerged from those of sacred science. Many great people are known to have worked in both spheres making impressive discoveries that have changed the course of history. Paracelsus, Isaac Newton, Pythagoras, and Thales are just a few of them. Physicality has developed the ability to assess and pursue their works in the physical field but has not been able to do the same for their spiritual works.

This does not make those spiritual works wrong or worthless. With the development of new kinds of instruments, it is quite possible as the Temple of the People suggests that physicality gathers evidences for phases of realities unknown to it so far. Such has been the history of physical science and it would not be reasonable to affirm that this is no longer possible.

The junction between both sciences will certainly be made someday if it has not already been made. Electromagnetism seems a promising field of investigation on that subject. However, it is of utmost importance to underline that the human being is the highest instrument possible. This is why many moral, ethical, philosophical, religious, and spiritual teachings offer methods of development to render the human able to perceive and live realities so far unknown.

Pure physicality cannot yet give a direct proof for the existence of divinities, but carried by the wings of philosophy it can offer striking orientations as will be demonstrated in the last section of this chapter and in the chapters 15 and 16 devoted to the discussion on the existence of God and the gods.

Spiritual science and the epistemology of the divine

As it has been shown, spiritual science was once part of religion in the West. It is still part of a religion like Hinduism which comes from the East and is also found in many African Traditional religions. This explains why more and more people are attracted to these religions. Like physical science, spiritual science has several disciplines. A discipline can be strongly developed in a spiritual school or religion while being weak in another.

In Hinduism and African Traditional Religions, spiritual science is power, as physical science is known to be. *An evil will with power in either fields can create damages to nature and harm human beings. A religion based on blind faith can maintain people in ignorance or in mental and spiritual slavery.* When a coercive spiritual force, like a spell, a ritual or a direct attack by a spirit is added, the destructive potential of spiritual science becomes more obvious.

That is one reason why spiritual science has been rejected and has made its way out of official religions in the West. No Christian would reasonably deny that Jesus was a spiritual scientist of a very high order even though it is impossible to find a person of that magnitude in the many religions which claim him as their center. Jesus and many others, some named in the Bible, used their power for good, healing and comforting; but others used it to destroy people.

The real question with spiritual science is if mankind can master it or not. Such is the problem posed by Lawrence Watt-Evans in his novel *The Summer Palace.* Watt-Evans is also the author of the fiction book *Touched by the Gods.*

There are so many authors, novels, cartoons, and movies in the genre of spiritual fiction and there are so many readers, viewers, and fans including skeptics and atheists! One might wonder whether the consciousness and unconsciousness are not solidly attached to the supernatural as the famous psychologist Carl G. Jung [1875-1961] acknowledged in his work *The Archetypes and the Collective Unconscious* and in *Psychology and Religion*[27].

For Jung, *the dreams and psychotic states of some patients prove that the psyche or the mind of a human being is not limited to his consciousness.* Because those dreams and psychotic states are uncontrollable, they cannot come from the consciousness and therefore originate in a part of the mind that is called the unconsciousness. The consciousness develops out of the darkness of the primordial unconsciousness, says Jung. Thinking existed long before man was able to say '*I' m thinking,*' he adds. If this is not a religious statement in a different language, what is it? Jung thus joins Descartes to associate the concepts of thinking and being.

Jung asserts that the unconscious is the mother of the conscious. Just as a human mother can only produce a human child whose deepest nature lay hidden during its potential existence within her, so the unconscious cannot be entirely chaotic accumulations of instincts and images. It is also obvious that the unconsciousness functions spontaneously, he affirms.

Normally the unconsciousness collaborates with the consciousness, he continues; without friction or disturbances so that one is not even aware of its existence. But when an individual or a social group deviates too far from his instinctual foundations, he experiences the full impact of the unconscious forces. These elements in the discourse of the psychologist Jung are very close to the notions of sin, guilt, and divine justice or punishment.

So, unconsciousness functions with intelligence and purpose. In India it is called super conscious Jung reminds. The manifestations of the unconsciousness show *traces of personalities* or *archetypes*. The

---

[27]Carl G. Jung, *The Archetypes and the Collective Unconscious* (Bollingen series, 20 [Princeton, N.J.]: Princeton University Press, 1968), 275, 282, and 289.

archetypes *exist* within the unconsciousness in dreams, visions, fantasies, delusions, and so on. Jung distinguishes two kinds of unconsciousness: personal unconsciousness and collective unconsciousness. The archetypes of the collective unconsciousness are, according to him, connected to mythological ideas completely unknown to the layman.

For Jung, myths in psychology are statements about process in the unconsciousness and this applies equally to religious statements. The difference, he says, is that the religious statement is more intense[28]. *Just as the body is a museum of its phylogenetic history [the result of an evolutionary development since the time of remote ancestors], so is the psyche.*

Carl Jung continues his description of the unconscious psyche saying that it is not only immensely old but also capable of growing into an equally remote future. The state of self-control or ecstasy some masters and yogis attain is to him the state of unconsciousness or *universal conscience*. But the negative aspect of this, he says, is that there is a decrease of clarity and details. Consciousness becomes all-embracing but nebulous Jung concludes.

In all this, one can see that the notion of unconsciousness or collective consciousness or superconsciousness of Jung is close to the concept of God and that the archetypes he connects to mythology are related to gods, goddesses, or angels.

Jung, at the difference of other influent psychologists such as Sigmund Freud recognizes that spiritual elements are important in the economy of the psyche. That is why he wished to cooperate with theologians so that both sides can learn from each other.

Now it is appropriate to show how spiritual science can bring evidences for the existence of God and the gods. Those evidences can

[28]Carl G. Jung, *Psychology and Religion* (The Terry lectures.New Haven: Yale University Press, 1938), 300.

be found in the religious world but in very rare instances. They can only be of experiential and scientific nature to really satisfy. This brings to the introduction of the concept of *authentic spiritual experience*.

When people are born in the physical world, they have many experiences and use their intelligence, creativity, and imagination to influence their environment. But there is a limit to what imagination can do. No matter how smart or knowledgeable someone is, he/she cannot produce some realities of this world. Many things exist independently of the will of human beings.

Likewise, on the spiritual plane, there is a reality made of spiritual substance. As there is life, things, and laws in the physical realm, there are also life, things, and laws in the spiritual realm. As said earlier, there are lives, things, and laws before unnoticed by physical science and by the physical senses that have become gradually evident.

Spiritual science says that much more is possible; that there are still subtler forms of life, things and laws that physicality cannot yet access but which are evident to spiritual scientists. Therefore, an *authentic spiritual experience* is not something imagined or a hallucination of some sort as some accuse it to be. Though a thing imagined or a hallucination is a reality of some kind. There is a relationship between 'imagination' and 'reality'. 'Imagination' can affect 'reality' but a great number of realities though they can sometimes be modified by human imagination do not owe their existence to it. This could still appear unclear to someone who never had authentic spiritual experiences, but to those who had had them, there is no doubt.

Physical science is a means by which imagination affects physical reality. Rudolph Steiner explains how similarly imagination can also be used in spiritual science to affect spiritual reality. But his method though safe, seems slow to some people. This is certainly the reason why rituals exist: to create fast spiritual changes that in turn will influence physical reality. Rituals set in motion powers [beings and laws] in spiritual realms that the performer does not always master as Manly Hall pointed out in *The Secret Teachings of All Ages*.

In general it is the personal environment, the sacred space, inviolable by others, that is transformable more easily and at first. The core of that sacred space is the person herself. It is known that diet, physical activity, health care, and so on, shape the physical body a certain way and are combined with genetic [inherited] abilities and with the social environment to enable the individual to achieving outstanding results or not.

For example, to qualify for the Olympic Games as a sprinter, an athlete needs favoring conditions to be fulfilled in all those spheres. He has to be born in a family where there is the genetic possibly to have the required height. Next, personal training and caring for the body is required. If favorable training conditions are not gathered in a country, there is no real possibility to develop oneself, or if the sport is not as encouraged as it is in best nations in the discipline, it will be hard for the athlete to fulfill his/her dreams. Of course, there are some exceptions in which a quality is so strong that through it alone the dream becomes reality.

The same way, spiritual achievements need favorable conditions such as a good family and society but also self-discipline. Steiner and many spiritual schools or religions have emphasized self-discipline. Being born in a family or society of spiritual scientists can help quickly grow spiritually.

If a society is advanced spiritually, but is dominated by evil wills, it will be hard for new people to achieve mastery as described by Watt-Evans in the *Summer Palace*. Talented and promising students can simply be victim of predecessors who desire to remain the sole true connoisseurs, hiding the knowledge. This is not about those who are guided by the noble desire to protect apprentices from being harmed by walking the path too fast, it is about those who refuse to bestow the right knowledge on candidates that are ready either to maintain a personal supremacy or because the candidates refuse to compromise their dignity or goodness.

A typical example in which dignity or goodness is asked to be compromised is found in the outstanding movie *Babylon 5*. In the tenth episode of the fifth season, the fifteenth and sixteenth minutes show a situation in which Bexter, head of a legal organization gave an illegal and immoral order to his protégé Byron who should comply if he wants to be introduced to important people and enjoy great privileges.

So, "making progress" can require the shutting down or the corruption of one's own personality; which is simply impossible for some people to do, therefore they do not often get what should be theirs. The individual competing egos as well as the egos of organizations and institutions can prevent someone to harmoniously develop. In spirituality the issue is more sensitive than in earthly affairs.

One of Seeker's teachers one day said to him and to one of his colleagues after an experience in 2008: *'Do you see now that the world is not white or black but grey?'*

A second case in which dignity is in danger is when a recruit decides to be selective in his or her learning. This can upset the spiritual teacher. Let's take another example from the life of Seeker. One day, he decided to gain more knowledge in the art of healing people by methods taught in his native place. These methods are different from those taught by people of the country of Sinkun and which Seeker has studied.

Thanks to a friend, he contacted one of the medicine men of his native place. The friend took on him to offer a great gift to the healer whom he knew as a patient. He explained to his healer the reason why he had brought Seeker to him. The therapist accepted the proposal but asked for one initial condition: the sacrifice of an animal to set in motion the spiritual powers that will assist Seeker in his apprenticeship and beyond.

However, Seeker who was willing to make a lot of sacrifice to get the knowledge was not ready for a blood offering. It was simply against his personal spiritual code. But the healer explained that blood sacrifice was a "no go" requirement for his science to be imparted and Seeker was obliged to renounce it. Later he heard that there were other therapists who do not require blood sacrifice but he was busy doing other things at that time.

An objective of this volume and others to come is to promote a message of hope for all kinds of people playing any of the roles in the stories just narrated; a message that will contribute to remove several obstacles and enable a better development of spiritual scientists.

Coming back to how one can know about supernatural beings, *theophanies* [manifestations of God or gods visible or perceivable to humans] appear to be the *most direct proofs*. Many cases have been described in the Bible and in other religious or even scientific literature as evidenced in the works of many psychologists[29].

These works described out-of-body-experiences [OBEs] and near-death-experiences [NDEs]. A remarkable testimonial book written on the subject in the style of Emanuel Swedenborg is the *Guided Tour to the Afterlife* by Harriet Carter who is a lawyer interested in spiritual and esoteric matters.

Most of those authentic spiritual experiences were not achieved through a rigorous and scientific process that can be easily replicated. Instead they appear "random", as it is sometimes noticed in physical knowledge, before reason comes to organize them into a science. That science has already been developed to a certain extent under the name of spiritual science or sacred science.

---

[29]Nevill Drury, *The New Age: Searching for the Spiritual Self* (New York: Thames & Hudson, Inc, 2004).

The emphasis of religion on beliefs rather than on science has made the authentic spiritual experiences rare, misunderstood, and not often repeatable at will. Spiritual science as developed so far has it rules. It is common knowledge that for vision to take place the thing or being to see must exist and the means or elements for perception must exist as well and in good standing.

The development of the fetus in the maternal womb is central to acquiring good eyes in order to see once in this world said Steiner. The eyes do not see in the womb, but they are developed and pre-pared to see once outside.

According to spiritual scientists, the *pineal gland [third eye]* and the pituitary gland play an important role in the development of the ability to have evidences from the invisible dimension. These glands can be stimulated artificially with certain drugs such as the DMT [dimethyltryptamine] as stressed in the 7th part of the first volume of the documentary *Spiritworld* on Youtube. However, the method is not simple and can prove very dangerous.

The great vibratory capability of the third eye enables it to play the role of junction or intermediary that connects the physical sphere to the spiritual one in terms of perception. Seeker had had experiences that helped him agree that most descriptions on the third eye and pineal gland, especially in Yoga are trustworthy.

Hindus and Yogis know a great deal about the subtle body as did ancient Egyptians. Both spiritualities emphasize the third eye represented on the physical forehead between and slightly above the eyes. They also speak of the energy body, the chakras, and the kundalini [a kind of vital force]. Testimonies about the knowledge of the subtle body in African Traditional Religions are also frequent. What is additionally needed is that systematic theologians, philoso-phers, anthropologists, and spiritual researchers investigate more these African religions to put this special knowledge of theirs in written, meaningful, and useful form.

Spiritual scientists say that the subtle body like the physical one, takes some time to develop. To them, if it takes the average of 9 months for the physical body to prepare for life outside the womb, it takes the average of a life span to get the spiritual body ready for life in the afterlife after "growing" the senses and organs necessary for that life.

When he reached about 23 years, Seeker began to have experiences that confirmed to him the reality of Chakras and of a kind of energy similar to the kundalini. His first extra-physical experiences started when he was 20.

Several methods for the development of spiritual organs and senses have been described. Some are fast, others are slow. Some are safe, others are unsafe. Some are moral, others are immoral; like in physicality. When physical organs and senses are not adequate, some physical experiences can be impossible or dangerous.

The example of a blind man venturing in the jungle is very illustrative. Because the eyes are not what they should be, the individual does not have a full grasp of the reality of the jungle. It might then be impossible to perceive some beings of the jungle that can be dangerous and life threatening. This is why some schools delay the spiritual training.

Manly Hall in his *Secret Teachings of All Ages* presents the *Book of Thoth* of Hermes Mercurius Trismegistus as containing the knowledge that leads to the presence of gods. According to him, Hermes followed the secret instructions of the Temple and gradually freed his higher consciousness from the bondage of his bodily senses; and thus released, his divine nature revealed to him the mysteries of the transcendental spheres.

Hall continues affirming that *the pages of the Book of Thoth are said to be covered with strange **hieroglyphic** figures and symbols, which gave to those acquainted with their use unlimited power over the spirits of the air and subterranean divinities. When certain areas* *of the brain are stimulated by the secret process of the mysteries [which include certain drugs], the consciousness of man is extended and he is permitted to behold the Immortals and enter into the presence of the superior gods.* For Hall, it was the 'Key to Immortality.' Kabbalah is also a method used to contact gods or immortals called angels and demons.

According to legend, he continues, the *Book of Thoth* was kept in a box in the inner sanctuary of the temple. The parallel with the *Ark of the Covenant*, the *Tabernacle*, and the *Temple* of Ancient Israel is startling if one remembers that the Lord spoke to *Moses face to face as a one speaks to a friend [Exodus 33: 11].* There was but one key and this was in the possession of the 'Master of Mysteries,' the highest initiate of the Hermetic Arcanum [corresponding to Aaron and the High Priests of Israel]. He alone knew what was written in the secret book.

Manly Hall adds that no other information can be given to the world concerning the *Book of Thoth* and that the apostolic succession from the first hierophant initiated by Hermes himself remains unbroken to this day. Those who are particularly fitted to *serve* the immortals may discover this priceless document if they will search sincerely and tirelessly for it Hall assures.

For him, Hermes in his *Book of Thoth* revealed to all mankind the "One Way" [note the parallel with Jesus] and *for ages, the wise of every nation and every faith have reached immortality by the "Way" established by Hermes* in the midst of the darkness for the redemption [another word frequent in the philosophy of atonement through Jesus] of humankind.

Some can disagree that men should serve gods. When one reads the *Corpus Hermeticum* of Hermes as translated by Clement Salaman in *The Way of Hermes*, the impression that emerges is not a service to the gods.

Hermes might have taught that man should serve gods elsewhere but in the *Corpus Hermeticum*, he just mentioned the important role gods played in the creation of human beings[30] and his disciple Asclepius added that for Hermes, destiny means that *almost all humans are guided by the gods who are also in charge of the stars*[31]. He adds that irreverence to gods is the greatest offense against them[32]. Even Asclepius spoke of *respect and not service*. He also added that *there is a very few number of people who free themselves from the influence of spiritual powers and who are directly under the control of God "Himself" mainly through their **reason**.*

More importantly, Hermes declared[33]: '*Indeed, if we have to speak the truth boldly, the true man is above the gods or at least fully their equal in power.*' Also, in *The Secret Teachings of All Ages*, Manly Hall gives a piece of information that appears to oppose a service to the gods. He states[34] that in the ancient societies of Egypt, Assyria, and Babylon, *the philosophical elect abstained from getting involved in idolatrous ceremonials but thought that those practices were good for the sorts of minds existing in the mass of the population.*

Talking about the '*Initiation of the Pyramid*', Manly Hall informs that the initiate is given the power to *know his guardian spirit and the power to separate his spiritual body from the physical one.* He also reports that the initiate receives the Divine, secret, and unutterable Name of the Supreme Deity by the very knowledge of which *man and his God consciously unite.*

Hall and many other writers acknowledge the role played by the ingestion of specific substances in the process of contact of humans

---

[30]Hall, The Secret Teachings of All Age.
[31]Ibid., 77.
[32]Ibid., 76.
[33]Ibid., 51.
[34]Ibid., 157.

with the supernatural realm. They confirm that these substances in some cases have negative side effects.

Caitlìn and John Matthews described in *Walkers Between the Worlds,* like Rudolph Steiner, a meditational method to open the gate between the physical and spiritual realms and contact the gods. They insisted on the tradition of Hermes like Hall as well as on wisdom and building a personal body of light. There are several schools, institutes, or foundations devoted to spiritual research even nowadays and an internet navigation based on those words comes back very rich and orienting.

It is not reasonable that the scientists of the things physical try to verify the claims of spiritual scientists using solely the rules and laws of physical science. Their scientific nature should push them to conduct investigations according to a precise methodology developed by spiritual scientists. They would do well to remember that physical science was part of a body of knowledge pervaded by spirituality. If not, the result can only be as a dialogue between two deaf people. This is where philosophy comes in; to create a bridge or a favorable atmosphere between both kinds of science.

Philosophy as an epistemological mean to know the supernatural

The goal of philosophy is twofold: organize the information about the known in a meaningful way and investigate the possible from the known.

Possibilities are what beliefs really are and this shows the real nature of faith in its most common religious definition. Consequently faith can be proven right or wrong. When it is proven right it becomes positive knowledge or knowledge by affirmation or confirmation often simply called knowledge. When faith is proven wrong, it becomes negative knowledge or knowledge by infirming.

Normally no one should bother others because of the possession of knowledge. This is truer for those who only believe or have faith. Usually "faith" is described as 'positive thinking' or 'power of intention' as Karen Kelly put it in *The Secret of "The Secret"* or as equivalent to 'positive wish'.

There is no need to beg someone to drink in order to stay alive except out of reasoned love and even in that case there is a step where the most vibrant and unselfish love has to stop. One basic human right and duty is to ultimately make some personal and fundamental choices. Most of people have the required sense of judgment to drink when necessary because they are convinced not only of the necessity of this action, but also because of its goodness. Two mistakes of religion have been to ascribe the same philosophical value to knowledge and beliefs or faith and to harass people in order to do them good. If religion or spirituality is that good, those with an average intelligence will come to it naturally, without harassment.

There is a kind of faith not often mentioned, but known to some spiritual schools which is not belief, not even the certainty of knowledge, but is beyond them. That kind of faith is a kind of will. That will, can be seen as a kind of wish, a kind of desire; it can also be seen more exactly as a kind of *command*. Command, often used by spiritual scientists comes from the unity of wish and knowledge or from the unity of wish and belief. It is clear that the first kind of command is stronger and more efficient than the second. This is one important aspect of what Jesus meant when he spoke of moving a mountain through faith. *You know what you are doing, why you are doing it, and how you are doing it.*

It is important that a person agrees with or accept the work of a spiritual scientist. That is why there are records of evil spiritual scientists and even of the Devil requiring a pact, a belief, and an agreement for extraordinary events to take place. The fourth principle of black magic reported by Manly Hall[35] illustrates well this.

Evil beings use attacks, harassment, and refined lies in order to obtain the voluntary association of people. Sylvia Browne, the Gnostic psychic, calls that kind of malevolent individuals 'dark entities[36].' But good spiritual scientists just show some evidences of their knowledge, intention, and power. Nevertheless, a bad person always has the possibility to become good through personal efforts and help from others.

Ultimately it is good to let people freely choose their destinies even if it is risky for them. *No man or woman has the right to protect another man or woman from himself or herself by systematically inventing lies.* There are many ways to help, and if that does not work, at least, the effort would have been made in a really good way. If it was totally possible to protect people against themselves, there would be no suicide.

In fact there are many cases of suicide whether physical or spiritual that would not have been committed if people were not deceived or lied to. *A well designed educational system imparting adequate knowledge [physical and spiritual] in appropriate times is the real answer.* Avoiding in medical circumstances to give a patient bad news that can provoke a heart attack or a cerebral bleeding via high blood pressure for example is understandable.

If such a fragile person insists on knowing a shocking truth, his/her attention must skillfully be directed toward other interesting subjects and activities, games, stories, movies, and so on; so that the weak person does not get the time to come back to the dangerous subject. In case this fails, then lying, saying the contrary of what is,

---

[35]Hall, *TheSecrets Teachings of All Ages*, 318.
[36]Sylvia Browne and Lindsay Harrison, *Phenomenon: Everything You Need to Know About the Paranormal* (New York: Dutton, 2005), 87-90.

just not to kill the person, can be allowed and the truth restored when the health becomes better.

People should not cease this opportunity to appoint themselves doctors and declare other people able or unable to bear a truth. The doctors in question are those who truly know how to heal, know the rules of the profession, and can scientifically diagnose such weakness of the body and/or of the mind.

The term 'doctor' here does not designate exclusively someone trained in the allopathic medicine developed in the West and exported but any professional able to heal without harming no matter the region of origin, whether trained in a university or not, and able to follow a precise rational methodology [allopathic, homeopathic, traditional, etc...] to obtain multiple and replicable healings. Every doctor not officially trained has however the duty to make his/her methods public and prove their efficiency in front of an ad hoc health comity and society in general.

Whether the patient suspects something or not despite the convincing performance of the "liar", the damage cannot be as if he/she knows the real truth. A part from such a medical reason, lying in any situation should not be accepted. The contrary is at best a failure of the educational system which must quickly be corrected and at worst institutionalized evil.

In case there really is a lack of knowledge on a subject, that deficiency must be acknowledged without shame and the field opened for investigation. This recognition will draw the attention of more minds and enable answers to be found as quickly as possible by talented persons. If the problem is hidden, the talented mind might not be aware of the problem and the solution would take time to appear as well. This can be the cause of useless suffering for many.

If there is a student who often asks questions which are only answered at levels of education ahead of him/her, he/she should be introduced to the benefits of patience and the laws of digestion and assimilation of information or knowledge. At the same time, the student should enter a program of education adapted to the specific needs expressed as in situations when some students are permitted to skip levels of education or undergo specific trainings.

It is not good to keep a relationship with someone through lies. This is neither authentic nor lasting. When people profoundly disagree, they should try to solve the problem through individual and/or collective reason or wisdom [the appropriate use of love is part of reason or wisdom]. If there is not enough reason to end the difference, there should be enough to categorize the issue as vital for common life or not.

When a disagreement is about a vital subject that the available reason or wisdom cannot immediately end, people should separate and seek likeminded. Violence should never be an option. This explains the joy the God of the Old Testament receives in relationship with humans who are "His" image [Genesis 1:31], why Adam was happy to see Eve [Genesis 2: 23] and why that God was obliged to separate temporarily from Adam and Eve in Genesis 3: 24.

This is the kind of attitude advocated by Fritz Perls, a famous psychiatrist and psychotherapist of the 20th century when he said: '*You do your thing and I do mine*'. Until the whole truth is established, the unity of the whole world should not be expected and even if the whole truth is established the difficulties to practice it must be met.

After that kind of high education, people will come to see the real dimension of each other and that of the universe and will build authentic and proper relationships. Before that, '*you do your thing*', '*with those like you if you want*', '*provided it harms no one.*' This is where law and justice come in. When education gets better, law and justice get better and vice versa. When education gets better both in theory and practice, less harm is caused and less justice is needed until the perfect stage of education and knowledge is reached. This is the idea expressed in Jeremiah 31: 33 and Hebrew 8: 10.

In a theology class that Seeker attended one day, a lady spoke of the fact that God uses wise people to create things and make life easy for human beings both physically and spiritually. This declaration is true, but the guides should also not use that knowledge to dominate, and enslave others.

In the work of evil, more destruction of the individual can happen if his or her agreement is given because, it allows reaching the very core of his/her being: the soul or the psyche. Evil beings work freely and easily in those who have given them their faith or trust, will, and agreement, the same observation is valid for God and good intelligent beings whether visible or invisible.

That is one reason why Jesus told people that their faith has saved them. This is a manifestation of free will. Since a person needs to trust certain people in social life, it is better that this trust be placed in *really* good people. Again as affirmed in many religious scriptures, for example 2 Peter 3: 9, an evil person can work on him/herself to and become good.

A doubtful person is a battle ground between evil forces and good forces. Each camp tries to win him/her to its side. But even physically, spiritually, or mentally enslaved or dependent people can switch side at any time especially when they are given a solid opportunity.

If religious people and spiritualists make their discipline attractive enough, it is possible that the most skeptical and atheistic minds come to their school and say: '*Can you teach me more so I can teach others, maybe even better than you do?*'

Graham Hancock and Michael Cremo, two eminent physical scientists, after they had immersed themselves for a while in the teachings of some ancient civilizations came to the conclusion that there is a dimension beyond the physical one[37]. Michael Cremo even came to believe in God.

One cannot end the description of the place of philosophy in the quest of the knowledge on divinities without remembering that all the great philosophical minds of Greek antiquity acknowledged God and/or gods.

The role of philosophy is not to directly show deities but to point toward them; the final job is the responsibility of spiritual science.

This chapter has offered some general views on the possibilities of knowledge of the divine. The next chapters will tackle the major theological issues of religion, spirituality, and secular philosophy making an extensive use of the Bible as well as other scriptures and reason.

---

[37]http://www.youtube.com/watch?v=o6Za8fMjo8U and http://www.youtube.com/watch?v=_zwec9sdQUo&feature=PlayList&p=E735 768B8DB1C231&playnext_from=PL&playnext=2&index=42 (accessed April 4, 2010).

Chapter 11

Scriptural and logical evidences that Jesus did not have a pre-existent life as an angel, and how his divinity should be understood

J ESUS is without doubt one of the most popular persons, if not the most popular in human history. That the western calendar is centered on him is significant. While doing his research, a seeker might come across a reading or two that deny the existence of Jesus. At the opposite, an overwhelming mass of historical data including from non-religious sources testify that Jesus was a real person who lived on earth. This question is often discussed in scholarship, mainly theological scholarship under the topic of *The Historical Jesus*.

Researchers such as Manly Hall [20th century], Jordan Maxwell [20th-21st centuries], and others explain with proofs that the gospels are astrotheology in disguise. Concerning its content, astrotheology can be traced back to the Mesopotamian civilization and several other ancient religions and spiritualities. Concerning the form, the word 'astrotheology' started appearing in spiritual writings from the 18th century according to Wikipedia.

Hall, Maxwell, and others have for example replaced the term 'son' in the gospels by 'sun' and have obtained a message with an astrological meaning. To them, Jesus represents the sun and his disciples the twelve signs of the zodiac with Judas symbolizing the sign of Scorpio.

They declared that the next great work of God according Jesus will occur in the Age of the sign of Aquarius, around 2100 years after the beginning of the Age of Pisces during which the teachings of Jesus prevailed. To them, the fact that Jesus told his disciples in Mark 14:3/Luke 22: 10 to follow the water bearer is his indication that Aquarius [the sign of the water bearer] will be the next Age for a new divine providence. Indeed Aquarius is the next sign that the sun enters after that of Pisces according to the *precession of the equinoxes* and Pisces is acknowledged by many as a symbol of Jesus. So, for Hall, Maxwell, and others, Jesus is not just the sun, but the sun in Pisces.

Even when his historicity is acknowledged, the accounts about Jesus' life vary and sometimes contradict one another. Apocryphal literature and institutions such as the *Jesus Seminar* even challenge some of the views of Jesus presented in the New Testament.

Whether Jesus has truly existed, whether he has been invented to convey astrological instruction, or whether he was a real person who lived a life that was astrologically meaningful, the fact remains that several religious people have understood the New Testament as describing events that really took place and therefore ascribe an important value to the subjects of the pre-existence and divinity of Jesus in their daily lives and in their plans for the future.

The question of the pre-existence of Jesus is a theological, a philosophical, and a scriptural one. That of his divinity is another fundamental question that mankind must finally solve. Indeed it has been at the center of the opposition between many Christians and many Muslims. The former consider him as divine even though the modality of this divinity varies while to the latter, he is a prophet of God.

For clarity purposes, the issue of the pre-existence of Jesus will be discussed here while that of his divinity will be one of the objects of chapter 16.

Formulation of the thesis of the pre-existent Jesus

There are theologies in which Jesus existed as a divine being before his birth on earth. In many of those theologies he is said to be the archangel Michael. Several biblical passages and arguments are brought forth to support that declaration. One of these argumentations has been organized the following way:

1.   From the heavens, God transferred the life of his powerful spiritual son into the bosom of Marie [Galatians 4:4]. Before his human birth, he had a spiritual body invisible to man [John 4 :24] and used to occupy a position that he often talked about [John 17 :5, 8 :23, 6 :62, 8 :58, 3 :13, and 6 :51].

2.   Before his coming on earth, his name was 'The Word.' That title indicates that he used to serve in heavens as God's spokesperson.

3.   He is called the first born of God and His unique son [John 1:14, John 3:16, Hebrews 1:6]. This means that he was created before all the other spiritual sons of God and that he is the only son directly created by God.

4.   According to the Bible, this first born son cooperated with God to create all the other things [Colossians 1:15-16]. Hence when God says: *'Let us create man in our image,'* he was talking to that son

[Genesis 1:26] who was living with Him since an unknown number of years [Proverbs 8: 22, John 1:3].

What is the Bible? What is its origin, its responsibility in theological polemic, and what is its real dimension?

Before showing what is wrong with the theory of the pre-existing Jesus and before offering an alternative, it is important to establish some facts about the Bible. This presentation could have found a good place in the chapter on epistemology and the knowledge of divinities especially in its first section that deals with religion.

A presentation on the Bible is more appropriate here because it has a direct application, the determination of the truth about a particular aspect of the nature of Jesus, which has been controversial over centuries. Talking about the definition and the origin of the Bible would help understand why various people based on it have been disagreeing with each other for a very long time with terrible consequences for human society.

In *The Lost Symbol*, especially in its last chapters, Dan Brown presents the Bible as a great and important book that people should read. He is absolutely right. However, other scriptures are also important as demonstrated and should be read for a broad spiritual education. Moreover, seekers should keep in mind that this great book can have shortcomings. The following lines will present some of them.

The free dictionary gives five definitions of the Bible which are all interesting for this section and are presented as followed:

1.

a.   The sacred book of Christianity, a collection of ancient writings including the books of both the Old Testament and the New Testament

b.   The Hebrew Scriptures, the sacred book of Judaism

c.   A particular copy of the Bible

d.   A book or a collection of writings constituting the sacred text of a religion

2.   Any book considered as authoritative in its field

The reason that probably explains the definition 1-a is that the very term 'Bible' is famous because of the Christian religion. In this context it is a collection of books organized into the Old Testament [OT] and the New Testament [NT]. The OT is the name given to the Hebrew Bible or Hebrew Scriptures by Christians and this is what the second definition tries to acknowledge by speaking of the Hebrew Bible.

This Hebrew meaning could have been the first to be given if the editors of the free dictionary have first considered the ages of the two kinds of Bible: the Christian one and the Hebrew one.

The Hebrew Bible speaks of events from a distant past to those of a period situated a few centuries before the era that began with Jesus as a marker. A thing important to know is that some of the writings of the Hebrew Bible or OT were the records of contemporary events like the *history* of the kings of Israel at the same time when others biblical records are writings concerning remote periods long gone before the birth of the writer.

For example, many believe that the Book of Genesis was written by Moses. But that book narrates events about Adam and Eve which occurred thousands of years before Moses and its last descriptions are about a period that was 400 years before him. Some call this type of records *revelations about the past* made by God to Moses. Others think that Moses also copied from other documents. Still others hold the idea that several parts in Genesis could not have been written by Moses.

Finally, there are those who think that the value of the Hebrew Bible for the development of humans is so important that it is ok if the origin or the author of each book cannot be formally established. Since the research behind this volume has not been able to solve the authorship problem and since the focus is to speak of proven facts or at least logical and reasonable ones, it appears wise to engage in theological analysis based on the OT, being aware of this limitation.

A part from history and information about the past, the Hebrew Bible contains other kinds of writings. There are *revelationsabout possible futuresand exhortations* toward various individuals and people to behave well in order to make those futures as good as possible; this is the *prophetic message.* There are also the gathering of thoughts about the events of life and their meaning; this is the *wisdom or philosophy* that appears in books such as the Ecclesiastes, Proverbs, and Job.

At last, there are parts of the Bible which are records of religious or spiritual *beliefs and practices.* Those practices and beliefs include worship, rituals, commandments, prayers, songs like those of the Psalms etc...

Christians adopted the Hebrew Bible because they believed it explains everything God has done before Jesus and because they though it explains many passages of the NT. Hence, they called the Hebrew Bible the OT and make it simply the Bible by adding the NT.

The NT is also subject to the same handicaps that the OT is subjected to. For instance things that Jesus has said and done were put in writing form only several decades after the event of the crucifixion. Several of those records were made by people who were not disciples of Jesus during the period they covered. Mark, Luke, and Paul were among them.

At the time of the NT, the OT already existed after centuries of gathering of books of spiritual or religious importance. The books that will later be part of the NT happened to also have multiple and different versions of some same stories.

The way Jesus met his first disciples is different when one considers the Gospel of Matthew and the Gospel of John. Concerning the Eucharist, it was Paul and Luke who were not even participants of the Last Supper who told that Jesus asked the Eucharist to be celebrated in remembrance of him [Luke 22: 19, 1 Corinthians 11: 24]. Paul and Luke were companions as shown in several passages of the book of Acts.

Matthew and Mark did not make such a mention while John does not even speak about the sharing of the bread and the wine. But he does speak a lot of Jesus as the bread that came from heaven, whose body must be eaten, and whose blood must be drunk [John 6: 53]. Peter Ouspensky has written in *In Search of the Miraculous* that according to George Gurdjieff, it was the actual blood and flesh of Jesus which was drunk and eaten in small quantities by all the participants of the Last Supper in a magical ceremony in order to keep an astral or psychic connection and a relationship with him after his death[38]. Gurdjieff, at a time of his life called himself an esoteric Christian.

A third problem the NT has is the presentation of inaccurate theological statements and doctrines. Some of them are from Paul. Those mistakes can be dealt with in detail in another work.

Though everything that Paul said is not wrong, he made several declarations which have been very influential but also untrue after deep analysis. An illustration dwells in 1 Corinthians 15: 47-49 where

---

[38]Peter D.Ouspensky, *In Search of the Miraculous: Fragments of an Unknown Teaching* (New York: Harcourt, Brance & World, 1949).

he states that Adam did not have a spiritual body but an animal one in contrary to Jesus who had acquired a spiritual body.

According to the definition of 'spirit,' one cannot imagine that Adam did not have a spirit. Additionally, the breath of life that God breathed into his nostrils [Genesis 2: 7] was spirit. 'Breath' and 'spirit' are often synonymous terms as acknowledged by the passage of the introduction the Dalai Lama to the *Tibetan Book of the Dead* quoted earlier in the section on Buddhist deities and also in the poem *'Les Morts ne sont pas Morts' ['The Dead are not Dead]* of Birago Diop]. Ecclesiastes 12: 7 confirms that before Jesus and his work and before Paul, some people were aware of a spirit in a human being that returns to God after death. The nature of that spirit will be ana-lyzed in the following chapter as well as in the next volume.

Though the Bible is authoritative according to the fifth definition, it also presents another handicap which is the existence of several different versions due to various translations especially in English. The reason behind those variations is sometimes errors in the copy-ing process, but more and more, differences in versions are the results of differences in the understandings of the various translators and/ or editors.

That is why the third definition speaks of the Bible as one of the copies of a collection of spiritual texts. 'Version' is another word for 'copy' which better introduces the part of human subjectivity involved in the making of this important document. Some think that the Bible has been dictated to the writers. Others prefer to speak of inspiration, and still others of revelation or vision.

Lastly, a few words should be said about how the Bible was finally constituted. **The compilation of the first Bible was the work of the Gnostic Marcion** [85-160 C.E.] who has been accepted for a long time as a Christian before his excommunication. Marcion was finan-cially rich, bishop and son of bishop according to some, and had had the means to collect sacred texts.

In his endeavor, *he rejected the Old Testament on the ground that its God is cruel and different from the God revealed by Jesus*. Fond of Paul, he only included his letters [the first Christian writings] and the Gospel of Luke in his Bible. This is understandable because as Hyam Maccoby and Seeker's professor of New Testament stated, the message of Paul has Gnostic connotations.

Disagreeing with Marcion's views, the other authorities of the Early Church gradually elaborated their own official version of the Bible including in it more books than Marcion. Nevertheless, they rejected books known today as the apocrypha. Recently, many of those books have become better known and many scholars have been able to perceive wisdom in some parts of them.

The goal of this section is not to affirm that God has not "spoken" to people. The purpose is to draw attention on the biases involved [not necessarily due to bad intention] in the writing of the Bible which are susceptible to affect the very nature and the impact of a divine message. *With this acquired vigilance, seekers would approach the Bible and any other spiritual document being ready to receive the divine message while doubting suspicious passages and getting rid of them.*

This is to say that for the sake of the manifestation of the truth, all versions should be considered and analyzed and none of them should claim the monopole of divine revelation. Paul himself recommended people to use their common sense [2 Thessalonians 2:2/ French version Louis Segond]. In the 21st Century King James Version, readers are advised not to be shaken in the mind. Paul also asks in 1 Thessalonians 5: 19 [New American Standard Version, English Standard Version, 21st Century King James Version, Louis Segond] not to quench the spirit.

The spirit that should not be quenched here is not the Holy Spirit but the spirit of a human being. The proof is that two verses later, *Paul adds that one should test or examine everything that is said holding what is good. In other words Paul encouraged people to use their critical mind.* Also, today's seekers appear more equipped than the seekers of old times such as the people of Berea [Acts 17:10-11] maybe because they have more information and the advantage of analyzing the Christian and general history for the past 2000 years.

At the light of this analysis, the doctrine of the pre-existence of Jesus will be considered without yielding absolute authority to any *version* of the Bible whatsoever, but appealing to scripture with the common sense and the critical and reasonable mind.

Seeker knows that sometime *believers* can find themselves prisoners of words, or entire religious philosophies. The main reason is that, despite their internal doubts, people tend to stick to their belief systems because something good in them has originally attracted them and they do not know what else to do if they abandon those ideas.

As religious people, they are deeply aware that something is wrong with the world they live in and that the solution cannot come from mere physical science. They find themselves obliged to belong to a spiritual or religious community to face the horrors of life and make not only this world a better place but offer a possibility of eternal liberation to those who suffer.

After a time of practice of their systems of thoughts, the believers crystallize their psychology and, as said in the introductory chapter, it becomes very hard for them to change. Fortunately for some, they crystallize themselves including in their personal thoughts, the awareness of things they could disagree with, or keep an open mind as an element of their crystallization. Those are the seekers who first break the emotional attachment to their faith of origin to give way to reason or at least to a superior reason.

In several cases, people cannot imagine a future outside their religion and give up on many issues hoping they will be fixed in due time or in the afterlife. Sometimes certain people are so attached to a faith that questioning a core doctrine will simply jeopardize their lives even on the economic plane. Friends, families, careers, and so on are at stake. Those elements are so essential for life that few dare to allow themselves to think reasonably from the beginning to the end by fear of losing them.

Seeker knows how comfortable it could be not to have to fight that kind of fight. What seekers of all degrees, advanced or beginners should understand is that they should first obtain complete religious, spiritual, and philosophical information. Then, they can choose whatever path they want. The necessity of a perfect book or knowledge for guidance in life makes many believe that such book already exists under the form of the Bible. But the truth is that humanity is still searching.

Why is the pre-existence of Jesus an incorrect theory?

Galatians 4:4 does not say that God has transferred the life of His powerful spiritual son into the womb of Mary but that God *sent* His son, which is very different. Before He *sent* Jesus, God has *sent* prophets like Elijah [Malachi 4: 5]. None of them has been transferred from heavens into the womb of a woman but all were born like every human being. Jesus was sent the same way, as he himself states [Matthew 21:34-37].

If Galatians 4: 4 does not plead in favor of the thesis of the pre-existence of Jesus, other verses such as John 17:5, John 6 :62, John 8: 58, John 3: 13, John 8: 23, and John 6: 51 do. The three first ones *can* authorize affirming that Jesus had had a pre-existent life. The last three add that this existence was in heaven. Let's start the analysis with the second group of verses.

John 3:13 'No one has ever gone into heaven except the one who came from heaven, the Son of Man who is in heaven.'

Some Bibles omit the last part 'who is in heaven.' This changes the analysis that one could make based on the verse. Indeed this last part can enable a conclusion in favor of the pre-existence of Jesus or not according to its absence or its presence. The reading of several Bible versions in English and in French shows that some maintain the last part while others do not. Among the translators who omit the last part, some give the precision that there are ancient manuscripts which have that part. The reason of the difference in the translations of this verse dwells in the fact that the original text of the New Testament has been lost and in reconstitution of the testament from the citations and commentaries written by some authors based on the original texts. The problem is that the last part of the verse figures in some citations and commentaries and not in others and modern translators inherited it according to the manuscripts they used. However, all hope to solve this problem is not lost because the verse expresses an idea which is in the general framework of the New Testament. If the spiritual researcher or the philosopher succeeds in finding other verses of the New Testament in the line of John 3: 13 with its last part, this will constitute the proof that that part should indeed be maintained and therefore that the pre-existence of Jesus is an incorrect theory. Additionally, the first part of the verse alone is sufficient to reach a conclusion after analysis. These tasks have been conducted by seeker; which enable him first to analyze the verse with the last part showing how that part is against the pre-existence theory, second to show how the first part guides in the same direction, and third, demonstrate how this understanding harmonizes with others biblical passages while the pre-existence is not and is against common sense or logic.

The word 'heaven' has several definitions. For the current needs, three of them will be called upon.

a.   Visible space above our heads

b.   Dwelling place of the divine, of the souls of the righteous after their death

c.   God, divine power

These kinds of heaven can also respectively be called firmament, spiritual world, and divinity [goodness, purity, love, power, justice, and so on].

What kind of heaven is John 3:13 talking about? Since the matter being discussed is of spiritual nature, the first meaning cannot be considered. Let's analyze the verse based on meaning b. The deduction is that Jesus has descended from the positive spiritual world to incarnate in the bosom of Marie and that while he lived on earth he still lived in heaven from where he came. It is this meaning that corroborates the pre-existing Jesus.

According to scripture, angels visit earth from heaven and go back once they accomplish their missions. When they protect people, they are often invisible. They show up sometimes on earth but do not have residence on earth.

No angel has ever incarnated in the womb of a woman. When people on earth die, they leave the earth for the spiritual world. Some, while still on earth have had like Paul [2 Corinthians 12: 2-4] the opportunity to visit heaven and come back. No one ever lived in both worlds simultaneously as this verse would imply if meaning b is chosen for the term 'heaven'. Those who have a physical body live on earth [body and spirit], take care of earthly businesses but can occasionally have contact with the spiritual world and beings. Jesus lived the same way.

The transfiguration was one of the times he directly contacted the spirit world. Most of the time he took care earthly matters in his ministry. He had double sight and could perform miracles, but Moses and others did too, and they did not come as transferred angels.

Hence, the argument that the body of Jesus was living on earth while his spirit lived in both heaven and earth simultaneously is not valid.

In the beginning of the verse being analyzed, Jesus affirms that no one has ever gone to heaven. If heaven is the spirit world, the declaration will not be true because there are several cases in which people went to the spirit world before the time of Jesus. The prophet Elijah is an example [2 Kings 2: 11]. The transfiguration of Jesus [Luke 9: 28-36] which shows Elijah and Moses discussing with him is a confirmation that Elijah had really been in the spiritual world.

The presence of Moses who is known to have died [Deuteronomy 34: 5] testifies that the spirit world is a place where people go at their death. This means that Elijah too simply died and that his death was depicted in 2 Kings 2 in a symbolic way. The chariots of the Hindu gods can help understand the meaning of the chariot which took Elijah into heaven. In the Fon culture of Benin, the paraphrase 'The king went to Allada' is often used to speak of the death of that king. Allada is a well-known geographical place in the country.

All these arguments demonstrate that meaning b for 'heaven' in John 3: 13 also cannot be accepted.

When the verse is red with the third meaning, there is nothing il-logic but only symbolism as frequently employed by Jesus. The verse then signifies that Jesus is of divine nature. This does not make him a pre-existing angel especially when meaning b has been rejected. Jesus said in one occasion at least that he is one with God; here he is repeating the same message in a different way.

The correct meaning of John 3: 13 is: '*No one has ever been divine except the one who came from the divine, the Son of Man who lives a divine life.*' The last part is the most important emphasizing the high spiritual achievement of Jesus.

John 8:23But he continued, 'You are from below; I am from above. You are of this world; I am not of this world.'

When Jesus uses the term 'world' or 'worldly', he means 'profane', 'not sacred', and 'not divine'. He uses 'world' or 'below' in opposition to 'heaven' or 'above' as did Hermes when he said: '*I am thankful to God for putting even a taste of the knowledge of the Supreme Good into my nous because this Good cannot exist in the world*[39].'

Consequently, John 8: 23 is just confirming John 3: 13 just analyzed.

Jesus also declared that his disciples were not of this world as he is not [John 17: 14]. This does not mean that the disciples were also incarnated angels but that they belonged with Jesus to a different spiritual and ideological sphere.

John 6:51 'I am the living bread that came down from heaven. If anyone eats of this bread, he will live forever. This bread is my flesh, which I will give for the life of the world.'

To solve this mystery, it is good to study most of the 6th chapter of the Gospel of John and add John 4: 34. Indeed Jesus begins the talk on the bread from the 32nd verse of John 6 and ends in verse 63. In verses 35 and 40, he shows that to eat of the bread of life is to come to him and follow him.

This is how his flesh is eaten and how his blood is drunk. In verse 63, Jesus emphasizes that his word is spirit and life. If both the word and the bread are life givers, then there is a possibility that the bread mentioned in John 6: 51 is the word. It becomes more than a possibility when one knows that one follows Jesus [eats his flesh and drink his blood] by listening to and following his voice or word [John 5: 24-25].

---

[39]Clement Salaman, and Hermes. *The Way of Hermes: Translations of The Corpus Hermeticum and the Definitions of Hermes Trismegistus to Asclepius* (Rochester, VT: Inner Traditions, 2000), 38.

Another indication that bread is the word can be found in John 4: 34. Jesus states there that his food is to accomplish the will of God. However the will of God is expressed in his Word, an attribute of divinity. So, the word is food.

Finally Matthew 4: 4 and Deuteronomy 8: 3 teach that the word is the spiritual bread sent from heaven and different from ordinary bread. In John 6: 51 Jesus also uses the term 'world' as 'lifeless', 'not divine'.

This explanation saves from believing in cannibalism as a way of salvation no matter how sacred the flesh in question is. Therefore, John 6:51 means that Jesus represents the divine word that gives life to the profane and lifeless world.

The second group of verses that can be understood as in favor of the pre-existence of Jesus: John 6:62, John 17:5 and John 8:58

John 6: 62 '*What if you see the Son of Man ascend to where he was before!*'

John 17: 5 '*And now, Father, glorify me in your presence with the glory I had with you before the world began.*'

John 8: 58 '*I tell you the truth,*' Jesus answered, '*before Abraham was born, I am!*'

The following verses are of the same order: *John 1:1-17, 1 Colossians1:15-18, Proverbs 8: 22, Psalms 33:6, Hebrews 1: 13.*

In Hebrews 1: 6, Jesus is said to be the first born of God. But in Colossians1: 15 it is added that he is the **first born of all the <u>creation</u>**. *Therefore, he is a creature of God too* as advocated by Arius, the ancient Egyptian presbyter of Alexandria [256 C.E.-336 C.E.]. Romans 8: 29 and Hebrews 1: 9 state that Jesus is the first born among several brothers while Philippians 2: 5-9 and Hebrews 5: 5-7 tell that it is because of the quality of his life on earth that God anointed him. He has become the author of salvation having been perfected [Hebrews 5: 9-10]. He could thus be called God [Hebrews1: 8-9], superior to angels [Hebrews1: 4], and could seat at the right of God [Mark 16:19].

If Jesus really existed before the beginning of creation and if everything has been made by him and for him, he would have been superior to angels from the start and would not wait incarnation for that to happen. That the archangel Michael is superior to his fellow angels cannot serve as argument here because the book of Hebrews and other passages of the New Testament clearly speak of the primary role of humans and Jesus regarding the elimination of sin.

In 2 Chronicles 18, King Solomon acknowledges that the entire heavens cannot contain God. As it will be shown in the chapter on anthropomorphic divinities, the true Supreme God has no right and no left in the literal sense. A correct understanding of the 'Old of the days' sitting on his throne will be given then.

God is beyond space and time. Therefore Jesus could not have sat literally at his right. Being at the right simply means being number 2; after God. This is a symbolical way of saying the same thing as John 3: 13. Jesus is then able to share the glory of God. Being the true heir of God, everything that has been God's becomes his.

That it is God Himself who created the world and not a probable son is also evident in Ephesians 3: 9, Jeremiah 51: 15 and Hebrews 2: 10-11. He created alone [Isaiah 44: 24], meaning that eventual craftsmen are not the true creators. How then can it be understood that God created everything by Jesus as stated in John 1:3 and Colossians 1:16?

Genesis 1 tells that God created by *saying*. In other words, he created using his Word [an attribute, trait or feature, not a person].The creation by the Word is confirmed in Hebrews 11:3 and Psalms 33:6. Because Jesus represents the Word of God, the bread from heaven as said, one can say and writes that everything made by the Word of God is made by him. However, Jesus is not literally the Word of God. That Word is the expression of the Divine Mind under the form of thoughts or words. That Word is Reason as Manly Hall presents it. It is good to give more explanation about the Reason or Law or Logos of God.

Proverbs 8: 7-8 shows in context that the Wisdom or Intelligence of God is expressed through His Word. Wisdom, Intelligence, Science, Thinking, and Justice are tightly linked [Proverbs: 8:10, 12, 18, 27, 28, 29, 30, 31, and 32]. To say that God created by His Word is the same as to say He created by His Wisdom. Proverbs 8: 22 informs that Wisdom was at the beginning with God before anything else He created and in Proverbs 3: 19 it is written that by wisdom God founded the earth.

Word and Wisdom can be at the beginning with God only by being part of God, as His attributes. Hence, one does not need to explain that there were three persons in one God at the beginning and that God the Father was talking another God or the two others Gods In Genesis 1: 26.

An undeniable link with John 1:1 has been established. Since word expresses wisdom, everything appears clear. Wisdom, under-standing, knowledge, and science were all involved in the creation act of God [Proverbs 3: 19-20].

The following diagram illustrates how Wisdom and Word are attributes of God and are not angels or members of a Triune God. *Even though a particular angel can embody a particular attribute of God, that angel is not that attribute.* God is said to have given great wisdom to an angel that later rebelled and fell [Ezekiel 28]. Even though that angel symbolized the Wisdom of God, his wisdom is different from the Divine Wisdom itself. It is also certain that this fallen angel is not Jesus or Michael.

```
                          Wisdom

          Intelligence        Word

God  ──────────▶Thinking──────────▶ Logos ──────────▶Created being

          Reason              Science
```

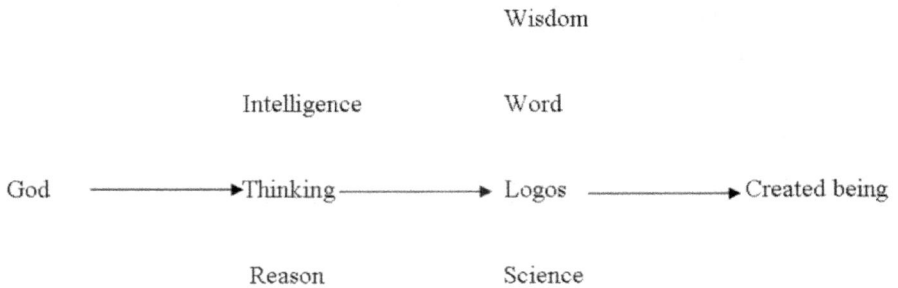

In one sentence it can be said that God speaks according to his wisdom after reasoning to create. *Every human being also has a wisdom that is expressed through a word with the use of reason or intelligence.* **The intelligences, wisdoms, words, knowledge, and philosophies of some human beings are better than those of others at least temporarily.**

The wisdom, reason, knowledge, philosophy, and word of Jesus were and are still better than those of many humans but they remain lower than those of God. That is why he himself confessed not knowing like the angels the time of his return on earth [Matthew 24: 36, Mark 13: 32]. That is why he thought better to accomplish the will of God than his own [John 4: 34]. His earthly life long, Jesus tried to distinguish the Word of God from his own as shown in his prayer n the garden of Gethsemane.

So, there is more than enough reason to say that Jesus was compared to the Word of God because his own word was close to that Word, at least in eyes of the writers of the New Testament.

Hebrews 1:2 stresses that it is through the channel of inheritance that in a way everything has been created by and for Jesus. This can be said about any human being who follows God at least as much as Jesus. The same way, Jesus had a glory with God before the world began and was [symbolically] before Abraham.

A way to understand why Jesus was before Abraham is by considering Jeremiah 31: 9 which states that the Lord is Israel's father and Ephraim is his first born.

According the story of Genesis, Ephraim was the second son of Joseph who was himself the eleventh son of Jacob. But Jacob, also called Israel, raised Ephraim not only as his own son and tribe in Israel, but as the first in importance though he predicted that the line of Judah his fourth son would play the major political role and though the Tribe of Levi was later ascribed priesthood functions.

The phrase of Jesus *'Before Abraham was, I am'* is also correct from another angle of analysis. God, the Original Being, is 'I am' according to Exodus 3: 14. Therefore 'I am' is before Abraham.

Humans were made to manage nature [Genesis 1: 26-28], for a time inferior to angels [Psalm 8:5], but destined to grow and surpass them as the *man* Jesus did [Hebrews 2: 5-8]. Man also has the authority to judge angels [1 Corinthians 6:3]. According to Hebrews 2: 5, God has not put the world under the dominion of angels but man.

The teaching of Sylvia Browne about a council of advanced humans guarded by the top angels also corroborates the preeminence of mankind. It is logical that mankind be preeminent having both the possibility to experience eternal spiritual life like angels and physical life like animals. As Browne says contradicting Swedenborg, humans and angels are from two different species. They are indeed two different spiritual species as there are various animal species. Here are serious additional proofs that Jesus was not an incarnated angel and not the archangel Michael but there remain several other scriptural proofs that can be produced.

The Qur'an speaks of man [Adam] as the superintendent of God that all angels shall revere [Qur'an 17: 61]. All angels revered him except Iblis. This idea is absent from the Book of Genesis and seems to also be absent from the entire Bible. However, in Hebrews 1: 6, this idea finds confirmation. The verse says that God introduced his firstborn again into the world. The firstborn in question that angels should revere here is Jesus.

The word 'again' suggests that a firstborn has been previously introduced. This previous firstborn could have been Jesus, but with all the proofs being given, it makes more sense that the first firstborn is Adam. If Jesus was a pre-existent being, who made everything, he could not have been introduced into the world including angels even once; it is the world that would have been introduced to him. These explanations are also the base for 1 Peter 1: 20, John 3: 3 and John 3: 34. Here appears another argument against the Christian concept of Trinity.

Jesus worked hard trying to embody the Word, the Will, and the Teachings of God. Adam according to the Qur'an [2: 30-34] proved worthy to receive respect and honor from angels because he was able to produce the names of things taught him by God. Since Sikhism has said that the Teachings of God can be considered his Names, it appears that *Adam achieved an advanced knowledge of the things divine and that his fall was from a high position. Every human being has the potency to achieve the same level as Adam or Jesus and even go beyond as Jesus clearly stated [John 14: 12].*

If Jesus is first born, then he was before Abraham; meaning he had reached a level of mastery or divinity higher than the one achieved by Abraham.

Since Jesus does not have a pre-existing life, to whom was God talking to in Genesis 1: 26? Many times in Genesis it is clear that the Angel of the Lord represented Him and appeared to some people. But a careful reading proves that *even when God is directly mentioned, it is always an angel-like being, or to put it simply an angel who is appearing, speaking, walking, or acting.* Hence the use of the plural like in *Genesis 1: 26* is coherent: *an angel representing the Supreme God was speaking to other angels.*

This point will receive further attention in the chapter on the anthropomorphic God. There are several scriptural, logical, and experiential proofs that there is a God beyond angels, the Most High, Incomparable that will be discussed in chapters 12, 13, 14, and 15. It suffices here to present *Job 38: 7* as the proof that everything angels have done during the process of creation was under the direct authority of the God.

Angels were His assistants in various ways. And since *they owe God their very existence [Nehemiah 9: 6, Psalms 148: 2-5, Ezekiel 28: 13]*, God remains in charge no matter the angle [*angel*] from which the issue is tackled. That the *acting Gods* of the Old Testament were in fact angels may explain some mistakes of religions and spiritual schools. *Angels are not demons, but they can make mistakes trying to follow the will of God.*

Jews in the 1st century were amazed with the knowledge of Jesus who did not study according to them [John 7:15]. But Jesus replied that his doctrine was from God [who taught him like Adam]. How was he taught then by God? Some people may be satisfied with the Holy Spirit explanation [John13:10].

Others may insist that he has studied with masters of Egyptian Mysteries, still others that he managed to receive the teachings of Hinduism in India, or that he studied with John the Baptist. The truth is probably in between; that he studied but was unique because of the particularity of the spirit he received from God at the conception, at the baptism, and many other circumstances. The possibility of angelic revelation to Jesus like to the prophet Daniel should also be considered. It is possible that other men would have used the same spirit differently.

Finally Jesus is not the archangel Michael for the additional scriptural or religious reason that death entered the world though one *man* [Adam] and was supposed to be removed through one *man,* Jesus [1 Corinthians 21, 1Timothy 2 :5, Romans 5 :19]. If Jesus was an angel incarnated, this would signifies that humans like Adam could not do the job and that God, the Supreme Being, in "His" Infinite Wisdom created them by error. *Every High Priest is taken* **from among men** *and appointed for men in things pertaining to God [Hebrews 5: 1].*Jesus was High Priest [verses 5 and 6].So he was taken from among men. He was a man.

What this chapter has discussed is whether an angel became a human or not; not that men at death become angels-like or angels as in the accounts of Swedenborg.

Chapter 12

Why the Holy Spirit of the Bible is not a person and why the concept of Trinity makes sense philosophically but not theologically

THE Holy Spirit is a religious and spiritual notion. However, this discussion should interest agnostics and atheists as well at least because the explanations will be offered in terms they are more familiar with.

The schools of spiritual thought can be classified into two general categories according to their views on the Holy Spirit. There are those to whom the Holy Spirit is a person and others to whom the Holy Spirit is a divine energy or force. Before introducing these two main concepts, certain terms frequent in the theological, psychological, and philosophical jargons require explanation. If that definition of terms is not properly made, confusion will cloud the knowledge on the topic of the Holy Spirit.

Some prerequisites: explanations about spirit, soul, mind, nous, consciousness, unconsciousness, superconsciousness, subconsciousness, preconsciousness, memory, dream, goodness, evil, intuition, inspiration, insight, energy, matter, and person

In the chapter on epistemology and divinities, precisely in the section on the science of physical things, a definition of the term 'spirit' has been given. Spirit was defined as a state of substance of high vibration and low concentration in opposition to physical substance commonly called matter. Spirit was then to be understood as energy. But there are two other definitions which should be added.

The first is 'spirit' as a person. In the physical world, there is a particular organization of substance under the form of the human body recognized as a person. The same way, there is an understanding of the word 'spirit' as a particular organization of spiritual substance or spiritual matter under the same form of the human body, but in the invisible realm; a being also recognized as person by religion and spirituality.

The second new definition for 'spirit' is spirit as principle(s) like the spirit of wisdom, the spirit of understanding, the spirit of counsel, the spirit of might, the spirit of knowledge, the spirit of fear of the Lord [Isaiah 11: 2].

When the Merriam-Webster dictionary online defines the *soul,* it offers a description that shows its equivalence with spirit as principle(s). Indeed *the soul is spoken of as an immaterial animating principle, an essential part, a moving spirit, active in rational beings but also having to do with human emotional and moral nature.*

The soul also in context can mean a person or the spirit of a person after death.

The free dictionary online also has a beautiful definition for the term: *'the soul is the animating and vital principle in humans, credited with the faculties of thoughts, action, and emotion, and often conceived as an immaterial entity'*. It is important to notice the appearance in this definition of the qualifying term 'vital' which means 'life sustaining' and that of the intellect, emotion, and will.

As such, soul then is equivalent to *mind* since the mind is according the Merriam-Webster dictionary a complex of elements in an individual that feels, perceives, thinks, wills, and especially reasons.

Hence, it is obvious that the terms 'spirit', 'soul', and 'mind' can be interchangeable designating the same thing and having different significances in other contexts. *For clarity purposes in this context, spirit would mean the spiritual or subtle body and 'soul' would mean mind plus spirit [what is said to survive after death].*

It is also necessary to give here, a clarification about the definition of the *'nous'*. In the Jonas Hans version of the transcription of the vision of Hermes Trismegistus, the term 'nous' appears as describing God, a human being, and other beings as well. The superlative 'Nous' is for God as shown in the beginning of the 6th section of the text: *'Then Poimandres said to me: ...That light is I, Nous, thy God....'* In the 16th section, Jonas Hans equates nous and mind. In Manly Hall's version, 'nous' is directly rendered as 'mind' from the beginning.

In the text of the Poimandres, the functions of the nous clearly show that it is the mind. Hence Dan Brown is right when in the novel, *The Lost Symbol*, he explains the term *'noetic'*, roughly translating 'nous' as 'inner knowledge' or 'intuitive consciousness' though the first phrase 'inner knowledge' encompasses a reality greater than that referred to as 'intuitive consciousness'. In addition the inner knowledge is in turn a smaller reality than the mind as the following lines will show. That is probably the reason why Dan Brown speaks of rough translation.

Jonas Hans presents the Nous as light and life in the sections 6, 9, and 12 of his version of the text of the *Poimandres* but Manly Hall makes a difference between Light and Mind [Nous, Intelligence]. To him, both are distinct attributes of God. The two approaches, that of Hans and that of Hall, are correct when 'light' is taken figuratively for example as the opposite of ignorance or something positive or good.

But in the literal sense, there is a difference in the two versions. The word 'Light' is not sufficient to describe the Mind because of its imprecision. Other realities such as the Word are also known, even by Jonas Hans, to be luminous. Therefore the Mind cannot be reduced to light. Moreover, it should not be presented as Light when one wants to be very precise and avoid confusion. This precision requires that Light be described as a separate reality linked to the Mind or other entities such as the Word. That is why Hall's version is clearer.

However, Hall's words raise a fundamental question. Is the Light co-eternal to the Mind as its "body" and as Hall seems to indicate, or is it a "product" of the Mind, generated by its activity as some could understand reading Genesis 1: 1-3? According to its definition, the mind*in the most restricted sense* is a qualitative reality rather than a quantitative one. Therefore, Light which is a quantitative reality is not a product of the Mind, but another attribute of God.

There are several kinds of lights and a form of light can generate another. Accordingly, the light of Genesis [a quantitative reality] came from the Original Light [also a quantitative reality] under the injunction of the Mind [a qualitative reality]. That the Original Light is co-eternal to the Universal Mind can be inferred from *Psalms 104: 2 and 1Timothy 6: 16.* But this is a scriptural and religious argument rather than a logical or philosophical one.

With the introduction of the mind, other notions such as con-sciousness, unconsciousness, subconsciousness, preconsciousness, and memory quickly show up and ask to be explained.

Consciousness is the part of the human mind that is awake or aware as shown by the definition of John Locke given in the introduc-tory chapter. *Unconsciousness* is the part which is not. The mind animates and guides the physical and the spiritual persons. Both the consciousness and the unconsciousness do.

Information circulates between the consciousness and the un-consciousness in both directions. A person might be aware of certain things at a time and not be at another that comes after. Then it is said that the person has forgotten. Psychologists will say that at the second time the person is unconscious of the given reality. In the opposite direction, there are things that the person becomes aware of, but he/she has never learned them from the environment whether nature of other humans. Dreams are also known to be purveyors of such information. This information is capable of fading again in the unconsciousness.

It is the same mind that animates and guides the physical body which animates and guides the spiritual body. It is just that specific functions are at work or are active in each case as when the same brain influences different parts of the physical body through the production of various hormones.

When a human is born, first the animation and guidance of the physical and spiritual bodies by the mind are far more unconscious than conscious. With the development of the person, the conscious part of the mind broadens both about physical reality and spiritual reality.

When the mind is more unconscious than conscious, its function is more automatic, has less free will and less inclination to mistakes and to evil. But when the mind becomes more conscious or more aware, its free will increases and it animates and guides according to its own understanding and will, opening the way to mistakes and evil when those mistakes are too big or too voluntarily hurtful.

The conscious intellect, the conscious emotion, and the conscious will have their counterparts in the unconsciousness. An evil mind uses those traits negatively. The evil intellect is oriented toward plotting the doom, the destruction, and the weakening or the dishonoring of others. The evil emotion is inclined to unfounded jealousy, destructive desire, and a lot of egoism. The evil will is prompt to act against others.

But what the evil mind often ignores is that all its actions have negative consequences on itself. No evil man for example likes dishonor, but it is the undeniable consequence of its actions. Good minds do not appreciate the evil one and even the other evil minds deep in themselves do not appreciate the evil mind either.

One of the definitions the free online dictionary gives to the term 'memory' is that of the faculty of the mind that stores and recalls past experiences, sensations, thoughts, knowledge etc...

Everything that is stored had once been in the consciousness whether coming from experiences with the outer world or from the inner world. There are three kinds of information in the memory when it is considered from the perspective of time: those which can be remembered immediately, those which are remembered with efforts, and those which are hard to remember and which make their way back to the consciousness when involuntarily triggered in specific circumstances. One could add a fourth kind of information that is never remembered, but if it is bore in mind that the specific trigger has not yet been operational, the three first categories would suffice.

Hence, if the individual is born with an "amount" of unconsciousness which progressively diminishes as said earlier, this unconsciousness is also enriched by the earthly life of the person through the consciousness and the memory. Memory then appears to occupy a "territory," a place, in both the consciousness and the unconsciousness.

Some may include the information that comes from the unconsciousness but has never been part of the consciousness in the memory and speak of memories of past lives introducing the concept of reincarnation. But reincarnation is such a complex notion that it is better to evoke it in another work.

What the understanding of memory introduces is the confirmation of the possibility of a record of life events in the mind as stated by spiritual teachers whether advocate of reincarnation or resurrection. That record is said to be displayed as a movie once the person dies and goes to the spirit world. When one thinks of radio, TV, and video waves that transport information and can be stored on USB *memory* keys, this idea does not sound odd.

The information of the memory that are remembered with effort are said to be part of the *preconsciousness*. It appears then that memory in fact has three territories: the unconscious, the preconscious, and the conscious.

As mentioned earlier, it was the psychologist Carl Gustav Jung [1875-1961] who elaborated the concept of unconsciousness. He spoke of the personal unconsciousness and the collective unconsciousness called *superconsciousness* in India. However, the definition of the superconsciousness is closer to that of God than to Jung's collective unconsciousness which simply is the aggregate of personal unconsciousness without its own personality.

In reality, the Superconsciousness is the Universal Consciousness in the sense of being aware of everything. The Superconsciousness is not just a sum of information but is a person with Intellect, Emotion, and Will. The Indian Superconsciousness is God as shown by encyclopedia.com.

The *subconsciousness* was a term used by Sigmund Freud [1856-1939], another largely respected psychologist and teacher of

Jung. Subconsciousness is defined sometimes as the absence of awareness [see the freedictionary.com] establishing the unconscious of Jung and the subconscious of Freud as synonymous terms. But the subconscious is also defined as 'not wholly conscious, partially or imperfectly conscious' and is therefore similar to the preconscious. Hence, in context, the subconscious can be either the preconscious or the unconscious, or both.

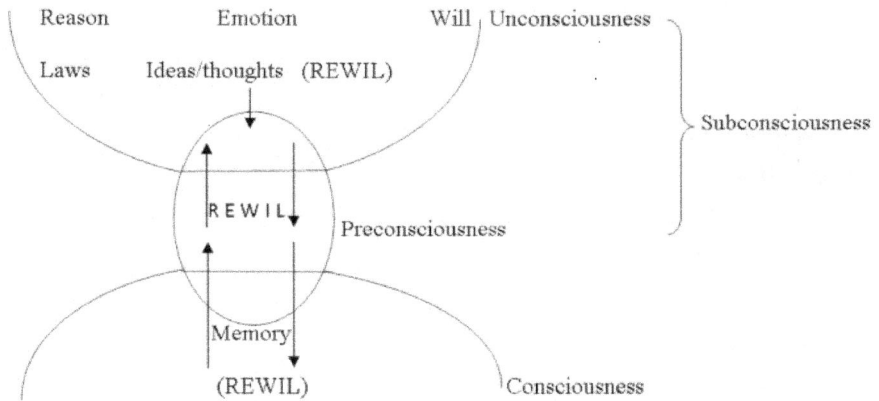

Illustrative symbol or representation of the human soul or mind : the scarab

It is strange how this representation of the human mind resembles the scarab which has a very important meaning in several spiritual teachings. This representation of the mind shows that in case of death, what separates from the physical body cannot just be 'pure consciousness' as Dan Brown seems to suggest[40] unless the famous author has used a particular definition of consciousness different from the one presented here. This remark is important because clarity in terminology allows clarity of understanding and makes spiritual quest a little less difficult. The mind is more than pure consciousness.

According the description of the *scarab* by egyptianmyths.net, during and following the period of the New Kingdom in Ancient Egypt,

---

[40]Brown, *The Lost Symbol*, 399.

scarab amulets were often placed over the heart of the mummified deceased. These heart scarabs were meant to be weighed against the feather of truth during the final judgment.

Speaking of the *Egyptian Afterlife and the Feather of Truth*, egyptian-history.suite101.com adds that what is actually weighted is the soul's heart. Writing on Insects.org, Yves Cambefort in his article *Beetles as religious symbol*, reminds his readers that to ancient Egyptians, the sacred scarab was the symbol of the immortal soul.

In Ancient Egyptian philosophy, since the scarab is the power which moves the dung ball which is like the sun, there must be a god, a powerful soul that moves the sun. The name of that god was pronounced the same way as scarab in Ancient Egyptian and was Khopri or Khepri. The rising of the sun every morning symbolized resurrection and immortality. There is a vast literature which goes in the sense of a correspondence between the human soul and the scarab.

Of course, it would be correct to consider Aksak, the big scarab, creator of the world described by Cambefort, as the Big Soul or the Universal Soul or Mind, or God. Furthermore, Khopri is the name under which the god Atum was also known. In the ancient Egyptian creation myth, Atum was alone at the beginning and created everything out of "Himself". Hence ancient Egyptians had the concept of a creator God, originally alone, who is the Soul of the universe or Universal Mind.

The Soul of God is different from the other souls in the sense that God knows all laws, ideas, thoughts, wills, emotions, and reasons. Therefore God has no unconsciousness and is aware of everything that has been, is, and could be. God is the Universal Consciousness or the Superconsciousness.

Coming to the phenomenon of *dream*, the free online dictionary again provides, certainly as many other dictionaries, an amazing definition. A dream is said to be a series of images, ideas, emotions, and sensations occurring involuntarily in the mind during certain stages of sleep. One can also add a series of "sounds and speeches" heard not by the physical ears but by the ears of the spirit and the mind.

Dreamers, even the most skeptic and most atheistic would acknowledge that they actually hear and see in their dreams but not with the physical organs of sense. Images and sounds are still present in the mind in many cases even after the dreamer has awakened. This is how people remember their dreams.

It is important to stress the involuntary character of dreams even though the possibility of voluntary or induced dreams should be explored. This shows that consciousness, in most cases, undergoes the dream. Sometimes, dreams are connected to things experienced and other times they are connected to nothing the dreamer can remember to have experienced. Hence, the dream is an activity of the mind involving both consciousness and unconsciousness.

Many spiritual people see in dreams based on the unconsciousness a way that spiritual entities and sometimes God use to teach. The God of Abraham contacted him that way several times.

An explanation about the mind cannot satisfactorily end without a few words on terms such as 'intuition', 'inspiration' and 'insight.'

Many define *intuition* as understanding or knowledge or perception of the truth with no apparent effort or use of reason. This definition poses the important problem of the verification and assurance that can occur only in the realm of the consciousness. By excluding consciousness and reason, it makes the task of verification and assurance impossible. What comes from the unconsciousness is by definition unknown and cannot be classified as understanding, knowledge, or truth.

The intuitive perceiver who does not make use of reason has no means of knowing the true nature of what is perceived.

Therefore it is one of the definitions proposed by the free dictionary, which considers intuition as impression that appears the most appropriate. This term renders well the unreliability or fallibility of intuition. So, if an advice ought to be given, it should be to strengthen and broaden the consciousness and reason and not focus primarily on the intuition.

The concept of *inspiration* implies that there is an inspirer whether God, a spirit, another physical person, a book etc...

Insight is the ability to perceive clearly and should not be considered as intuition which is just an impression.

There is a relationship between the three kinds of spirit defined so far. The spirit as principle(s) [soul or mind] can be carried by the spirit as energy which can be carried by or be organized as spirit as person. The Universal Soul and the individual souls, the Universal Spirit and the individual spirits, as well as the Universal Physical Body and the individual physical bodies mutually influence one another.

The Holy Spirit in the Old Testament

Very few passages in the Old Testament associate the words 'Holy' and 'Spirit.' The ones this research has found are:

Psalm 51: 11 *'Do not cast me from your presence or take your Holy Spirit from me.'* and

Isaiah 63: 10 *'Yet they rebelled against Him and grieved his Holy Spirit.'*

In those two passages, there is no indication to state if the Holy Spirit in question is soul, spiritual body, or energy.

Fortunately, several other parts in the Old Testament help in elaborating an opinion. Several times, the *Spirit of God* is mentioned.

In the biblical books preceding that of Numbers, 'spirit' in the expression 'Spirit of God' generally means 'Divinity.' But a new notion appears in Numbers 11: 16-29. The Lord came down and spoke with Moses, took of the spirit that was on him, and put the spirit on 70 elders and leaders of Israel so that they may bear the burden of the people with him. When the Lord did this, and the spirit rested upon them, they started to prophesy. Joshua, the assistant of Moses was jealous for Moses who replied to him that he wishes all the people to have the spirit of God and be prophets. This is a saying of a real man of God.

A saint does not use wisdom, knowledge, and power to enslave or continuously rule people but seek that they too be raised even if this means he/she will have nobody to rule. Moses' declaration to Joshua not only tells what type of society should be, but informs about his own desire to get rid of the burden of the people. *A true man of God understands leadership as having no choice other than bearing the burden of the people and end with that situation as fast as possible after raising the level of the people.*

The operation that consisted in putting spirit on the 70 elders is a transfer of energy and power. The power that enabled Moses to do everything he did was now given to 70 elders in a lesser measure to do a less important but supporting work. That the power involves energy is evident in the fact that it rested on them and that it enabled Moses' face to glow [Exodus 34: 29-35].

Everything done by the Spirit of God or Divine Energy is done by God. God and the Holy Spirit cannot be separated. The Holy Spirit is an attribute of God, an aspect of "His" personality and not another Divine Person. If the Holy Spirit should be spoken of as a person, it is better to speak of God directly. To avoid any confusion on the road of spiritual education, it is better to use a precise terminology.

That the Holy Spirit of God is power and energy is obvious in Judges 13: 25 [like electric power], Judges 14: 6 [strength], Judges

14: 19 [power], 1 Samuel 10: 10 [gift of prophesy], 1 Samuel 11: 6 [indignation], 2 Samuel 23: 2 [divine word], 2 kings 2: 9, 15 [transferable energy and power], 1 Samuel 17:14-16 [fear and depression calmed by music].

God breathing in the nostril of the man Adam [made of clay] and making him become a living being is an indication, as stated earlier, that breath is everything required at the subtle level for an autonomous human being to live.

The Holy Spirit in the New Testament and the mistakes concerning the Trinity

By considering Galatians as foolish [3: 1-5] and telling them that they did not receive the Holy Spirit and miracles by obeying the Law of Moses but by believing the message heard about Jesus, Paul demonstrated an ignorance or a forgetfulness in the matter of the existence and manifestation of the Holy Spirit in history. Indeed, the Holy Spirit had been given many times in the Old Testament period.

One important example that precedes and parallels the Pentecost in Acts 2 is the Pentecost [collective reception of the Holy Spirit] that happens in Number 11: 16-29 in the time of Moses. A reason why Paul did not notice such a phenomena in his own time is that Israelites have disobeyed God several times and had fallen from grace. Especially it was difficult to remark a person similar to Moses among the Jews of the 1st century.

Hence, in contrary to Paul's beliefs, by obeying the Law given through Moses, people can receive the Holy Spirit. People like Moses and Jesus are just channels of the Law and the Word of God, so that it can reach people in need of spiritual development without harming them. That is why their quality as servants and lovers of God and mankind is important.

They serve as buffer to make divinity more accessible to the common people. They worked hard to be able to bear the voice of God and see "His" light in order to help others do the same. But in reality, it is the Word, the Law, the Wisdom, the Reason of God [as Hermes suggested], ultimately God, that creates, recreates, or restores.

If Paul really knew about or remembered these things, he would not have developed his theology on Jesus the way he did.

Parallels that explain the nature of the Holy Spirit as energy and power are everywhere in the New Testament. The Pentecost in Acts 2 parallels the one in Numbers 11. The other gifts of the Holy Spirits are spread but Paul summarizes them in 1Corinthians 12: 7 [wisdom, knowledge, faith, healing, prophesy, discernment, speaking strange languages, interpretation]. The Holy Spirit is also associated in the New Testament with fire [Matthew 3: 11.], inspiration [Luke 12: 12], flames or tongues of fire [Acts 2].

An example of the gift of healing by the Holy Spirit can be found in Luke 8: 43-48 when a bleeding woman touched Jesus with the intention, the wish, the desire, the will, the faith, the misunderstood command, to get cured. A force came out of Jesus and healed her without producing the same effect on other people who were also touching him but unwillingly or with a particular purpose.

The positive pole was already set in Jesus, the woman just set in herself the negative pole for the force to move and Jesus acknowledged this by telling her that her faith has saved her. The faith of the woman was not completely blind because the previous demonstrations of Jesus plus the urgent need to get cured and be relieved have given eyes to her faith which became knowledge living but a small place to doubt.

If the Holy Spirit is not a person, why did Jesus asks in Matthew 28: 19 to baptize in the name of the Father, the Son, and the Holy Spirit?

Such baptism does not necessarily mean that the Holy Spirit is a person. The fact that some among early Christians understood things that way does not change reality. One should not be impressed by the term 'name' to make theological mistakes. Jesus has a name. Animals have names [Genesis 2: 19-20] and things also have names. That the Holy Spirit has a name does not make it a person.

Actually nobody in Christianity and the Unification Movement seriously tried to give a personal name to the Holy Spirit "who" is supposed to be a feminine person. One could expect names such as Deborah, Sarah, and so on, but no one ventured seriously on that theological path among Christians and Unificationists. The Hindu goddess Shakti replacing Brahma in this role is a good candidate for the position of Holy Spirit as a person though some might argue that even Shakti is the personification of energy and not a real person.

The importance given to the Holy Spirit in Mathew 28: 19 is to stress its role in the well-being of humankind. In John 3: 5, Jesus associates Spirit and water as essential for rebirth and salvation. In Matthew 3: 11, it is question of baptism with water and the baptism with the Holy Spirit. In this latter verse, Matthew simply adds 'Holy' to 'Spirit' with reason. One could have the right based on this to constitute the Duality of 'water and Spirit' [both being things]. But it would be making the same mistake as those who have set the notion of Trinity.

It was shown how the Holy Spirit transforms people and makes them better. This is how rebirth occurs. The Holy Spirit renews people [Titus 3:5]. Jesus being close to God can use the power of God as his. Rebirth for Jesus is symbolic, not literal in the traditional physical sense.

Some have avoided the idea of physical father and the physical mother for the rebirth but have declared necessary a spiritual father and a spiritual mother in the person of Jesus plus the Holy Spirit thus falling into another trap. Indeed, Jesus after his death remains a person but the Holy Spirit has never been a person in contrary to the affirmation that it is a feminine spirit. The couples God - Jesus and Universal Mind - Holy Spirit [not Jesus- Holy Spirit] make more sense in the theology of rebirth.

Water renews things and people by washing them and baptism of water is associated with *repentance* that helps individuals *get rid of ideas of guilt and forgive themselves.* This is a cleansing of the soul and the spirit or of the robe at a certain degree. But it is not enough.

To be really renewed one needs not only to be emptied, get rid of negative ideas and feelings like hatred, and even negative energies; but be filled with positive energy associated with love, prophesy, wisdom, and so forth. This role is also fulfilled thanks to the Holy Spirit directly or indirectly through teachings like those of Hermes, Jesus, Moses, good books and so forth.

From another perspective, if the Holy Spirit was a person and member of the Holy Trinity, it would be illogical that "She" occupies only the 3rd place because her role would correspond to that of a mother. Why would a son be inferior to his father but superior to his mother? *The Holy Spirit is mentioned after the Father and the Son to stress the order of intervention of the Divine Attributes in the process of every creation and recreation: Mind-Word-Energy or Father-Son-Holy Spirit. This is salvation.*

The Universal Soul works through the Word to make people receive the Holy Spirit or reviving energy. Since the time of the Old Testament, God was working in such a manner. That is why even non Israelites such as Balaam have been filled with the Spirit of God. They have been able to see clearly, hear the word of God, and behave with righteousness. Balaam received words from God as did Israelites. God did not wait for the time of the New Testament to send the Word and the Spirit. This salvation has always been available and Jesus tried to improve it.

The Father-Son-Spirit that Jesus spoke of is the equivalent of the Nous-Word-Light or Mind-Word-Light of Hermes.

Talking about Jesus in the preceding chapter, it was demonstrated that the Word is an attribute of God and not the person of Jesus who was also a receiver of that Word. Therefore, the Trinity Father-Jesus- Spirit as the Godhead is not a correct theological notion. It has meaning only in the philosophic sense that three elements form a trinity. From gathering three elements to declaring that they are God, there is a huge step which should not have been made.

The concept of God-Word-Spirit of Blavatsky is not theologically true either because the Word and the Spirit as attributes of God are part of God and should not be different elements of a Trinity that includes God.

Finally, even the Trinity Mind-Word-Light is not the Godhead. According to the vision of Hermes, the Word which is Reason is a result of Thought. Therefore, the Thought has the right to be included in a Trinity before the Word and if the Word should be included in any Godhead, that Godhead will not be a Trinity but a "Quatuornity". If one decides to acknowledge all the attributes of God, then it would be better to speak of *Infinity* and the notion of Godhead would be meaningless. Therefore the concept of Trinity has no important theological significance.

Browne like others clearly and correctly associates the white light and the Holy Spirit; for example when she describes the Dark Side in her book *Phenomenon*.

The Holy Spirit in the Qur'an

The Qur'an speaks of the Holy Spirit as author of revelations [16:102] and also of the angel Gabriel as Holy Spirit and author of revelations [2:97]. There are two ways of understanding this. The first is that the Holy Spirit is the angel Gabriel in the sense that Gabriel is a spirit and is holy. The problem with this view is that it is not satisfying when one reads the Bible-related verses [2:87, 2: 353, and 5: 110].

Indeed it is difficult to accept based on the Bible for example that is was Gabriel who came on Jesus in the form of a dove, that it was him who was divided on people on Pentecosts etc...The way this contradiction can be solved is to accept that there are two meanings for 'Holy Spirit' in the Qur'an: one that is Gabriel, a spirit who is holy and the Holy Spirit as it is described in the Bible. The two kinds of Holy Spirit can make revelation, thus there is no contradiction.

The Holy Spirit in other religions and spiritual traditions

To ancient Egyptians, Amun is an invisible *force* in the wind, the breath of life. In the mythology of Taoism, the Primordial Heavenly Lord, Yuanshi Tianzu, existed within the galactic void for millions of years without change, and is described by some as the First Cause, the primeval spirit without beginning and without end, the source of all truth whose doctrine leads to immortality and who was formed from the *original breath [qi]*. The qi in Chinese is translated as "*energy flow*", a life force, a vital force.

Hence, it is correct to infer that the Mystery religion of ancient Egypt and Taoism know about the reality of the Holy Spirit. The descriptions of Brahma, Shakti, Agni, Vayu, and Indra show that Hindu religion and philosophy have the knowledge of a vital force or energy that is invisible and at the base of all creation.

In *Isis Unveiled* of Theosophy, the seeker is told that the aether is the breath of the Father, life-giving principle and the *Holy Ghost*. The Temple of the People composed of theosophists teaches that the

Holy Spirit is the Holy Fire, the tongues of flame, a consuming fire, prana, a life force, a form of electric energy, the creative fire.

The market of spiritual energy: goodness and the Holy Spirit versus evil and dust

Simon the magician was able to see the difference between the Holy Spirit and the source of his own power. But he made the mistake to think that it could be purchased [Acts 8: 18] as he certainly did for his negative spiritual power. Evil forces have knowledge of the constitution of the universe [they once helped in the process of creation]. They know how to make conversions between different types of energies. Since they can no longer have direct access to the light of God, to the Holy Spirit, they have become eaters of dust [Genesis 3: 14].

One form of evil spiritual energy conversion and transfer is human sacrifice. There are many stories on the pact with the Devil in the Western world as previously said. In sub-Saharan Africa, some people are aware of promises made by some magicians to evil forces and the going of these magicians to the cemeteries to perform strange rituals to gain power. That is a reason why the God of ancient Israel forbade his people to adopt the worship of gods in imitation of Canaanites who used to practice child sacrifice [Deuteronomy 18: 10-14]. Sikhs say in their *Pearls of Sikhism* that the miracles performed by Yogis and Sidhas are different from divine intervention. If the power of the Yogis is acquired as described above, then Sikhs are right. But if it is the Holy Spirit of the Supreme God which is at work, then the Sikh affirmation is not correct. Many Yogis pray, fast, and respect others like Jesus did. It is possible that there are also evil Yogis as there are good and bad people that can be found in all religions, spiritual schools, and scientific disciplines.

The psychic centers, the chakras, and the kundalini which are basis for the function of the psychic body can be activated through evil procedures. Dust [Genesis 3: 14] is an inferior form of energy. In the world of the Devil, nothing is given for free. This is spiritual business.

'If you want something that I can do, you pay with something that you have, can have, can steal, or can accomplish that I want.' 'You live in a world of high concentration of energy. I live in a world where people know how to influence the events of your world. You want things to happen to you; I want energy from below since I can't have it from above. Deal?'

The explanation of the book of Enoch about how different spiritual sciences have been taught humanity by fallen angels and the description of spirituality as business between devotees and gods in Sumer confirm the scenario just presented.

In that system, only high ranking individuals, those very close to the Devil, see the bottom of the pot after they have been sufficiently corrupted not to be disgusted by that repugnant bottom. Most business partners are left in ignorance or are covered with lies so gigantic and so refined that simple minded people do not know the true condition of the world.

The Devil holds his closest partners hostage. In turn, these partners, openly or not, hold their subordinates hostage until the most innocent soul who wants to do good but is not well informed serves the visible and invisible empire of evil. Simon the magician thought he could purchase the Holy Spirit the somehow.

According to scripture, spiritual science is universal and comes ultimately from the Supreme God who conveyed it to angels to some extent. But some have turned against God and have begun to use their knowledge in anarchy. They put everything they had forth to implement as fast as possible, an empire of evil on earth. At the time of the flood, all the inclinations of the hearts of men were toward evil. The Holy Spirit cannot be purchased but given more and more intensely through a life of devotion to the Supreme God the Ultimate Owner; a devotion to truth, justice, wisdom, peace, love etc....

The particular authentic spiritual experience of Seeker with the Holy Spirit

Yoga and Hinduism teach about the vital or energetic body with its important components that the chakras and nadis are. They also teach about the kundalini and describe it as a vital energy at the base of the spine that rises through the main and central nadi and the seven principal chakras.

Seeker has had the experiential confirmation of the existence of the chakras and some of their characteristics, functions, and relations to the pineal gland but he did not experience a kundalini rising from the seventh chakra but rather a vital energy of soft and pleasant electrical nature that often comes and fills him from the top of the head [the first and main chakra] to the base of the spine following a trajectory almost central, but slightly on the right and of opposite direction to that ascribed to the kundalini. Sometimes the power just rests at the top of his head like in the different Pentecosts.

One sensation given by the descent of the energy is joy and ecstasy different from sexual ecstasy, but really wonderful. During that state of bliss, Seeker understands how Jesus was full of joy thanks to the Holy Spirit [Luke 10: 21]. Other sensations are strength, confidence, and love [agape].

Another experience lived by Seeker is the tremendous power of love like the one represented in the picture of the Sacred Heart of Jesus that Seeker experienced as originating from the heart chakra. He knows that the spinning lotus is not just symbolic but also literal [at the spiritual level] and that Rudolph Steiner's description has a great deal of truth.

Hence, Seeker has had and continues to have the experiential proofs that there are a lot of truths and realities in what religious and spiritual scientists teach. His testimony is worth what it is; to be accepted or rejected. Some scientists of the physical things think that the experiences ascribed to Gautama Buddha, Jesus, Yogis, ancient Egyptians, and many others are mere physiological reactions.

But Seeker knows it is not the case because his experiences have been described with great accuracy by religion and spirituality, while physical science, medicine, and physiology said nothing about them. Maybe someday physical scientists would be able to prove these facts. That would be part of the process of junction between spirituality and physicality.

In the documentary *KGB psychic files*, on Youtube, a kind of psychic energy is shown to have been photographed in living beings and well developed in the hand of some gifted human beings. Seeker knows that this is not an invention or an imagination.

He wants like Moses that all human beings experience the things that have happen to him and more. That way, he can learn from them too. He is conscious that much more progress needs to be made by all.

One amazing side of his experiences is that they usually can be reproduced at will.

Chapter 13

The anthropomorphic God and gods

SINCE the night of times, the question of the anthropomorphism of God has been present in human minds. The image of *the old man sitting on his throne* has nourished the imagination and the consciousness of billions of human beings. However, other voices have spoken of *God as Principles, Universal Mind, or Universal Soul,* an invisible power pervading the entire universe. Formulations of this second understanding of God are found like the first in the Bible but also in the teachings of Hermes Mercurius Trismegistus. Those teachings are dear to Hermeticists and Neo-Platonists.

Today, these two ideas of God compete in the minds of men and women of all religions and all spiritual schools. There is a fundamental difference between the two kinds of God. The way one would relate to an old, all mighty man, the Ancient of Days, sitting on his throne in heaven and surrounded by his court, is certainly different from the relationship one would have with a God *without* human form, an all pervading Soul.

Arguments for and against the literal [physical or spiritual] anthropomorphism of divinities

The earliest pantheons have portrayed deities in the form of men and women irrespective of their ranks. To Sumerians, ancient Egyptians, Greeks, and Mayan, gods were like human beings including the most powerful among them or the first that came into existence. Apsu, the Sumerian primeval deity was killed by Enki, the god of wisdom and both were human-like. Marduk, the most powerful god of that pantheon was begotten by Enki and his wife Damkina. Marduk was made king of all the deities and is represented on Sumerians tablets as a man approximately between 40 and 50 years.

In ancient Egyptian mythology the most powerful god, the sun god Re was associated with Amun, the primeval deity, invisible force and also a sun god; under the name Amun-Re. Images of Re and Amun show them as men. Also the primordial Greek sky god, Uranus and Zeus, the most powerful god of Greek pantheon were in human form and behaved like men except that they had supernatural abilities.

Despite the fact that each god/goddess is associated with a principle or many principles of the universe, he/she was still portrayed like a human being. These observations are also valid for the Mayan, the Taoist, the Hindu, and the Zoroastrian pantheons.

The description of the Court of God in books like Enoch [chapter 46], Job [1:6], Daniel [7: 9], Zechariah [3: 1-5], and Revelation [4: 1-11] has contributed to shape the anthropomorphic idea of God. The book of Enoch contains like the book of Revelation apocalyptic and christocentric events so precise that it raises serious doubts concerning its authenticity as a book that dates from the time of the patriarch Enoch who lived very far in the past.

In fact, the image of the Ancient of Days on his throne with his court is of symbolic nature. In visions and dreams given by God, the elements that are shown are often symbolic and not literal. The dreams of the Pharaoh explained by Joseph [Genesis 41], Joseph's own childhood dreams [Genesis 37], the dreams of king Nebuchadnezzar of Babylon explained by Daniel [3: 1-18, 4: 1-37], Daniel's own visions of the four beasts representing four kingdoms [7: 1-28], and the vision of the Ram and the Goat symbolizing the Kingdoms of Persia [Iran] and Greece [Daniel 8] confirm that symbolism.

The symbolism of the Ancient of Days dwells in the fact that God is the oldest person, the wisest and affectionate guide.

The atmosphere of court, with sometime [Zechariah 3: 1-5] an attorney and a prosecutor [Satan] is to stress the kinds of powers that exist in the universe. No matter how much evil there is, God remains the Absolute Judge and no one accused, harassed, or tortured by Satan will be punished in hell if the good God does not decided so in accordance with the life the accused has lived and not according to the sayings of Satan alone. *The Supreme God does not need Satan to tell who has done what and when. Everyone reaps what he/she has sown.*

In reality, there is no such a thing as a literal judgment in heaven or a literal Lake of Fire for the second death, and so on. There is no literal sword in the mouth of the messianic figure presented in Revelation 19: 11-15.The sword symbolizes the word of God as the passage itself suggests.

By reading the book of Genesis, one can discover that there are many instances in which the angel of the Lord is clearly mentioned as acting in the name of God [Genesis 16: 7-12/Exodus 3: 2/ Judges 13: 3]. But even in almost all the other situations, it is certain, based on the scripture that it was still an angel that acted on behalf of the Supreme God.

The God of Abraham showed himself to him as an angel, an anthropomorphic being. *But that God was not described as old.* That the God of Abraham is like a man can be seen in Genesis 18 and that he was not different from an angel is evidenced in Genesis 19: 1. Indeed if three beings appeared to Abraham as men belonging to the same species and if two of them were confirmed as angels, there is little doubt that the third was also an angel. The God of Jacob was also an angelic being [Genesis 32: 24-30]. A man fought with Jacob and he was convinced to have seen God.

Sometimes, the biblical authors used the expressions 'the angel of the Lord' and 'the Lord' in the same passage and event [Exodus 3]. In Judges 13, despite their knowledge that it was an angel of the Lord who appeared to them; the parents of Samson were convinced that the angel was God.

Some authors of the New Testament showed that they were aware that God gave the law to Israel through angels [Acts 7: 53, Galatians 3: 19].

The God that Jesus talked about had no humane form like the God of the Old Testament. Jesus' God was in him and the disciples and inversely [John 14: 8-11 and 16-17]. That is why Jesus could not show the Supreme God to Phillip while it is known that the God of the Old Testament [a powerful angel] could appear to people. The God Jesus taught about is not the God of the Old Testament. The God of Jesus is far greater. In fact that God who is the Supreme is Incomparable. This explains why Jesus refused to follow some traditions of the people of Israel and insisted that the entire law can be summarized into two: love the Supreme God and love fellow humans.

From all the preceding, it can be said that the Supreme God never showed "Himself" in reality to anyone as Jesus certifies in John 6: 46 and as 1 John 4: 2 confirms.

The only exception could be the period of primordial history before Abraham from Genesis 1 to Genesis 11. This part of the Bible is a real puzzle, an enigma that can give serious headache to researchers who try to unveil its mystery. The fundamental question here is: *'Who was the God of Adam, Enoch and Noah?'*

Let's analyze the God of Adam through the following table based on Genesis 1-3.

Theories Passages	1	2	3	4
Genesis 1:1-25	Anthropomorphic God (A G)	Invisible God (IG)	I G + AG	I G + AG
Genesis 1: 26-27	A G	I G	I G + (DA-Demiurge angel Aa + angels Ab, Ac, Ad, etc)	I G +(AG Demiurge-Aa-L + Ab, Ac, Ad, etc...)
Genesis 1: 28-31	A G	I G	I G + (AG-D)	I G +(AGD-Aa-L)
Genesis 2	A G	I G	I G + (AG-D)	I G +(AGD-Aa-L)
Genesis 3: 1-21	A G # Serpent (Satan, Lucifer)	I G + GA # Serpent (Satan, Lucifer)	I G + AG (Aa, D) # Serpent (Satan, Lucifer)	IG + AG (Aa) # L (Satan, serpent)
Genesis 3: 22	A G	I G	I G + (AG-D)	IG + (AG-Ab, Ac...)

The table summarizes four paths one can follow while trying to uncover the identity of the God of Adam.

According to the first theory [strengthened by the image of Ancient of Days in Job, Daniel, Zechariah, and Revelation], God is an anthropomorphic being. "He" has a form like an angel or a human. This understanding of God is well spread. Nevertheless, it presents one serious shortcoming when one remains in the Old Testament itself.

In the sayings of King Solomon at the apex of the wisdom given him by his God, he says in 2 Chronicles 6: 18 after building the Temple: '*But will God really dwell on earth with men? The heavens, even the highest heavens cannot contain you. How much less this temple I have built!* '

An anthropomorphic being like the angel that appeared to Abraham occupies a very small portion of physical or spiritual space. The declaration of Solomon shows that the God he had in mind at that precise moment is not such a God. When one leaves the context of the Old Testament, the first serious obstacle to theory 1 is the words of Jesus and many other important figures of the New Testament [1 Timothy 6: 16, 1 John 4: 12].

The author of Psalms 104: 2 declared that God is dressed in a robe of light while that of 1Timothy 6: 16 adds that God lives in a brilliant light and no human can approach Him. Those to whom scripture is an important authority can see here another proof that the Ancient of Days is a symbol. Additionally, **from a logical perspective, the idea of the Invisible All Pervading God explains better the omnipresence of God**.

Theory 2, God as Invisible All Pervader encounters an objection in the Old Testament itself in Genesis 1: 26 and Genesis 3: 22. These passages show that God as Invisible [physically and spiritually] is talking to other intelligent beings. How this happened and all the protagonists should be identified. Hence, theory 2 is incomplete.

Theories 3 and 4 find their justification in the attractiveness of anthropomorphism. It is the idea that a form is important in the implementation of some aspects of the work of creation. This argument is supported by the fact that God acted in the Bible often through angels, prophets, kings, Jesus, and so on. Hence, supporters of these two theories would want to see God, the Invisible All Pervader as using a central form [a highly wise angel or a collective of angels: the Demiurge of the Gnostics] to accomplish certain types of work.

Another support for theories 3 and 4 is that the "God" of Genesis 1: 26 is silent concerning the superiority of humans comparing to angels. This superiority at least in terms of predetermination is evidenced in 1 Corinthians 6: 3, Hebrews 1: 5-8, and by the declaration of Hermes Trismegistus[41]. But in Genesis 1: 26, only the superiority of man to nature is mentioned.

The advantage of theory 3 over theory 4 is that the anthropomorphic walking and talking God of Genesis 3: 1-21 is not Lucifer who has never been portrayed as the main angel of the Supreme God before the fall. In theory 3, Lucifer is just one of the main angels of God in harmony with Ezekiel 28, Isaiah 14, and Revelation 12. He was certainly not a person that represented God and told Adam and Eve not to eat the fruit which is the case in theory 4. God certainly warned them through another angel who was member of the Demiurge who is called the Lord God.

Angels who represented the Supreme and Invisible God as Anthropomorphic Gods Aa, Ab, Ac, and so on could be Michael who often confronted Satan in the name of the Invisible All Pervader, Gabriel, Raphael etc... By using the indefinite article 'an,' Judges 13: 3 [Con-

---

[41]Salaman, *The Way of Hermes*, 51.

temporary English Version, French Bible Louis Segond] confirms that God has many envoys that "He" can send and not just one.

Considering Yahweh or Jehovah as an angel like Helena Blavatsky is not necessarily a good idea. The name 'Yahweh' came forth in the Bible for example when an angelic being made a self-introduction as Yahweh in the beginning of the book of Exodus. Since the appearing angel spoke to Moses as God and called himself Yahweh, Blavatsky definitely considered him the "angel Yahweh," the creator God who walked in Eden.

But a different analysis of the message of the angel shows that he is just a representative of the Supreme God who is beyond him. Whether the angel really wanted to appear as the Supreme God or not, the meaning of 'Yahweh' in Exodus 3 seems to be 'I am'. In that case, the name is too great to be that of a lone angel. 'I am' can only be the Supreme God, the All, the true origin of everything. **In Exodus, it is said that Moses would be as God for Aaron. This shows that a person who is not God can present him/herself as such. Hence, an angel can present himself as Yahweh without being the Supreme All Pervading God**.

Anyhow, there was a very important angel called the Lord God who oversaw the creation of the world including Adam and Eve, who was challenged by Lucifer the serpent, who walked in the Garden of Eden, walked with Enoch and Noah, and appeared to Abraham and to many others. That powerful angel had other angels that support him [the angels of the Lord] and Satan can also come in front of him as shown in Job 38: 7 and Job 1: 6-7. So, descriptions about the Ancient of Days can teach lessons about the Supreme God as well as the God of the Old Testament. Seekers should therefore remain vigilant.

An extensive search has not been able to determine the meaning of the word 'Yahweh.'

If that word means 'I' am' then it does not correspond to any angel no matter his power or pretentions. But if the word means something else then it could correspond to the Lord God of the Old Testament member of the Demiurge who is also known as El-Shaddāi [God Almighty] or El-Elyon [God Most High].

The fact remains that anthropomorphism is not compatible with omnipresence, omniscience, and omnipotence. **Since the God of the Old Testament is not Omnipresent, Omniscient, and Omnipotent; this explains his mistakes. But it is also clear that that God is better than the other gods who ask for human sacrifice and encourage immorality.**

Coming back to theories 3 and 4, Isaiah 14: 12-15 tells about a being, a bright star, son of the morning, who wanted to rule over the stars of God and be like God. Angels are known to be stars as shown in Hindu mythology explained by Theosophists and also in ancient Egyptian mythology. But the lesson taught by Isaiah does not stop there.

The being in question is equated with the King of Babylon [Isaiah 14: 4]. Babylon is also associated in Revelation 17 with the empire of evil and sin. The king of Babylon is the direct representative of Marduk, the god whose main temple was in Babylon. In addition, the Babel tower project took place in Babylonia [Genesis 11: 2]. The God of the Old Testament destroyed that project because it is dangerous that humanity gathers around the evil principles of the other gods.

The Babylonian creation myth speaks of the tower project, a stage-tower raised at Esagila to reach Apsu [the sky]. Marduk [king of the gods] and Enki [god of wisdom] are closely associated and it is even said that Marduk finally took the attributes of Enki. There is little doubt that Marduk who asked the gods to become their king, is the bright star of Isaiah 14 represented by the King of Babylon whose kingdom is associated with evil in Revelation and with the dangerous Babel project.

The Book of Ezekiel [chapter 28] speaks of a being who has pretended to be God, the prince of Tyre, a man, wiser than the Prophet Daniel but who will be destroyed. The same chapter continued from the verse 12 with the description this time of the king of Tyre, filled with wisdom, exquisite in beauty, a created angel [a cherubim], who was in Eden the Garden of God, blameless until the day evil, excessive pride, and corrupted wisdom were found in him. This king of Tyre also has the characters of Madurk-Enki-Serpent. The fact that Marduk as well as Satan convinced other gods or angels to work with them, should not get out of sight.

Two kinds of gods can be studied in the Old Testament. A number of benevolent *angels* or anthropomorphic gods helped the God of the Old Testament who was also an angel but a very powerful one in creating and guiding humanity. But there were *some among them led by Satan or Lucifer* who later used a wisdom that became corrupted to push weak humans into error and established an evil tradition that enslaves and brings suffering. They are malevolent gods.

When a particular wisdom is corrupted, power can maintain an acceptable situation until that wisdom is restored. This is what explains the intervention of the army in some less advanced countries. The problem is that when "might" too decides to become selfish, the situation is far worse and can result in massacres. Therefore it is preferable that wisdom never gets corrupted or that might maintains unshakable loyalty that would help with patience, wisdom to get rid of its corruption. *What is even better than might is a superior wisdom that acts swiftly when a particular wisdom is corrupted.*

Jesus taught about the Universal Soul that cannot be seen in contrary to the powerful angel who acted as the God of the Old Testament. Indeed that powerful angel has been seen by Moses and seventy three elders of Israel [Exodus 24: 9-11].

The God of the Old Testament has two main aspects. In the vision of Daniel and the book of Enoch, he is described as old but not as such by all the people he appeared to including Abraham, Jacob [who fought him], Moses, and so on. So the heavenly court in the Old Testament can be a real situation or a symbol like in Revelation 4. It is also possible that the God of the author of the book of Revelation was still the powerful angel of the Old Testament since one cannot say for sure how much of the teaching of Jesus he understood.

What is clear is that at least two remarkable men in the ancient world [Hermes and Jesus] pioneered a new spiritual understanding which consisted in talking about a God far more important than the most powerful angels, fallen or not, called Gods or gods.

The Universal Soul or All Pervading God is the source of all beings including powerful angels such as the God of the Old Testament. That Omnipresent, Omniscient, and Omnipotent God helps all intelligent beings [angels and humans] in their development. Goodness, mistakes, and evil depend on how those intelligent beings use well their free will.

So, by associating with other angels to create the heavens, the earth, and humans, the powerful angel of the Old Testament called Lord God was using his gifts from the Universal Source to help that Source further make concrete beings. This is the origin of the idea of the demiurge.

In the process of implementation of the Will of the Universal Soul, the hierarchy of beings is not determined by their moments of creation. The evidence can be seen in the fact that humans are better than minerals but are partly made of them. Similarly, the fact that angels existed before humans and helped in their creation does not mean that there are better than humans.

Angels participated in the creation of humans like mineral but their action is most remarkable at the soul or mind level since they themselves are souls or minds that emanated from the Universal Soul or Mind.

In their development, humans start by not having much control over the minerals that help build their physical bodies, but as time goes, they come to make a better use of minerals.

Similarly, thanks to angels, especially the human soul or mind grows. This is what astrology or astrotheology teaches by showing how spiritual beings in conjunction with the stars, the planets, etc…orient the behaviors of human beings. Astrology or astrotheology is taught in the writings of Hermes, in several creation myths and ancient scriptures as well as in the Bible [Job 38: 31-32/ Matthew 2: 1-2]. The Qur' an speaks of the zodiac in Surahs 15: 16 and 85: 1 [Yusuf Ali's version] but mentions neither its association with angels nor its influence on humans. Two prominent post-modern teachers and researchers on astrotheology are Manly Hall and Jordan Maxwell.

Again, as time passes, humans reach a level where they find errors in the management of angels and have brighter ideas on how to improve themselves and the rest of creation including angels. Jesus realized this. That is why his spirituality included a lot the chasing of demons or fallen angels.

However, there are records of spirit banishments before Jesus, mainly in the Kabbalistic and Hermetic traditions. But Jesus went several times after spirits that he had not personally called thereby initiating a new way of dealing with the gods. Like Hermes, he taught about the All Pervading God who cannot be compared with any spirit, angel, or demon including the God of the Old Testament.

Today, the failures of demons, the mistakes of angels, the sayings and the works of Hermes and Jesus show that the human potential is beyond that of angels as described in scriptures. Therefore, it is humanity's duty to listen more and more to the Universal Soul and manifest more of the potential of the Original Being.

Other arguments for the Invisible All Pervader God

According to the authors of <u>Psalms 104: 2</u> and f <u>1Timothy 6: 16</u> God lives in a bright light that humans cannot approach. This gives a metaphysical and concrete dimension to God and explains the light of John 1: 5, 6, 9, and 11 which characterizes primarily God "Himself" and secondarily through inheritance Jesus. How Jesus is the incarnation of the light has been discussed in details in chapter 11.That explanation shows the possibility for any man or woman to also incarnate the light [philosophic light or wisdom or illumination or understanding on the one hand and the energy of the Holy Spirit on the other hand]. Hence, he/she can be a true brother or sister of Jesus [Romans 8: 29, Colossians 1: 18].

Saying that God dwells in the light means that the Universal Soul who is the first kind of light, a qualitative one [Intelligence, Reason, Wisdom, Love] dwells in the second kind of light, a quantitative one [Energy of the Holy Spirit, primordial substance or matter, light in the literal sense].

This means that the Universal Principles of Good, Wisdom, Intelligence, Beauty, Love, Truth, Will; in short the Divinity or Supreme God, is present in all forms of matter. But the perception of that presence varies as many spiritual schools have taught.

This language is the same that Hermes Trismegistus spoke. To Him, God is the Mind of the Universe or Universal Mind or Soul whose prime creative and life giving trait is the Nous or Intellect or Reason.

Gross matter shines less than spiritual matter which even shines less than the light in which God dwells. That is why humans cannot approach that light, too intense, too bright, and too powerful. This light if it is experienced too directly by the ordinary man would kill him as high voltage electricity would. That is why the physical body of man in spiritual science is gradually prepared to bear more and more intense light through the practice of truth, wisdom, righteousness, love and so on. The spiritual body is prepared as well.

Through that kind of training, human mind develops its capability to set energy in motion and thereby transforming personal life and the environment. This is how physical substance comes to respond to the mind more and more directly.

Why Moses' face shone and why Jesus was able to transfigure becomes more evident. The reason why evil forces of darkness fear the light, God, and Jesus Christ is also made clearer.

Emanuel Swedenborg described a division of heavens according to the intensity of light with the highest heavens corresponding to the highest intensity and brightness. That men must prepare to withstand and live in bright light is evidenced in his report on 'not so bad people' who thought there were very good and wanted to live in higher heavens after they have shed the physical body. The opportunity to do so was given to them, but they almost died trying and run back or down as fast as they could.

Now a problem posed by Emanuel Swedenborg must be solved. He mentioned that Jesus is the God of heavens, who appears in those heavens as the sun and gives light to the other human beings who believe in him. He added that anybody who holds a different idea, like that of the Invisible All Pervading God could not live in the highest heavens.

Two major objections go against those declarations. First, Swedenborg spoke as if Jesus himself did not recognize the authority of a God, his Father, his Teacher, the Will of whom he accomplishes and not his. With his teaching, Swedenborg rejects several words in the New Testament and gives the impression of presenting his own Jesus, different from the one that manifests in the gospels.

The second objection to Swedenborg's affirmation that there is no God above Jesus in heaven does not reject his experience but finds a different explanation to it. His experience could be considered authentic because of Jesus' high spirituality, love, truth, and under-standing. Jesus himself declared that there are ways to achieve an even greater wisdom, truth, spirituality, and efficiency than he achieved [John 14: 12]. Jesus can appear as a sun comparing to people who did not reach his level.

Many, especially in Christianity, instead of working on how to be-come a source of light, prefer to work on how to reflect the light from Jesus. A cosmological argument shows how Jesus can have brothers and sisters equal to him, with their own brightness; being gods as he is [John 10: 34, Psalms 82: 6]. It has been shown that the true desire of God is that all humans become prophets or suns. Messianism is a misunderstood concept that will be explained in chapter 16.

In old times, a great number of people did not know about the composition of the visible universe as people do today. It is now public knowledge that there are several billions of galaxies each with billions of stars or suns. A sun is a star. It is just the distance of observation that made some people think that stars are of lesser brightness and size and of different nature comparing to the sun of the earth. In fact there are stars brighter and bigger than the sun of this solar system. Sirius A, for instance, is 23 times as luminous as the sun and considerably hotter.

If there were more humans to achieve great results, even greater than Jesus as himself recognized, it is possible that Swedenborg would have seen a different heaven. May be there have already been such people and Swedenborg just went into the spiritual solar system in which Jesus is the sun because he was Christian.

In the teachings of Hermes and in ancient Egyptian mythology, the Sun is the *symbol* of the Supreme All Pervading Creator God, not Jesus. Stars also symbolize angels in mythologies. The reason certainly is because some religious thinkers thought that the sun is bigger and more luminous than the Stars. Therefore it is the context that defines how a message with such symbols should be understood.

Based on their perceptions of physical reality, ancient thinkers have established religious and philosophical correspondences. To understand them, one must access those perceptions as they have been recorded or more exactly the meaning of those records. To evaluate the accuracy of ancient thoughts, new ideas based on better perceptions thanks to progress and the merit of the age should come forth. That is why a response is given to Swedenborg here. Light or the sun or stars can symbolize different realities depending on the experiences and knowledge of those expressing ideas. These experiences and knowledge vary according to several factors including the time or era.

The point of this argumentation is not to stir agitation and rebellion against Jesus or any other spiritually advanced human being commonly called master, but to simply engage people philosophically and encourage them to develop themselves and enjoy the full potential of being humans.

Again the desire of God is for all to be bright stars and manage the rest of creation, not that a human being has dominion over another. When this happens, the planets and other entities surrounding each human-star will not be other humans, but beings of different species and realms corresponding to the idea of Genesis 1: 28-30 and Qur'an [17: 61] according to which God established mankind as superintendent.

Those who have tried to abuse other humans, even to a slight extent, should repent and take the bright path, the path of the *'True Master of oneself and contributor to the development of the Universe.'* Evil is not necessary for happiness. In the contrary, it is the biggest obstacle to true happiness.

God is the Existence that sustains suns or stars and everything else. Now that astronomy has showed there are billions of stars, to take one star, for example the sun of the earth as the exclusive symbol of God appears inappropriate. It becomes obvious that the sun should represent a particular angel, god, or human; maybe the angelic God of the Old Testament who tried to embody the will of the Supreme God or Universal Soul. Hence, the doctrines of ancient religions based on sun worship should be reassessed.

Nevertheless, since light is part of the Supreme God and since God made angels, humans, and the rest of the universe with light; any source of light including the sun, an angel, a human, and so forth can help meditate on God.

In *Isis Unveiled*, Theosophists give an inspiring explanation of God. In their first principle, they reject the idea that the Supreme God has a human form. In their second principle, they acknowledge the Logos and the Demiurge.

Their idea of a collective Demiurge is acceptable. Theosophists assimilate the Logos to the Demiurge, but the Logos is subtler than the Demiurge. The Logos is the Word, the Divine Science, and the True Spiritual Science that helped even for the coming into existence of the Demiurge. In their third principle, Theosophists affirm that intelligence, soul, and consciousnesses unite within energy or matter and guide it. In their fourth principle they affirm, with reason, the eternity of matter and energy.

The Temple of the People, a theosophical offshoot, sees ether, as subtle energy. In the *lesson 64* of the first volume of its teachings, it acknowledges the place of light and defines God in manifestation as one great life principle that lives, moves and has His being in matter, force, and consciousness [human consciousness].

Thinking of God as a principle is correct but some can misunderstand this point. They can take God just for a force that can be used as shown in the cartoon *Shaman King*. The idea of the anthropomorphic God is not rejected to fall into that trap.

As the Ultimate Intelligence, Emotion, Will, and Energy, God is a person, meaning a consciousness, Consciousness, Superconsciousness, the Universal Person in which as Paul said we have our beings; existing, living, and moving [Acts 17: 28]. Hence, Divinity is not simply a Principle, but a Person, a Mind, a Soul [universal] or Consciousness with Principles. Speaking of God as Principles organized as Soul or Mind is clearer than presenting God as a Principle [at the singular].

In a way, everything including mankind exists within God, as part of God and contributes to define the reality that God is. Through creation the Original Unique Person, has become many. Hermes expressed the same idea saying that God is bodiless and yet everybody is his. He is all that exists[42].

The Original Unique Person was Mind in Energy. Through creation, parts of Energy have been individualized and some of those parts [for example humans] have also received minds or souls. What remains of that Original Unique Person after creation is the God-in-relation-to-creation. That is why God has been reduced by some created beings to the Universal Mind or Universal Soul, a being separated from them.

God is both present in the Holy Spirit as well as in the other forms of energies, lights, matters, or fires. But the Holy Spirit is the Remaining Original Energy that responds more quickly to the will of the Universal Mind. The Hindu saying that God created the world and entered it; with however a significant part out of it is thus clear.

Therefore, there are two ways of thinking about God. The first one includes creation and corresponds to a modification of the Original Unique Person; the second is the God in relation, formless without

---

[42]Salaman, *The Way of Hermes*, 35.

the forms given to created beings, and who acts swiftly through the Holy Spirit or Holy Fire.

God is perceived according to the level of spiritual development of human beings. Some cannot perceive the Divine; but even in the most evil beings, God is present but quiet, almost inaccessible, and waiting to be revealed through personal work on oneself.

Humanity is still striving to understand the God present within creation. It is harder maybe useless for now to try to understand the God beyond creation. This is how the unknowable and the knowable God can be explained.

Chapter 14

The Fatherhood and Motherhood of God

God as Creator, Parent, Male and Female

IN the two preceding chapters, the Fatherhood and Motherhood

of God have been explored from the angle of the Father, the Son, and the Holy Spirit. It was shown how the conception of an anthropomorphic God such as the Ancient of Days is incorrect and how His Fatherhood can be symbolically admitted. The Holy Spirit also has been proved to be Divine Energy, the motherhood of which is also symbolical from a certain philosophical standpoint. How Jesus is the first born has also been seen.

An additional explanation will now include the analysis of the verb 'to beget' and the fatherhood and motherhood of the gods of ancient civilizations and Old Religions. This discussion will also include the analysis of the phrase 'the sons of God' in Genesis 6:2, 4; Job 1: 6;

and Job 38: 7 as well as that of the concept of androgyny or hermaphroditism.

To beget, apart from pointing to the parent-child relationship also means to cause, to produce, and to create. Therefore whenever a saying within or outside the Bible does not appear logical with the terms 'father,' 'mother,' 'son,' and 'to beget' at the first degree, that saying makes sense when the term is understood in the sense of 'to cause' or 'to create.'

Hermes declared that the Father's nature is to create[43] clearly showing that *the very Fatherhood of God is to be understood in terms of creation.* To beget also means to have a philosophical child as a result of education whether general, spiritual, or religious like in the case of Paul in Philemon: 8-10.

In ancient civilizations and old religions, there is a cause and effect relationship between natural phenomena and this relationship is transferred to the gods that represent them. That is how a god is the father or son of another. For example, since there is air between the sky and the earth, ancient Egyptians considered Shu, the god of air as the force that keeps earth and sky separated and therefore as the father of Nut, the goddess of the sky and of Geb, the god of earth.

Since to father can mean to create, the biblical passages that speak of angels as sons of God could be understood.

In some cases, a son in disgrace is no longer considered a child; he remains a son when he follows the will of the father. In Job 38: 7, the angels are sons of God because they were doing what was expected from them. In Genesis 6: 2, 4, some angels were still sons of God because though they were about to lose that status, they had not lost it yet. In Job 1: 6, after the fall, the sons of God [the faithful angels] were separated from Satan who was no longer a divine son.

---

[43]Salaman, *The Way of Hermes,* 29.

As Hans Küng rightly says[44], Jesus was not the first to know God as Father as many believe. Kings David and Solomon and Israelites at least knew that before him [1Chronicles 22: 10]. The God of Solomon knew he already had a father in the person of King David, but still he wanted to be a father to him. To create and to father in language are very close concepts figuratively and also literally. Indeed, Solomon was born from the flesh of his father David and mother Bathsheba. The flesh of these parents came from their parents' and ultimately from God.

The bodies of animals, plants, and minerals also have the same origin. But God is not called their Father. It would make sense though that God be called the father of animals, plants, and mineral at the light of the explanation given. However, this attitude would not separate enough mankind from the other beings to the taste of some. The notions of fatherhood and motherhood seem more appropriate for the human sphere. In that case, the mistake not to make is to restrict God to humanity. God is more than the Father of humans. He is the creator of the entire universe and its population.

Küng finds striking that in matriarchal cultures, in place of the "Father God", there is a "Great Mother" out of whose fertile womb all things and all beings emerged and into which they return. He believes that the nature of a society conditions the kind of God it has. He is also of the opinion that the Fatherhood of God is to be taken symbolically or analogically. For him as for many other scholars, the God of the Old Testament does not present only masculine characters but feminine traits as well.

Küng draws attention on the fact that God was the Father of Israel *which was His firstborn son*, particularly the King of Israel. He then advances that the title of Jesus as 'Son of God' does not mean a

---

[44]Hans Küng, *Does God Exist?: An Answer for Today* (Garden City, N.Y.: Doubleday, 1980), 672-673.

miraculous procreation. Küng advocates for more recognition of God as mother.

Sylvia Browne, the Gnostic psychic, succeeded in not making the Holy Spirit a Mother God rather identifying it with the Light of God. She also supported the concept of Father God and Mother God thus acknowledging almost an Androgynous Ultimate Reality. She speaks, in *Phenomenon*, of the Father God as the Intellect of the universe and of the Mother God, named Azna as the Emotion of the universe.

In describing Azna, she introduced the image of a woman holding a sword but she gives no representation of the Father. Her description of God is different from the one presented in the chapter on the anthropomorphic God and in this volume in general.

The notion of God is part philosophical and part experiential because there is the knowable God and the unknowable God and because the knowable God is progressively revealed or progressively known. Hence, the brainstorming between revelations and beyond is of philosophical nature while the revelations or knowledge already accessed constitutes empirical data.

The experiential part is made of the revelations of people like Hermes, Jesus, the authors of Psalms 104: 2 and 1 Timothy 6: 16, the experiences and writings of Seeker, and so on. The philosophical part is the understanding or the explanation of the revelations and the estimation of the nature of new possible revelations. This is speculative philosophy and as such it is not knowledge. Nevertheless, it is not blind faith or a leap of faith and is more than it because it has a logical foundation.

Under the reserve of further experiential information, it can be said based on logic that the concept of Father-Mother-God of Sylvia Browne has some flaws. Indeed, though God is mysterious in many ways to humans, it cannot be logically said that the Father God is the Intellect and the Mother God is the Emotion. Some could quickly jump to the conclusion that the Father God has no emotion and that Mother

God has no intellect. This would be rejected on the ground that the Father God and the Mother God would then be pure single principles and that God would not be a person.

One of the broadest definitions for the term 'person' is given by the free online dictionary. It qualifies as a person, the composite of the characteristics that make up an individual personality; the self. Dictionary.com speaks of a self-conscious being or a rational being.

The core that characterizes a person is the intellect, the emotion and the will, plus other characteristics such as the thought, the word, creativity, and so on.

If God the Father in Browne's theory is pure Intellect and God the Mother is pure Emotion, then each of the other Divine Principles would have to be a God. Thus, there would also be a God representing the Will. Some could bring the Word or Jesus Christ in here but that will not do since Jesus Christ himself acknowledged he came to do the Will of the Father. If God the Father has a Will, "He" is a *Person* and not a pure Intellect and "He" should not be deprived of Emotion either. Thus, the concept of Father God as pure Intellect and Mother God as pure Emotion cannot be accepted.

A second way of understanding Browne is that God results from the unity of two persons and would be dual instead of triune for example. The idea sounds attractive especially when one remembers that Adam and Eve are the image of God, as two separated beings, with the purpose of unity. But Adam and Eve, together, can be the image of God even if God is not Dual but Unique.

Additionally, two Persons in one poses the problem of two Wills. This opens the possibility for clashes between one Will directed by Reason and another governed by Emotion. The problem would be complicated by the fact that Emotion has a certain reason and Reason has a certain emotion because the Father and the Mother are Persons but with one dominant trait each.

In the case of the Dual God, two Persons as the Godhead, one could say that Reason would appeal to the certain reason of Emotion and Emotion would appeal to the certain emotion of Reason for absolute and mutual understanding and unity [God as One] to happen. The point is that Reason or Intellect, 'God the Father,' would always win because there is no emotion, no love or hatred without some reason.

Browne herself acknowledges in *Exploring the Levels of Creation*[45] that the intellect gives direction, while emotion activates to go in that direction. This brings back to the old saying to "*Think before acting.*" However, it ought to be added that before to go in a direction, the will intervenes after the emotion and before the act.

There is a reason for everything. What makes certain people think that reason is not everywhere is that in some cases, the reason is not apparent or obvious, but hidden or unknown to the thinker who is ignorant concerning a great number of subjects. This is one of the reasons of the existence of research: to determine the unobvious reasons behind phenomena.

Many other people affirm that love is the primordial principle or force. Philosophically, there is some truth in this statement; however the affirmation is not absolute. In fact, the relativity here is so important that all in all, reason still emerges as the prime principle.

This nebulous statement deserves some explanation.

There is a difference between the creation of life and the enjoyment of life. For life to be created, the first requirement is knowledge, reason, intellect, truth, science, law, or wisdom. The affirmation of Jesus in John 6: 63 that the word [logos, science, reason] is spirit and life is illustrative enough. Some might also want to consider John 5:

---

[45]Sylvia Browne, *Exploring the Levels of Creation* (Carlsbad, Calif: Hay House, 2006), 144.

24 which states that the word is also resurrection. To enjoy life, the most important thing is love.

That there is an appropriate way to love is a fact. What determines the appropriate way to love then? It is the word, wisdom, logos, reason, intellect, law, knowledge, science, or truth. Love has no value without life, especially without the life of the mind. Love or emotion plays a role in the generation of life especially human life. But the life of the parents ultimately, the first parents [religiously Adam and Eve] cannot be without the word [see Genesis 1].

Once life begins, what makes it worth living is predominantly love but intellect or law or reason is required for its beginning. What is the worth of the love of a crazy person? Let us be reasonable, let us nourish the mind with truth or wisdom or knowledge, then let us love. It is only that way that our love will truly exist.

Since reason would always give the direction as Browne too acknowledged, Mother God in her theory would always obey Father God and will not have a Free Will; or Her Free Will would be an illusion. This would be a problem to many worshipers and certainly to feminists. But the feminist question in general will be dealt with in another work.

An attempt can be made to stipulate that the situation of dominance is temporary and that Mother God would evolve toward the perfection of Her reason while Father God would evolve toward the perfection of His emotion. This would lead to the finality of two Gods, Independent from each other, Self-sufficient, alike in perfection, in purpose, and goodness.

The question now is: why would the Dual God go through an evolutionary process to be two Identical Gods instead of the Unique God simply existing with Perfect Reason and Perfect Emotion from the start?

Any of the two dual theories of God as two Principles or two Persons opens the ways to triune and "quatriune" Gods etc..., considering more and more attributes of God. For Example an association of the Intellect, the Emotion, the Will, and the Word would give a "qua-triune" God that can be called "Quatuornity". This directly leads to the forms of polytheism, particular kinds of henotheism, or different forms of pantheism.

The second possibility of an evolutionary process resulting in two Supreme Gods is a total waste of time. So, the dual theory based on Sylvia Browne' s idea is without foundation. According to the report of Hermes, the Universal Nous told him that God is One and that a plurality of Gods would be absurd[46].

In *If You Could See What I See*, Browne describes Father God and Mother God as Male Principle and Female Principle[47]; but she also identifies Mother God with Azna, or Theodora, or Sophia, or Isis, or Hera; a person and the most important goddess in some cultures. Again, she gives no name and no representation for Father God and states that He usually chooses not to hold a form for very long. Some might expect at this point that Browne introduces Osiris, Zeus, or another major male deity as Father God, but she does not.

On the same page Browne compares the Father to the head and the Mother to the heart. What this volume would have expected from her is that she states that the head and the heart belong to the same person, not each to a different person with two Gods at the end. But such a declaration may push to want to know if the Unique God is Male or Female. This is the understanding that the idea of the andro-gynous God will offer.

The concept of androgynous God was expressed by Hermes. This idea is also expressed in the ancient Egyptian creation myth which calls the god Atum, the *Great He-She* that was alone in the

---

[46]Salaman, *The Way of Hermes*, 55.
[47]Sylvia Browne, *If You Could See What I See: The Tenets of Novus Spiritus* (Carlsbad, Calif: Hay House, 2006), 183.

beginning, created the universe, and is the Soul of the Universe. Since Hermes Trismegistus was from ancient Egypt, it is possible that he was the author of the myth or that he studied it. So *Atum as universal mind is male-female.*

This concept of androgynous God is in harmony with the notion of God as a Person, a Unique Person, with one Intellect, Emotion, Will, Word etc…, *as explained in the chapter devoted to Jesus [partially by the diagram].*

An androgynous or hermaphrodite being according to the dictionary is a being with both male and female characteristics.

Wisteme on its website and in *What animals on earth are androgynous animals,* speaks of complete androgyny or complete hermaphroditism in which impregnation takes place without assistance and cites the molluscous of the classes of *Conchifera* and *Tunicata* as examples.

The other situation of androgyny presented is that in which impregnation takes place by mutual application of the sexual organs of two individuals. The snail and the slug are such androgynous animals. There are also androgynous plants like *Arum maculatum* also called Adam and Eve that are androgynous having male and female flowers on the same root.

According the Spiritual Science Research Foundation, angels can be either male or female but the highest among them do not identify themselves with any gender[48]. To Sylvia Browne, angels are androgynous; there are no male angels and female angels[49].

Hence there are proofs of the existence androgynous animals and plants, and statements that there are androgynous spirits [to verify by

---

[48]Spiritual Science research Foundation, "*Angels: a spiritual perspective*" http://www.spiritualresearchfoundation.org/articles/id/spiritualresearch/spiritualscience/angel#36 (accessed July 14, 2010).
[49]Browne, *Phenomena*, 15.

each person in his/her development].There is also an extensive literature about androgynous human beings who have existed in the past on earth, for example in the writings of Madame Blavatsky. But again, this affirmation requires proofs.

With these examples from the animal, vegetal, and the spiritual kingdoms, the idea of the androgynous God appears credible. Among all the concepts of God, it is the only concept supported by revelation to Hermes, testimonies of psychics, logic, and solid evidences from physical science, in this case zoology and botany.

The Nous or Mind of Hermes is androgynous means that there is the Intelligence, the Information, the Ideas, the Essence, the Emotion and so forth... of masculine and feminine beings in God. God is the Male-Female Universal Consciousness.

However, the Hermetic androgynous God is different from the Hindu hermaphrodite God. The Hindu notion, the union of Shiva and Shakti corresponds *partially* to the Nous and the Light while the Hermetic one corresponds *completely* to that union on the one hand and to the union of plus and minus *within the Nous or Mind "Itself"*.

Actually it is Vishnu who is the Universal Intellect in Hindu philosophy. Therefore Shiva would need to unite with Vishnu to come close in meaning to the Nous of Hermeticism. Moreover, some aspects such as the anthropomorphism and masculinity of both Hindu deities make the parallel only partial.

Now the question that should be asked is if human spiritualists ever wondered how the angels call God.

Angels, according to scriptures do not have children; therefore the expressions 'Father God' and 'Mother God' should not mean as much to them as it means to humans. Having themselves children, the latter have come to value the parent-child relationship above everything else. Therefore they have come to think of God as Father and Mother or Parent and of themselves as His-Her children.

Though scripture in John 8:44 calls the Devil, 'father of lies,' as said in the beginning of this chapter, this fatherhood is not literal but symbolic. It has also been said that calling God 'Father', 'Mother' or both or parent is a way to say that God is the author and the origin of all beings.

In reality, no human has seriously tried to say that God is Father or Mother the way men and women are. Seeker has had the thought that something must be the most valuable in the angelic realm and that they must call God or relate to God through that reality. He suspects that thing to be light, knowledge, and wisdom; and that this is the reason why the spiritual schools or religions who are guided by the Immortals [whether angels or demons] emphasize those elements.

But what name of God can be inclusive of all created beings? The word 'God' is not bad but something more can be done.

Beyond the Fatherhood and the Motherhood of God: The 'I AM' concept in religion, spirituality, and philosophy

According to Exodus 3: 14, God said to Moses His-Her Name is '*I AM WHO I AM*' or simply '*I AM*'. Hermes[50] affirmed that God is all that exists; therefore "He" has all names and that is why "He Himself" has no name.

In the report of his vision, Hermes says that God is the Nous [or Intellect] of the Mind in the Light. Since a person is considered as mind and body and also as spirit, his/her name should include all these realities. God as whole is "I AM", the Creator and the Created united.

---

[50]Salaman, *The Way or Hermes,* 35.

Several Israelites, Jews and many others believe that the name of God which was given in Hebrew has been lost due to the respect of the commandment that states people should not take the name of God in vain. At the same time Manly Hall affirms that some schools still possess that knowledge which gives them great power.

This introduces the question of the sacred alphabet. What alphabet is the most sacred, since the world has many of them? Words generally have two forms: the written one and the spoken one [image and sound]. Since there is a Divine Word, there must be a Divine Alphabet and a Divine Language.

Many spiritualists such as Emanuel Swedenborg think that the Divine Language was spoken by Adam and angels and that it has been gradually lost due to human corruption. They think it was a symbolic language that became less and less symbolic and less powerful in Egypt and Sumer and that the Hebrew Language that later appeared, after the Arabic and at the same time as the Aramaic and the Phoenician, is even less powerful.

At the light of these elements, what value to give the name and/or title of God in Hebrew? Emanuel Swedenborg thought the ancient language will be regained while Sylvia Browne insists on telepathic communication between angels and humans. Before the time in which definitive answers to that issue can be offered, it is of prime importance to remember that sounds and images serve as conveyers of ideas which characterize realities.

Concerning the reality of God the best way to conceive and relate to Him-Her is through the 'I AM'. 'I AM' indeed summarizes everything that has been, is, will be, and could be. 'I AM' is understandable in any language as conveying the idea of the Ultimate Reality.

According to Sikhism, the names of things are simply the Word of God which is equivalent to the 'Speech' of Hermes; which humans uses in association with the Nous or Intellect or Reason to manage the cosmos.

Any secular philosopher who thinks deeply about what has been expressed long ago in Exodus 3: 14, thus in the Bible, would come to the conclusion that spirituality and religion are not total ideological messes.

Good philosophers can come to point out wonders in old scriptures, but they also have the duty to identify what does not make sense, and even add new ideas to them. Good psychics or mystics can endeavors to prove that every supernatural description mentioned is not an invention. They have been doing so more or less successfully. But the works of all these contributors needs to be united and accelerated.

The 'I AM' concept is a scriptural and philosophical notion so true that it authorizes to see the supernatural encounters of Moses not as a myth or something that never happened but as genuine spiritual experiences. If it was through thinking or meditation alone that the author of Exodus 3: 14 made its statement "inventing" all the religious story of ancient Israel, it would mean that there can be philosophical statements of outstanding nature in spirituality and religion.

The concept of 'I am' is also emphasized in the Hindu creation myth.

From the experience of Moses and the scripture of Exodus 3: 14, one can establish a connection with Hermes, Ancient Egyptian religion, and many other spiritual systems via the thoughts of the philosophers René Descartes and Blaise Pascal introduced at the beginning of the introductory chapter.

Philosophically, Descartes and Pascal made it clear that the 'I am', the existence of a human has to do fundamentally with the thinking part or the mind. Long before them, Moses the religious, spiritual, and receiver of divine revelations had offered the possibility to see the Whole Universe, physical and non-physical as the 'I AM'. Hermes Trismegistus also long before Descartes and Pascal has emphasized the importance of the Mind, not just the human mind as

them, but also and above all the Divine Mind, that Thinks too and
produces the Word or Reason or Wisdom using Nous or intellect.

Scripture tells that God has made the glory of King Solomon
through divine wisdom and Solomon has called wisdom and intelligence the tree of life in the book of Proverbs [3: 13-18]. This confirms
the previous reasoning that Intellect is the real giver of life and preeminent over emotion.

Crystalink on its website describes the ancient Egyptian god
Thoth as the Mind of Re, the supreme god. Thoth was called 'Lord of
Divine Words' involved in arbitration, magic, writing science, and
judgment. He was considered the author of all works of science,
religion, philosophy, and magic and was declared by Greeks to be the
inventor of astronomy, the science of numbers [numerology], mathematics, geometry, land surveying, medicine, botany, theology, civilized government, the alphabet; the true author of every work of every
branch of knowledge, human and divine.

In all this, one can see that 'Thoth' was another name for 'Nous' or
the 'Divine Mind' of Hermes and that there is no separation between
the science of physical things and that of spiritual ones.

Paul, despite his mistakes was vigilant enough to recognize the
value of divine wisdom [1 Corinthians 2: 1-7], the power of common
sense [2 Thessalonians 2:2] and that of analysis [1 Thessalonians 5:
19-21]. John 1 and Proverbs 8 respectively placed the Word and
Wisdom at origins of the universe.

Gnostics value the gnosis, wisdom, and mystical knowledge; and
philosophers by definition are lovers of wisdom. Several religions and
spiritual schools emphasize the Divine Word and the Divine Law. One
can see why many philosophers have been spiritual and why many
spiritual people engaged deeply in philosophical thinking or meditation.

Thoughts, wisdom, reason, and words can be corrupted by negative jealousy and madness the prophet Ezekiel showed [28: 17].

Jealousy and madness' is another expression for 'sick ego' or 'out of balance ego'.

Hence the concepts of Mind, Soul, Thought, Word, Reason, Meditation, Intelligence, Science, Instruction, Discernment, and Wisdom are all interconnected and are the foundation of the Universe, spiritual and physical.

Coming back to the Fatherhood, the Motherhood, and the Name of God, since He-She gave the 'I AM' concept to Moses through angels, it appears that both the angelic and human sphere should relate to the Ultimate Reality through that notion.

'I AM' is the Ultimate. The Everything in which _we_ move and have our _be_ing. 'I' who spoke to Moses through the angel and 'I' [Francis, Moses, Michael, Gabriel, Elephant, Ant, Carbon, Hydrogen, Proton, Photon, and so forth]… AM part of the 'I AM'. When people say '_We are One,_' they are affirming the 'I AM'.

It is amazing that both the pantheistic and the anthropomorphic ideas of God are present in the Bible. But the 'I AM', the pantheistic view, is all inclusive.

'I am' is the microscopic ego. 'I AM' is the Macroscopic Ego. The Macroscopic Ego is the healing of the microscopic ego.

WE ARE ONE. WE ARE. I…AM.

Chapter 15

Existence and nature of God from religious, spiritual, and philosophical perspectives

On the existence of God

HOW science, philosophy, spirituality, and scripture cooperate
to lead to God has been explained in chapter 10. Now a case will be
made for the existence of God through arguments that are in harmony with the explanations already given on key theological concepts
such as the Holy Spirit, the anthropomorphism of God, the Fatherhood and Motherhood of God, and Jesus. The purpose is to answer
the fundamental question: *what God for the 21st century and the ages
to come?*

During the 6th year of his medical studies, Seeker has had the opportunity to discuss with two nurses from France on the subject of
God. They were doing their international internship and it was in
2002. Even at that time, most discussions with Seeker used to quickly

turn to the topic of God. He does not remember how this particular discussion started but somehow the two nurses realized that God was his favorite topic and that he thought he knew God.

In contrary to Seeker, the two ladies were atheists and enjoyed showing it almost as much as Seeker liked talking about God. The entire discussion went on in a friendly atmosphere. Cigarette in the hand, one of the nurses asked Seeker why he was so convinced of the existence of God because in Europe, the great majority of the population no longer holds such a belief.

Before giving his answer, Seeker shared with the young nurse his surprise that people do not believe in God anymore in Europe while in the past Europeans have brought many teachings concerning that God mainly through Christianity to several parts of the world including Africa. But he also expressed his confidence that God will find His-Her way back in Europe because it was still a continent of great intellectual people and because there are plenty of explanations on God that would satisfy their developed sense of reason.

On that, the other nurse assured Seeker that no argument would ever convince her and that she was sure she would have heard a variant of any argument he had to present. However, she encouraged him to try convincing her. Seeker then asked what the cause of her life on earth was. She answered she came from her parents. Then he asked where her parents came from and she replied they came from their own parents for sure. Then she realized that on that way the discussion would go on and on.

So she admitted that Seeker was posing the question of the origin of human kind, and then she thought about the origin of life. He told her that even before life there were things that existed and phenomena that occurred in order to allow its appearance and that *God is the last cause possible when one reviews all the causes behinds all phenomena.*

The nurses responded that they never heard such argument and asked him if he really wanted to make them admit that God existed and Seeker replied that it would be good to admit what their reason told them and the discussion ended. He could see that they were no longer as sure that God does not exist as at the beginning of the chat. But he also perceived it would be hard for them to really come to accept that Existence for two reasons.

The first reason dwells in the education they have already received which has shaped their psychology, or crystallized them. Since most people know that someone who accepts the existence of God and is honest with him/herself usually disagrees with certain life styles, Seeker thought in himself that it could be hard for the two ladies who were nice people to draw all the consequences of the existence of God.

The second difficulty that he found was that if they return to their home country, they probably would not find someone like him among their friends to stimulate their intellect towards God examining all arguments for and against Him-Her as he has trained himself to do. He was pretty sure that in case they express a desire or doubt in favor of God, most of their friends, relatives, and co-workers would find them weird, possibly ridicule and discourage them.

When he later read elaborated agnostic and atheistic philosophies such as the ones expressed in the book 'The Improbability of God' and summarized in chapter 7, Seeker knew he would have to make much more effort of reason and wisdom than in the discussion with the nurses if he expects any agnostic or atheist to seriously engage in a spiritual life with God at its center. The new details of his cause and effect argument are regrouped in the first section of his response to the concerns of atheists [see cosmological arguments].

In response to agnostic concerns

Does the human mind really lack the information or rational capacity to make judgment about the existence or nature of God as T. H. Huxley and the other agnostics think[51]? Is God unknowable or inscrutable as Herbert Spencer declared? Is it possible to maintain faith independently of empirical evidence as David Hume suggested? Such are the questions that this section will try to answer.

As mentioned earlier, empirical evidences are of two kinds: the physical ones and the spiritual ones. Physical evidences are perceived with the physical organs of sense helped in some cases by instruments. To perceive spiritual evidences, one needs spiritual senses which unfortunately do not have the same level of readiness in all human beings.

That is why many spiritual researchers offered methods for spiritual growth. The spiritual body is developed for the purpose of living in the afterlife. Paul's affirmation in 1 Corinthians 15: 43-44 that it is not the physical animal body that resurrects but a glorious spiritual body is thus understandable.

However, Paul wrongly thought that the physical body is transformed into a spiritual one at the resurrection while in fact the spiritual body grows with the physical body and separates from it at physical death.

For example it was only after 20 years that Seeker began noticing the manifestations of his spiritual body. One day, between 2005 and 2007, waking up from a dream, Seeker literally felt an energy body taking place back in his physical body, in every compartment of that body. He was able to feel at that moment two parallels bodies completely intermingling, one filling the other as electricity in gross matter.

---

[51] *The Encyclopedia Americana*, 2000 ed., s.v. "agnosticism."

In the dream, Seeker was giving a lecture on God, urging people especially one of his friends from high and medical schools to obey "His" laws. During the lecture a powerful force began attracting him toward a white luminous hole that had appeared above his head. The light was shaped like a doline or a funnel with the smaller hole up. Fearing that passing through that hole would mean his physical death, Seeker desperately asked God to let him live longer on earth to accomplish some important works. He came close to the hole and high above the ground before the attracting power diminished and started going back down.

It was during that descent that he woke up and noticed for the first time in his consciousness that his spirit was coming back and witnessed the mingling process with his physical senses almost completely awakened. It was an amazing moment with a sensation that dwelt with him until today. Later, he came across books describing similar experiences and knew it was one aspect that spiritual science can rely on, study, and reproduce.

One should not expect too much that people who have not developed a subtle body and organs of sense perceive and understand spiritual things. The two major chances they have are: first to be so advanced in the science of physical things that they reach the border or junction between the physical world and the spiritual world and begin to empirically sense spiritual things. The second opportunity, which is rare is that God bestows a grace according to His-Her sole discretion.

So, the simple answer to agnosticism will be in the form of a question. How can one perceive evidences he/she is not equipped to perceive? If agnostics were to have those experiences, far from being imagination as they can accuse them to be, they will also see that the human mind has the rational capacity to make judgments about the existence and the nature of God. That is why Paul said in 1 Corinthians 2: 14: '*The animal man does not accept the things that come from the Spirit of God, for they are foolishness to him, and he cannot understand them, because they are spiritually discerned.'*

It is possible to maintain faith without experiential evidences as Hume shyly suggested. But it would be better for it to be rooted on a very solid philosophy. Hence, philosophy or the quest of wisdom can provide enough indication to push the "animal man" of Paul on the spiritual path.

The same Paul in Romans 1: 20 and Hermes[52] suggest beginning the philosophical work that leads to more knowledge of God by considering the physical world and by remembering that a statue or a portrait cannot come into being without a sculptor or a painter. The Universal Nous [God] also told Hermes that "He" had made all things so that through them, "He" could be seen[53]. Thus, Hermes highly recommended contemplation of nature and thinking up on it [meditation].

The practice of spiritual science with a good heart and purpose will offer many evidences for the existence of the supernatural realm and God. As it has been demonstrated, it is not only possible to humans to know the divine and the supernatural, some actually already know part of it. What remains is to make more progresses and generalize them to the entire human race.

In response to atheistic concerns

Rational atheism and romantic atheism which react respectively against a confusing and a frightening God have good reasons. Several of those reasons directed against religion but also against spirituality have been acknowledged in chapter 10. The objective of

---

[52] Salaman, *The Way of Hermes*, 35.
[53]Ibid.,58.

this section is to try not to set aside any accusation made directly against God and present a new case for God as reasonably as possible. The following is a counter proposal to "*The improbability of God*" as summarized in chapter 7.

A- Cosmological arguments

A-1- The scientific case for a God who created the universe

It has already been said that supernatural evidences are collected and analyzed through supernatural abilities. However, one can still make a case for a God who created the universe by proving the wrongness of the use of natural evidences to make a case against God. The use of the cause effect-argument by Hermes, Paul [Romans 1: 20], and others will be placed back in its right dimension.

A-1-a- About the conservation of energy that is said to be against God

The existence of matter in the universe did not require the violation of the energy conservation [$E= mc2$]; therefore there has been no creator say the atheists.

The law of conservation of energy is true. But it has been shown that the original energy was, truly speaking, an attribute of the Original God, a kind of Body, because God is Nous [Mind] in energy.

A-1-b- Against the lack of imprint argument

This world itself is an imprint of the Creator. But if it is a supernatural imprint that is sought, maybe the microscopes, spectrophotometers, telescopes, and so on, are not what should be used.

A-1-c- Since there is no beginning, there is no creator?

How does the existence of previous universes infirm the existence of a God who is said to be the Alpha and the Omega [Revelation 1: 8], Eternal Being, without beginning and without End?

A-2-a- The cause and effect argument

During his discussion on God with the two nurses, Seeker unknowingly following Thomas Aquinas and others, has used the cause and effect argument. But in *The Improbability of God*, the argument has been rejected on the ground that the universe has no cause and therefore it is better to stick with that fact rather than create the obscure notion of God and affirm it is the cause of the universe. *Suggestion was made to simply consider the universe itself as God*, since there is no evidence of someone beyond it.

As said earlier, there is a reality within matter or energy of various degrees or forms that animates it and that is called the Universal Soul or Universal Mind or God.

This first God as Hermes called it is the *essential* part of God who revealed itself to people in the past and even today but not entirely. There is a knowable God who can be perceived and felt by those who can.

This little demonstration replaces the cause-effect argument in its proper formulation and could entirely convince those who ascribe great value to scriptures such as those of Hermes and the Bible.

But in addition, what can pure secular philosophy, pure physical empirism, and reason tell about the existence of a Reality that animates matter from within?

Whatever form of organized matter is considered, it obeys the instructions from a center within itself. Living cells, with nucleus are organized and function according to the information contained in the DNA of the nucleus. The DNA seems to contain everything needed to auto-replicate and cause the building of entire organisms.

The DNA also seems to be in contradiction with the principle of anterior cause. But since it is made up of smaller molecules, there must have been a time when the first DNA was not organized as such and a cause must have organized it. Some believe that that kind of organization just happened randomly.

Jainism is a religion that can be called the spiritual Darwinism or the religious Nietzscheism because it declares that men are Gods or Gods to be and that the universe does not need someone to create and manage it. Nevertheless, apart from what exist in nature, human beings create the things they need. If those things require creators, it is not correct to say that nature, which is more complex and more organized does not need a Creator.

Some may say that humans as the collective consciousness or collective unconsciousness are creators of the universe and that they have *forgotten* their works and identity. That would be a declaration without proof. It is better to just acknowledge that as far as humans know, they have not created universe.

The randomness in the theory of evolution will be further tackled later in this chapter. Here, it is important to notice that the adversaries of God are the "followers" of *Randomness*. After a series of events and realities which all have an anterior state or cause, evolutionists chose *'no ultimate cause at all'* instead of *'a ultimate cause misunderstood.'* Even according to the standards of the science of physical things or those of secular philosophy, the second attitude is better in terms of soundness, reliability, reasonableness, and fairness to the first. And there is further explanation to support that.

There was a reason why the first molecule of DNA was formed the way it had been. Part of that reason lies in the ability of the small molecules to form that macromolecule and in the ability of the atoms to form the small molecules. This shows that the potential of having a DNA existed long before the DNA actually manifested and that a specific pattern was successfully followed to that step. The pattern is explainable, replicable, and is not the succession of tiny little chances as evolutionists say.

Other phenomena apparently seem not to have causes like in the hen and the egg story and in certain physical mechanics like oscillations in clocks. But an attentive analysis always reveals the causes. Even microwaves, which are invisible to the naked eye, have a source. Thoughts which constitute extremely subtle realities originate from the mind.

Hence, observation shows that within the mass of energy, the little universe or microcosm that a human is, there is a mind [with intellect, emotion, and will, not randomness] that is behind the human activities. Why then would there not be a Universal Mind within the Mass of Energy or Macrocosm that the Universe is? *This is an existential question.*

The mind is invisible to the naked eye and determines significantly what goes on in and around the body. Why would there not be a Universal Mind that determines what is goes on in the universe including things humans ignore? *This is a functional question.*

If the origin of the human body is Matter, Energy, or the second God of Hermes, why would there not be an origin of the human mind, the Universal Mind or first God of Hermes? *This is a logical question.*

It is not reasonable to accept the existence of an origin for the human body which is of the same nature and refuse similar inference considering the human mind.

The problem many seem not to perceive when denying or seeking God is that the Mind is the essential part of God and that it cannot be approached; related to; or analyzed the way matter is. Energy [when not under the influence of a powerful will and intellect] is there to be analyzed, measured, tested, manipulated, used etc... But the mind does not accept that kind of relationship. The Mind values things such as respect, love, and proper way of doing things or truth or knowledge.

Even a baby cannot be treated as mere matter. How about a 7 years old child? How about a teenager? How about someone in the 30s, 40s, 50s and beyond? How about the Universal Mind, God?

A person with enough wisdom, after reading the two lines above and the preceding ones, would understand why God has to be related to in spirit [mind] as it is said in John 4: 24 and why truth, wisdom are important in the relationship with "Him." That is why people with greater truth or knowledge, wisdom, and love are closer to God. That is why they tirelessly seek the company of each other and enjoy it when it is gradually built. They "see" God, know Him/Her better, and learn why the pursuit of the wellness of the community or that of the world already includes their own wellness.

When virtues manifests in a relationship, from partners, mutual trust increases, more dear things are shared and the weak person is empowered.

The universe could be considered not as God but only as the body of the knowable God. A human being is not his body alone. Calling the universe God would be to ignore the internal Power that moves energy and all beings in the cosmos. It would be similar to calling a human being a body. Even atheists would find it difficult to be reduced to their bodies. Some might be reluctant to accept that they have souls; however they would easily admit that they have minds or psyches which are the same things as explained in chapter 12.

Since the mind is more important than the body, it makes more sense to reduce God to the Mind than to the universe.

Coming back to the arguments in 'The improbability of God ' where they were left, it is really strange that "science" admits an exception to the law of conservation of energy. Doubly strange is the purpose of such exception: to prove that God does not exist. Indeed the opposite argument of the conservation of matter has previously been used to prove the non-existence of God.

Why in God's name would electrons, positrons, and photons spontaneously emerge in certain occasions in perfect vacuum according to Heisenberg uncertainty principles? The scientific mind normally recommends admitting that a vacuum is not perfect if electrons, positrons, and photons can spontaneously emerge in it.

Physical science should reconsider its concept of perfect vacuum. Heisenberg's experience only shows that there is a state of reality, a state of being that "science" cannot yet analyze and assess. Efforts should be made to solve that mystery instead of making affirmations contrary to scientific rigor just to deny the existence of God.

Also, who is in God's place to know if His-Her omnipotence has to be shown by creating many universes? An atom with its nucleus and electrons can be considered a small stellar system. Molecules are aggregates of atoms and are the elements that constitute tissues which in turn assemble in organs to finally result in the emergence of man or woman. Based on this, can a human not be considered a multiverse?

Even at the macroscopic level, the solar system is just one of the billions of stellar systems that make a galaxy and there are billions of galaxies. If God were to create other universes, where would they be? If they were placed next to each other, how will a human being know where a universe ends and where another begins? The result will still be one universe in the human eye.

Who decides the size a galaxy or a universe should have? This is a question of perspective or angle of view. As surprising as it may appear, God has already shown that "He" is an almighty God by creating millions and millions of galaxies containing millions and millions of stars like the sun. If a galaxy were called 'a universe' and inversely, some could still ask that "He" creates many galaxies to prove "Himself".

A-2-b- A support for Hugh Ross

The theory of general relativity is after all a theory of relativity. It supports Hugh Ross rather than contradicts Him. Hugh Ross born in 1945 is an astrophysicist and a creationist Christian apologist who considered that before time as humans know it, God existed in his own time [see chapter 7].

The relativity of time is not just limited to special relativity and general relativity which are very technical notions. In simple language, the relativity of time can mean that time is different according to the angle [person] of observation. Globally, there is no difference between humans in their observation of time. But the situation changes when God is introduced. The following example illustrates the declaration of Ross.

Let's consider a man who makes some preparations, builds a room, paints it, puts in some furniture, a light bulb to serve as the sun, some flowers and mice, and finally adds an intelligent cat. Let's suppose that the cat which never leaves the room is smart enough to calculate as the man, the time that passes according to the regular periods during which the lamp in the house is on and off.

If the man never tells the cat about how much time based on the real sun has passed before the building of the room, how is that cat supposed to know that reality? For the cat the time in the room centered on the light bulb is what matters, but the man knows there was time before the building of the house, a time that is not determined by the light bulb but the sun. Hence, both will differently see time as many men and God do.

Human, time is according to the room and the light [the universe and the sun] says Ross, but God was before the creation of the universe and the sun and humans; as the man of the story was before the room, the light, and the cat. It is not acceptable that the cat who has never seen the man denies his existence just because of its own limited notion of time. Human too should not deny the existence of God because they only perceive time through the sun.

Actually it is very possible that our sun is not the first to be formed. This brings another level of relativity. Maybe the first star should have more right to determine time within the universe and each galaxy and stellar system can have its time as well. Even on earth, countries have different times and hours depending on their time zone.

God's time is different, much broader than that of today's humans. And that is one of the things that make "Him" God. If every law applicable to humans was applicable to God, how would God be God?

A-2-c- The argument of vacuum fluctuation
See A-2-a-

A-2-d-The Lee Smolin argument
See all the previous and following points

A-3-a- The argument based on the hostile nature of a singularity to the development of life

Sometimes God is accused not to be able to do amazing and surprising things in the supernatural sense. Here "He" is accused of doing so.

If it is true that a singularity was at the origin of the Big-Bang, and that it was unlikely according to scientists to develop into a hospitable world of living creatures such as man; why would God, who is supposed to know far better than man, not be able to impulse that kind of development or evolution? Who said that scientists know everything possible for God to know about a singularity? If such is the case; scientists are then each the all-powerful God or God is a human. It is not even certain that the universe truly developed from a singularity. In other words the singularity argument remains a theory.

There are so many things man does not yet know. Instead of continuing his study and increase his knowledge and wisdom, why does he challenge God with such a limited knowledge? God is supposed to have made the human being who is still a mystery to himself. Why does he think he can fully understand his creator when he does not fully understand himself? Why is it that some things he does not want to happen occur anyway, and how can he explain that things he wants to happen do not often happen? Even when man reaches the top of his capacities, the Supreme God will remain the Supreme God.

Houses are not spontaneously built and cars do not come to existence that way. Everything people use, from clothes to the toothpaste is designed by a real intelligent being according to clear principles, mathematical laws, physical laws, chemical laws etc... Why would the distance between earth and the sun that favors life not be calculated by God? Why would the life-sustaining water and air not be placed on earth by God?

A-3-b- The singularity argument (continued)

To answer this point of the atheistic argument, it suffices to bring a kind of modern parable that one well known religious organization, the Jehovah Witnesses is fond of.

Suppose the disassembled pieces of a washing machine in a big bag. How long will it take for a washing machine to spontaneously appear without the intervention of someone to assemble the pieces? The answer is never. There is not even a tiny chance for this to happen in billions of years. After a time, the pieces will even deteriorate and it will be even "more impossible" to have spontaneously a washing machine.

It is when the situation is most improbable to happen that a designer is most needed, to put order into chaos as stated in many creation myths or to bring form out of formless state as written in Genesis 1: 2.

So this argument cannot be used against God.

B- Teleological arguments

B-1- Arguments from scale and B-2- Entropic coincidences
See all the points above.

B-3- The theory of evolution

The theory of evolution has shortcomings and the scientists of physical things know or should know them. Let's see what is wrong with the argumentation of the author of the *Improbability of God* who made use of that theory.

First, let's consider the washed pebble's argument. The problem is that the sea and the laws of physics that enable the washed pebble to be belong to an original designer, God.

Suppose a man who places a seed in a container and sets up in a greenhouse the favorable conditions for that seed to grow in the soil for one year. Consider that he sets up a timer that would open the container during the sixth month and release the seed in the soil for growth. Now imagine another man who comes during the seventh month, sees the plant that has grown from the first seed, immediately plants his own seed, and observes the growth of a second plant. Would it be right to conclude that nobody set up the scheme for the first plant to grow?

The point here is the notion of programming and automation. Saying that a programmed and automatic system does not have a programmer because the programmer cannot be seen would be a mistake. Programming is not a sign of laziness but of smartness. The fact that someone is able to imitate the program or achieve the same result through a different method changes nothing. Therefore, the argument of the washed pebble compared to the lens to prove the inexistence of God is not acceptable.

Besides, defenders of the argument of the Designer do not say that the washed pebble was made by an optician, but by God. That is why He-She was able to set up the program [sea and physical laws] that can give birth to a washed pebble. The optician can create a lens, even through programming and automation, but not in the same way.

Second, the anthropic coincidences are not solely about the laws of genetic. A wide range of beings and phenomena in nature do not have a genetic material. Genetic arguments and the theory of evolution do not respond to the global question of the existence of a Designer for the entire universe. But even within the domain of life, genetic, and human beings; the theory of evolution of Charles Darwin and Alfred Russel Wallace and the way the author of the *Improbability of God* tries to use it is not without significant problems.

For this question of natural selection against design, what is the difference between 'sheer chance' and 'a whole series of tiny chance steps?' In fact the chance is even purer in the second case. A whole series of tiny chances steps is more unbelievable than a sheer chance. This is for the form of the argument. Concerning the content, why would there be just a whole series of tiny chances steps just once?

The idea of the All Pervading God, present within energy and matter can be a support for the theory of evolution because it explains unidirectional evolution. Actually, it is not even certain that man is a product of evolution as developed by Darwin and others.

Many credible scientists are bringing fourth arguments that mankind is not the result of evolution. A simple online research on 'arguments against evolution' will prove enriching. But before a definitive conclusion is achieved, it can already be affirmed that evolution does not contradict God. Whether evolution or not, the existence of God remains justifiable.

Third, let's talk about the lazy God in more details.

What man or woman would like to be doing the same things all the time? Why has society so many inventions? The answer is: so that they can devote their time to other important things. Does a television exists so that man can remake it over and over again or to find joy watching it?

What was the emotional state of the God of Genesis when he saw the things he made? He was pleased, happy, and even very happy in Genesis 1: 31. If that God is truthful, good, loving, and so on; how can he not be happy with truthful loving men and women?

If the problem of evil is put aside here, just to be tackled in the next section, what human being will ever get tired of his family, his friends, computers, games, nature, physical science, spiritual science and so forth? To be honest, there is an eternal program there. God did not plan to become lazy after creation but to live eternal happiness in relationship with his creation, especially human beings.

Besides who knows everything God does or does not do in order to speak of laziness? Who knows the "physiology" of God so perfectly as to say if the work of the Holy Spirit to help creatures [especially the billions of humans] grow is done without the Divine "Omnivigilance," "Omniconcentration," and Promptness to respond to their needs?

Who knows the process of incarnation of souls sent by God well enough to say He-She is doing nothing. Who knows if the suffering of generations of men and women, the madness of the Devil as David Zindell put it in his fiction novels *Lord of Lies*[54], the madness of his followers, and the pain endured by all the creation as mentioned by Paul in Romans 8: 22 cost God nothing emotionally and that He-She does not put His-Her Mind and Power at work to help them? Who can say that sending prophets or seers, teachers or instructors, and healers is being lazy? Who is master enough of his/her dreams as to say that nothing is taught in them and through them by the Divine?

C-The existence of evil is not incompatible with that of God

The inductive evil argument is not against God because the attributes of God have been misunderstood or not explained as they should be.

Evil is like a cloud that does not allow God to be perceived. That is why religion and spirituality put an emphasis on sanctification. Innumerable scriptural proofs show that God is against evil. Confusing cases could be studied and explained one by one.

---

[54] David Zindell, *Lord of Lies* (New York: Tor, 2008), 351.

If the denial of evil is not defendable, the response based on free will is. No opposition has been found against the free will argument. The reason is that it is very logical and fully explains why evil exists. It is the basis to prove the existence of an All-Powerful and Benevolent God. If mankind is not free to choose between good and evil, it is not free at all. People would be prisoners of good. God cannot give free will to humans and at the same time refuse any possibility for evil to appear.

Andrzei Woznicki agrees that Fyodor M. Dostoyevsky and others have already identified that in front of evil, freedom is the very foundation on which any justification of God and man could be based. This is also the opinion of Sylvia Browne who supports the accounts of Ezekiel 28 that evil appeared when originally "white" entities, good spiritual beings, used their free will wrongly [see *Dark Side* in *Phenomenon*].

Some would have preferred that God achieves his goal by making people good, with the possibility to exercise free will only to choose among good things. Of course the result would be a limited free will, like a computer; which comes to no free will at all.

Why is free will necessary then? The answer dwells in another question: how does a person feels toward family and friends on one side and a computer, a robot, and an android on the other side? In the absence of evil, there is no comparison: the first category of beings with a high consciousness and free will is preferred. The difference is so important that God chose to have a world in the way it is at the risk of seeing evil emerge and develop.

God "Himself" exercises "His" Personal Free Will for good. In Genesis 1: 31, God sees that everything "He" created was very good and in Genesis 6: 5-6, God is sorry because "He" put on earth, humans who have become very evil.

To those who consider the scale of evil, far greater than the scale of good, and who conclude that God has lost His-Her bet, it should be replied that there is a divine answer or answers to evil. But it is not the purpose of this work to go into details on that point.

It is true that non-belief can be considered widespread from a practical stand. But with a better understanding of God and how evil can be removed from people and the world, non-belief, theoretical or practical, reasonable or not, will regress and disappear. God's All Powerful character will then be recognized by those who have doubted it. That God does not use brute force to solve all problems is wisdom, not foolishness or weakness. God wants created beings to be free, but "He" also does not want them to use that freedom to destroy everything He-She has made.

Even though evil is rampant on earth in this époque, several people genuinely good can still be found and even among evil people, a great number if not the totality is striving to leave the prison of evilness. According to scripture and logic, if there were no hope to change the world into good, God will have, again no other choice than to intervene like in the story of the flood.

Fortunately, several noble souls have done various works to reduce evil and give a chance to those who aspire to be good. However, a lot more work still needs to be done.

On the Nature of God

Previous chapters have shown that God is Divinity or Universal Mind with Nous or Intellect dwelling in Light or Energy including the Holy Spirit. In addition to this basic understanding, many other elements have been given to describe God. Yet more remain to add.

The Urantia *Book* reminds the reader of Hermes, Psalms 104: 2, and 1 Timothy 6: 16 when it declares that '*the Creator covers himself with light as garment.*' It also adds that God is a Personality.

Confirming the non-anthropomorphic nature of God, the book recommends not thinking that the Father is like men in form and physicality and affirms that God is Spirit, a universal spiritual presence.

To the Urantia foundation, no one can approach God or *see* him. If God is Universal Mind, how is possible to *see* him? It asks. Can anyone *see* the mind?

The *Urantia Book* explains that the glory and spiritual brilliance of the Divine Personality are impossible of approach by the lower group of spirits beings or by any order of material personalities. It insists that it is not necessary to see God with the eyes of the flesh in order to discern him by faith-vision of the spiritualized mind.

Another experience Seeker had and has in his quest should be narrated here. From time to time, he sees a white light. As strange as it may appear, that light sometimes manifests as spontaneous flashes, sometimes as a steady light as one can imagine based on the experience of Hermes Trismegistus and then it vanishes after a few seconds or minutes. He has not yet seen any Dragon like Hermes [a symbol according to *Poimandres*] or angels like the prophets.

The light manifests at times of prayer and meditation or intense positive feelings. It is seen even by the physical eyes whether open or close and is not limited to the faith-vision of the spiritualized mind. It is tangible on both planes; the spiritual or energetic and the physical.

There is a third occasion in which a white light appears to Seeker in addition to the dream with the light in doline or funnel shape. It is bliss or ecstasy. This experience occurs at two different occasions. One is spiritual, the white light being accompanied with the penetration of a pleasing energy in the body from the top of the head associated with the 1st chakra to the base of the spine associated with the 7th chakra. Sometimes it happens in response to deep preoccupations of the mind and brings insights, sometimes in response to deep preoccupations of the heart and brings comfort. At those times it is spontaneous. But Seeker has later succeeded in willingly reproducing the experience.

The sensation of pleasure is a distinct component of the phenomenon and is not solely due to the insights or the comfort. That pleasure is of soft electric nature and comparable to sexual pleasure, but not exactly the same. Sexual ecstasy is the second case of ecstasy where the white light can manifest accompanied with pleasure and mainly outward energy flow.

Spiritual ecstasy or pleasure begins at the top of the head with the inflow of current, follows mainly the spine, and stops at the bottom of the back in the area of the bone sacrum while sexual ecstasy or pleasure when prompted starts in the genital and sacral spheres.

Seeker's experience of spiritual ecstasy reminds him of those saints who have been so satisfied with spiritual life that they renounced the pleasures of the worlds; mostly sexual pleasure. On that line of thinking, he cannot help but remember the Christian and Buddhist monks and nuns. He understands how Jesus felt the joy that comes from the Holy Spirit [Luke 10: 21/Contemporary English Version]. He knows he is experiencing something very important, not yet the appearance of a dragon whether symbolically or literally as Hermes narrated but, divine goodness, something because of which, a long time ago, he knew he could never doubt about the existence of the Invisible All Pervading God, the Supreme God.

The light that manifests is not a symptom of an illness such as hypotension. Being a physician helped him know that he was not sick or mad and reading Yoga, Hindu, and Buddhist scriptures was like reading on human spiritual physiology. He could then avoid worrying unnecessarily or go crazy.

Until he found all the explanations he needs, he is confident to be on the right way because he knows that the phenomena are certainly related to the work he has done and was doing on himself plus other factors he is not aware of.

Sometimes Seeker sees that the air around him is luminous and vibrates. Sometimes he can see that the light is coming out of his eyes. He knows that someday, he will understand the meaning of all these phenomena plus others he experienced but which are not narrated here.

In summary, Seeker did not see God but understood and felt Him-Her better with the additional help of his many readings and thinking. This conclusion joins that of Hermes and the one that can be drawn from an informed reading of the New Testament. Hermes said that God is seen by the Nous and the Heart, speaking not of literal eyes of the Nous and the Heart but of understanding and feeling.

As said earlier, many public figures of the New Testament including Jesus acknowledged that no one has ever seen God [John 1: 18,1 John 4: 12, John 6: 46]. In the last example, Jesus declared he has seen God. That kind of declaration is very rare from him. Usually, he speaks of knowledge of the Father as in Matthew 11: 27, Luke 10: 22, and John 7: 29, not "vision" of the Father.

Fortunately, there is a verse that helps avoid the confusion that could have arisen from John 6: 46 when Jesus declared he has seen God. That verse is John 14: 7 where Jesus shows that seeing the Father is knowing Him. There, Jesus is no more the only one who has "seen" God, but he attests that his disciples too have seen Him. In 1 John 4:7, one can read that anybody who loves knows God.

From the wide range of religious literature Seeker has consulted, the experience of Hermes appears to be the closest to a vision of God, followed by the experiences of Jesus at his baptism and transfiguration. In the case of Jesus, God manifested "Himself" through speech with the appearance of a dove at the baptism and the manifestation of Moses and Elijah at the transfiguration.

In the experience of Hermes God manifested to Hermes as a dragon which spoke to him. But the dove of the baptism of Jesus was not the speaking entity and symbolized the Holy Spirit which is not the Universal Mind that spoke. In addition to the speaking dragon, Hermes was given a clear vision of the divine light, a very important description of its nature and the role of the Divine Mind with His-Her Intellect [Nous] in the creation and the management of the cosmos.

Though it is said that God spoke face to face with Moses as with a friend [Exodus 33: 11], chapter 13 on the anthropomorphism of God and gods has shown that the God of Moses mentioned was an angel of God representing Him/Her. The angel could then speak to Moses face to face when all the conditions are gathered.

Literally, humans can see parts of God which are parts of the universe on the physical, spiritual, and mental spheres. To be fully seen or understood, God would have to cease being so big, so pervading etc…reducing the dimension of His-Her being; and this is impossible. What people should aim at is to see and understand with the intellect and the heart the parts of God in nature, angels, humans etc…and appreciate the moments when the God who is not part of creation manifests to them as He-She manifested to Hermes and Jesus. God can also choose different ways of manifestation.

Though some Buddhist schools do not believe in God, the Buddhist concept of enlightenment is close to the concept of seeing God both literally and in terms of understanding.

God possesses what it takes to create masculine, feminine, and hermaphroditic beings. He-She as the Universal Mind and the Universal Energy is their source. They are because He-She is. God as Universal Mind alone is the Essential Androgynous, the Ultimate Androgynous, and the Causal Androgynous.

According to Blavatsky and Theosophy [The secret doctrine I: Cosmogenesis, *Universal Soul*], God is the matter-moving Nous, the animating Soul, that is immanent in every atom, manifested in man, latent in the stone, and has different degrees of power. To them, this pantheistic idea of a general Spirit-Soul pervading all Nature is the oldest of all the philosophical notions. But Seeker and Hermes, probably others too, know it is not just philosophy, but something concrete.

The energy garment of God which is the origin of the cosmos is according to Hermes, the material God, the second God; also immortal[55]. But speaking of 'One God' as 'Mind and Body' or 'Mind and Body' is preferable to speaking of 'Two Gods.' The combination of the gods Amon and Atum of Ancient Egypt on one hand and that of the Hindu gods Shiva, Vishnu, Brahma, Shakti, and Prajapati give approximately the same idea about the nature of God.

God is the *All Pervading Omnipresent* as demonstrated. God is also *All Powerful*, but channels His-Her Power through Wisdom. God has a vast knowledge, far beyond human imagination but He-She is not all knowing because of the *free will* given to some created beings. *God knows all the past, all the present, and can predict the future in almost all cases because of His-Her knowledge of the law of cause and effect and also because He-She knows all the laws of the universe visible and invisible.* He-She is able to perceive the results of actions in remote futures.

Some consequences are unavoidable especially when the time of their manifestation is near. Other consequences can be prevented through the setting into motion of other influential agents that will impact the original cause on the process of its development. Good choices made even in desperate situations can change or reduce negative consequences, unless they are too late. Those familiar with the laws of medicine and health for instance can easily understand this point.

Awareness campaigns that encourage people to quit smoking in order to avoid a heart attack are based on that principle. God's Science is incredibly vast, but He-She has given to some creatures,

---

[55] Salaman, *The Way of Hermes*, 41 and 48.

the possibility to surprise Him-Her. Since men and women have free will, God can only guess with great accuracy of course, what choice a human being will make in a particular situation. But the final decision belongs to humans.

There is a proverb according to which man proposes and God disposes. This is true, because He-She accomplishes things according to the weaknesses or strengths demonstrated by people in their souls, hearts, prayers, and deeds. But the opposite is also true in the sense that God assigns missions, proposes destinies, but people follow or refuse. In many cases, the will of God is not discerned properly or not at all.

The *Holiness*, *Goodness*, *Eternal* nature, and *Invisibility* of God have also been established but the *Justice* of God still needs to become clear. The Justice of God is so bound to the problem of evil and human condition that it can really be understood only in a book centered on humans and not divinities.

Concerning form, *God is without form and with form at the same time* as explained in the chapters 12, 13, and 14.

In terms of love, God is *All Loving*. In term of wisdom, God is *All Wise*. Concerning peace, He-She is *All Peace* with the consciousness that force can be used as the last way to maintain a kind of peace.

Real peace cannot come out of the use of force even as a defensive method. Authentic peace only comes from education oriented toward truth, wisdom, and love. So, whenever force is used, there still remains a long way toward real peace, a way toward the healing of the hearts, minds, and bodies of those who have suffered and felt pain.

There is at least one additional character of God that is often discussed. It is His *changing* or *unchanging* nature. The answer is similar to the one given about the form of God. The part of God which is creation changes and a part of the God beyond creation also changes through His-Her part which is in creation according to the responses and development of the beings with free will. But there is a part of God, beyond and within creation that never changes. Certain things are of the responsibility of God and cannot be affected by human beings and angels including the God of the Old Testament.

Chapter 16

Existence and nature of gods from religious, spiritual, and philosophical perspectives

On the existence of the gods

SEVERAL of the preceding chapters have mentioned some civilizations of the past and religions of the present which believe in the existence of the gods. The different methods a person can use to come into the presence of those supernatural beings has also been explained. Finally it has also been demonstrated that the idea of the existence of such beings is philosophically sound. What remains for the skeptic readers is to have authentic spiritual experiences involving the divinities. However more description of the nature of the various beings that can be called gods according to the different scriptures and logic is still needed.

Nature of the gods

Angels and demons

Angels are supernatural beings portrayed in the literature of Judaism, Christianity, Gnosticism, Islam, and other movements who adopted some of their teachings. According to Revelation 12: 4-9, there are two kinds of angels: those who rebelled against God following Satan [1/3] and those who remained faithful to God led by Michael [2/3]. Angels who remained faithful to God continued to be called angels and sons of God while rebel angels became known as fallen angels, demons, devils, and so on.

In reality, even the God of the Old Testament is not the Supreme God who is Omnipresent, Omniscient, and Omnipotent. As shown, the God of the Old Testament was a powerful angel and could appear to people while the Supreme God cannot be shown and is in all as taught by Hermes Trismegistus and Jesus.

The seven primary supernatural beings called Amesha Spentas in Zoroastrianism are echoed in the Bible in the seven spirits of God [Revelation 1:4; 3:1, 4:8 and 5:6] and in the Seven Master Spirits of the Urantia Book. These Seven Master Spirits are said to be the primary personalization of the Infinite Spirit.

The seven spirits are said to preside each, one of the seven superuniverses of God and in any association of them, it is Master Spirit Number One who speaks for the Universal Farther and Master Spirit Number Three speaks for the Holy Spirit.

However the Holy Spirit is the Light or Energy which serves as garment for God, is without its own personality, and is moved by God the Father or Universal Mind from within. Therefore saying that Master Spirit Number Three speaks for the Holy Spirit may mean a different relationship than Master Spirit Number One speaking for the

Universal Mind. Definitive confirmations can only come from experience.

Concerning Demons, Jesus acknowledged the existence of Satan and his angels [Matthew 25: 41]. According to the book of Enoch, demons taught mankind after rebelling. Deuteronomy 32: 16-17 equates demons with gods who are not God and to whom sacrifices are offered. Paul in 1 Corinthians 8: 4-6 acknowledges that there are gods in heaven and earth represented by idols and to whom sacrifices are offered. He adds in 1 Corinthians 10:19-22 that gods are demons.

Hermes too was convinced of the existence of demons[56]. His student Asclepius taught that some spiritual powers who obey gods are evil; others, a mix of good and evil[57].

Demons like to be worshiped as Paul also shows in 1 Corinthians 8: 4-6 and as the numerous passages of the Old Testament about idol worship confirm. In the Old Testament, good angels accepted acts of worship but such is not the case in the New Testament where the worship is directed toward God [Revelation 19: 10, 22: 9]. Demons are able to make people prophesize according to their views [Jeremiah 2: 8, Acts 16: 16].

The definitive impression Hermes gives is that humans are at least equal to the gods as it was presented in the section on spiritual science in chapter 10. Sylvia Browne, the renowned psychic and author thinks that angels and humans are equal in the sight of God[58]. But despite her insistence on the equality between angels and humans [which is understandable from a certain philosophical standpoint] she describes a council of eighteen human Master Teachers also called Brotherhood or Avatars or Elders that makes humans

---

[56] Salaman, *The Way of Hermes*, 42.
[57] Ibid., 76.
[58] Browne, *Phenomenon,* 14.

more important or closer to God in destiny than the most important among angels. She says that a legion of Principalities [most advanced and most powerful angels according to her] stands behind those Master Teachers as a testament of their importance and that the council acts as God's voice on the Other Side.

It has also been shown in the chapter on Jesus that Paul believes that man has the authority to judge angels [1 Corinthians 6: 3].

All this establishes the pre-eminence of humans, not humans who chose to remains inferior to angels longer than necessary [Hebrews 2: 7/ New American Standard Version, Contemporary English Version] but those humans who have worked to raise their spiritual level becoming superhumans or deified humans as it will be further explained in this chapter. Hebrews 2: 9 confirms that such was the case of Jesus.

Angels are usually described as anthropomorphic beings and differently in some cases like in Revelation 4: 6-7 where supernatural beings with animal shape are introduced. Some of those beings have six wings like those that Isaiah introduced [6:2-4]. But in contrary to John in Revelation, Isaiah did not say if they were human-like or animal like.

One could assume that the anthropomorphic depiction is the correct one, the use of animal traits being symbolical as some humans are compared to wolves. The symbolism could go beyond words and reach images that are presented to the seer. Nevertheless the existence of intelligent spiritual beings with animal shape is possible.

It should be noticed that scriptures display a correspondence between angels and animals. If angels are far more intelligent than animals, they also possess instincts and emotions which make their actions not completely reasonable thereby causing mistakes. It is this observation that certainly pushed Hermes, Jesus, and Paul to understand that the human potential is greater. That is also certainly the reason why the people of ancient Israel including King Solomon could not understand the God of the Old Testament and made covenants with other gods despite the many good qualities of that God of the Old Testament.

Sometime, people deal with angels without noticing that [Hebrews 13: 2]. Angels are not omnipresent and are not all knowing. They try to follow the will of the Supreme Invisible All Pervading God. They are very powerful because the supernatural can affect the natural as it is written everywhere in the Bible. But angels are not almighty or omnipotent, only God is. Angels possess free will and can make mistakes. When they make very big mistakes and do not repent they are considered evil and are called demons.

Angels know many things unknown to humanity because they are spiritual and conscious beings. They are usually invisible to humans, but can appear to them. They are created beings [Ezekiel 28: 12-16, Colossians 1: 16] and have a beginning as concrete entities. But on the essential level, all beings including humans existed in God and in that sense, they are without beginning.

If angels have a concrete beginning it should be logical that they have a concrete end as well. But since their beginning was the Will of God, their end can also come only if He-She wills it. But does God want that? Nowhere in the Bible is the true death of angels described. Considering that some angels continued to exist even after their fall, one can conclude that they are to live for eternity.

The second death of men and angels, the Lake of Fire etc..., has a symbolic meaning and not a literal one. Revelation 20:14-15 talks about the second death in the sense that anyone whose name was not found recorded in the Book of Life was thrown in the Lake of Fire. The word 'recorded', here is important. The Book of Life is not an original book that God has and which contains only the names of those destined to salvation. The Calvinist concept of predestination is not correct.

The Book of Life is a book in which the names are *recorded* according to the good deeds [see verse 12]. Revelation 3: 1 affirms that the Church of Sardis has the reputation to be alive but is dead. Death in this verse is symbolic. It does not mean the death of a physical body, but a state of separateness from God, a state of major disobedience and opposition to God and his Word, a state of madness or hatred.

That is what happened to Adam and Eve after they disobeyed the God of the Old Testament. That God told them that they will certainly die if they eat of the forbidden fruit [Genesis 2: 17]. When they did, they died, not physically but like the Church of Sardis. Jesus confirmed that kind of death in Matthew 8: 22.

The Word of God [holy teachings] and the Holy Spirit are considered as fire. There are three kinds of baptisms: repentance [the baptism of water], education and teaching [baptism with the word, with knowledge], and the coming of the Holy Spirit [baptism with Divine Energy] with the purpose of renewing, making alive again even in the sense of preparing and nurturing a glorious spiritual body.

With that kind of help people are empowered to take the right actions and have their name recorded in the Book of Life. This is the first death of death or evil. Paul in 1 Corinthians 15: 54-55 is convinced that immortality and incorruptibility will be acquired by human and death defeated. Another way of saying this is that the death caused by a major violation of the divine law should die. It is within that context that the verse Revelation 20: 14 speaks of second death which is the Lake of Fire.

The Lake of Fire is a second divine dispensation, a second way to kill death after the first unsuccessful attempt to completely kill it. That is why death and the grave have to be thrown in the Lake of Fire symbolizing the *second death* of death.

Le Lake of Fire is not as destructive as one could imagine. It is in fact a purifying fire. God is certainly able to disintegrate any conscious energetic being; but He-She prefers to appeal to His-Her Wisdom and to help the wicked repent [2 Peter 3: 9].

The first death of death was predicted by Daniel [9: 24]. The Holy Spirit, the Holy Word, angels, Mary, the powerful Jesus etc..., were mobilized for that to happen. But despite that first dispensation, death has continued to reign. Some people ceased the opportunity to change and accomplished good things, proving worthy to be recorded as alive, and figure in the Book of Life, but others continued to violate the heavenly laws rendering necessary a second dispensation; that of the second death of death [the lake of fire].

The first death of death was supposed to be for all eternity [Daniel 9: 24] but even in that circumstance God respected free will. The Lake of Fire is another chance that God wants to offer even to the Devil himself, the beast, and the false prophet [Revelation 19: 10]. This shows God's intention to transform the empire of evil and its leaders into good. It could appear unjust but though God is a merciful God [Jonah 4: 10], He-She never said that people should not bear the consequences of their actions or that they should not work to clean them. Even human society punishes crimes not for pleasure but as part of the healing process.

People who violate the law of nature pay the consequence. The abuse of alcohol leads among other things to liver disease. Individuals who try to jump from the 15th floor of a building without parachute of any kind usually die. The violation of divine laws has consequences as well. One is to be condemned to dust eating [Genesis 3: 14] meaning that they are no longer able to access the wonderful food that the Word of God and the revivifying Energy of the Holy Spirit constitute.

It is certain that evil spirits are not really having a good time. They are like criminals who are still freely moving but they are sick as well. It is not wise to violate laws and go suffer in a prison or a hospital.

There is much more to say about divine justice. The purpose here is to shed a light on the death of angels.

The conclusion is that they do not die in sense of non-existence but in the sense of separateness from God which requires "treatment", the purification ordeal by the Lake of Fire and also a payment as when criminals pay their debt to society. It is well known that truth also burns and purifies in addition to the payment of social debts. It is rare to see people who are really proud to be evil. Most of the time, they do not want to appear as such as Browne pointed out describing dark entities. Only those who can no longer reason properly or who think of themselves as unpunishable show pride in committing evil deeds.

Nevertheless, it ought to be added that in reality, God has attempted to kill death more than two times. The mention of a second death by the book of Revelation is only due to the theological understanding of its author that there are two *global releases of the Word* to purify the world: the one at the time of Jesus and the time of the second death of death. However, at least the word of Noah for world salvation should be added.

In terms of love, angels can succeed or fail and their character is changeable. Like humans they should work to remain in the Light and Truth of God. One thing that gives confirmation to good angels that they were right not to follow the Devil and remain with God is the miserable state of the fallen angels and that of the invisible and visible empire they have built.

When a group of children is told not to put the finger into fire, some could obey for various reasons; but others could try their chance for reasons personal to them. When the faithful children see the burnings on the hands of the disobedient ones and their misery, they are even more convinced that they did the right thing.

Concerning the sex of angels, only male angels are described in the Bible except perhaps Zechariah 5: 5-9. The word 'perhaps' is used because the women with wings of the passage could be real angels or symbols like the woman in the basket who symbolizes wickedness.

Men visited Abraham and appeared also to other figures. Michael and Gabriel are masculine names and Paul talks in I Corinthians 11: 10 as if angels are only male figures. However, there are female supernatural beings in Zoroastrianism from which some biblical mystics drew much of their understanding. Three of the seven Amesha Spentas created by Ahura Mazda are female: Armaiti [on his left], Haurvatat, and Ameratat.

For Sylvia Browne, angels are androgynous meaning that they are neither male nor female but have the characteristics of both. The Spiritual Science Research Foundation expresses its answer differently saying that angels can be either male or female but that the angels of high spiritual level do not identify themselves with any gender. In *The Lost Symbol*, Dan Brown's character Mal'akh declares that Gods have no gender[59]. That there should be female or androgynous angels is not against logic. However, as for the case of angels in general, experience is required to prove or disprove the existence of female, male or androgynous angels.

Browne went as far in the portrayal of angels as to speak of their race which goes beyond and includes all races. While she gives as many other spiritual writers an angelic hierarchy [hers is of eight levels ranging from *Angels* to *Principalities*], she also asserts that despite the differences in power, angels are all equal.

A very broad and very rare description of angels can be found in Gustav Davidson's *Dictionary of Angels*. The book presents a wide range of angels whether loyal or fallen, their function and appearances in history [how mankind related to them], and their hierarchy.

---

[59] Brown, *The Lost Symbol*, 268.

In the cinema industry, more and more movies are offering cosmological explanations of the universe. Many convey pantheistic and evolutionary ideas. A movie like *Babylon 5*, though it does not speak of angels and demons, describes beings close to them. *Vorlons* are very similar to angels and the *Shadows* to demons. Both races master the science of invisibility in relation to the physical realm. *Vorlons* are like spirits made of white light and can dwell in the human bodies and the *Shadows* are hideous dark beings. The latter are systematically inclined to evil and destruction while the former are obsessed with order and discipline even if it means the massacre of planets with billions of inhabitants. These traits of the *Vorlons* make them not so different from the angels of the Old Testament.

To end this section, a few words must be said about Kabbalah that Manly Hall describes as a secret teaching encoded by Moses within the five first books of the Bible. In his description, Hall states that Kabbalah is a science taught by various powerful angels to several important biblical figures. According to him, the first initiates believed that the angel Raziel was sent from heaven to teach Adam, that Tophiel taught Shem, Raphael taught Isaac, Metatron Moses and Michael David. David and Solomon are said to have been the most initiated.

Hall adds that according to Christian D. Guinsburg, the teaching was passed down from Adam to Noah and then to Abraham who gave a portion of it to the Egyptians and eastern nations. Moses initiated 70 elders who also taught some other peoples within their nation.

Hall continues his description stating that the Kabbalists have divided their science into five parts: natural, analogical, contemplative, astrotheological, and magical Kabbalahs. Magical Kabbalah seeks to gain control over demons. But those five parts can be reduced to three by combining analogical and contemplative Kabbalahs on the one hand and the astrotheological and magical Kabbalahs on the other hand. Moreover, the entire Kabbalah can be reduced to its most important part which is astrotheology and magic; therefore to the management of the universe by angels and demons.

Another main aspect of Kabbalah that must absolutely be mentioned here is that it believes in a Supreme God without substance, essence, or Intelligence.

According to Seeker, it is clear that Kabbalah is astrotheology under a different name. It is also clear that Kabbalah is a polytheistic system that acknowledges several gods [angels and demons]. From two different perspectives, pantheism can either be polytheistic or monotheistic whether the Supreme God is considered as having Intelligence or not.

So, even though Hall is right stating that Kabbalah is a pantheistic system, it is in reality a *polytheistic pantheism* because its Supreme God has no Intelligence. This said, the strange relationship between Abraham and his father Terah concerning their going to the land of Canaan mentioned in chapter 9 will now be explained.

Terah was clearly a polytheist as shown. He suddenly left his place of birth in Mesopotamia to go to Canaan without any reason given in the Bible. Having died on the way, his son Abraham continued on the same quest this time after God has asked him says the Bible.

Since the God of Abraham was known to his relatives including his brother Nahor and his nephew Laban, one can understand that the God or Lord of Abraham was one of the powerful angels or gods known in that family which had kabbalistic knowledge.

One can also say that the Lord of Abraham who was among the many gods that his father worshipped tried to become the Unique God acknowledged by humans. Certainly, the departure of Terah for Canaan was the order of one or several of his gods. But the Lord of Abraham succeeded in being acknowledged by him as the Sole God and he then took entire control of the Canaan Project thanks to Abraham's faith and that of his descendants.

That Lord later appeared to Laban who was Abraham's nephew, Isaac's cousin, and the uncle of Jacob to warn him not to attack Jacob who was fleeing away from him [Genesis 31: 24].

At the time of Moses, angelic forces helped the twelve tribes of Israel vanquish the army of ancient Egypt and massacre entire populations to settle in Canaan. Once again, a group of angels working for goodness and peace on earth used genocide as solution instead of an educational program and accepted slavery [Lev 19: 20].

The God of Saul, first king of ancient Israel, and also God of David ordered them to kill a great number of people even though that God explained that bloodshed through wars was not appreciable [1 Chronicles 22: 8/ 28: 3]. One should also notice that that God also confessed to have exterminated David's enemies in front of him [2 Samuel 7: 9].

King Solomon was according to many the greatest initiate of Kabbalah. Though he started well with his God taking wisdom from him and building him a temple, he ended up not listening exclusively to that God and came back to the polytheistic system that Abraham abandoned [1 Kings 11]. In addition he married 700 wives and had 300 concubines. Solomon's polytheism was a conscious and voluntary choice despite the warnings of his God. He challenged his God.

Seeker's thinking is that Solomon knew Kabbalah so well that he could deal with a great number of spirits. His knowledge must have showed him like to his ancestors before Abraham that his God was one among several angels and that there was no reason not to use the services of the others as well. That is why he continued worshipping other gods despite the warning of his God whose reason was probably the misconduct of several other gods or angels.

In his anger, the God of Solomon told one of his enemies, Jeroboam, that he will help him take ten tribes out of eleven from the son of Solomon if he obeys him and does what he considers right [1 Kings 11: 38]. Obviously, the main God of Solomon and the other gods had different ideas about what is right.

What transpires from the attitude of Solomon is that he consciously decided not to be as "gullible or naïve" as Abraham or David. He must have written the book of Ecclesiastes in a moment of great doubt. The book was written by someone with a lot of experience, who has seen many things, and has been disappointed. That is why he declares that great wisdom and great knowledge bring sadness [Ecclesiastes: 1:8].

Even though this declaration is globally incorrect, it has the merit to show the importance of having good remedies if one wants to discover hidden diseases if not the result is despair like in the case of Solomon.

In Ecclesiastes Solomon fears his God, finds wisdom valuable and useless at the same time, and considers wealth, political power, and work as futile. He finds many injustices in life, thinks that life is meaningless, and that everything ends with physical death. At that time, Solomon was confused; talking meaningful words in some passages and displaying a huge lack of wisdom in other passages. Solomon was probably aware of his state but decided anyway to pass down his experiences to future generations.

In the light the preceding data, Kabbalah or astrotheology is not the main solution for establishing peace and happiness on earth principally because of the limits of angels and demons displayed in history. What it has offered the world is a situation of conflicts, wars, nationalism, tribalism etc…that most of humans dislike.

One cannot say that the people of ancient Israel is guiltier than any other because most of the nations of the past have massacred others too; often after consulting gods or spirits. That is why most of them had gods of war. Humanity in its whole is responsible for finding the way to overcome the limits of angels and demons and reach a greater wisdom and practical goodness.

Potentially, the relation between humans and angels is more interesting and more mutually beneficial than that between humans and animals. *It belongs to humanity to find the way to benefit from the help of angels without being led by the tip of the nose.* As Paul said, humans really have the potential to analyze, judge, and select the works of angels. The time is ripe for such a philosophy to be formulated.

Annunaki, Igigi, and Nephilim

Annunaki and Igigi were the gods of Mesopotamian civilization. They are described as anthropomorphic supernatural beings behaving like humans; sometimes in a good way, sometimes in a bad way.

Two important differences exist between the Annunaki and angels. The first is that Annunaki have a material side like humans who are created from their blood.

The second difference is that angels [the supernatural beings of the Bible] are not said to have created humans as their slaves in contrary to the Annunaki and Igigi though in the Old Testament human worshipped good angels too. Biblical verses that speak of the superiority of man over angels are written by humans. If the angelic Lord God of the Old Testament asked to be worshipped, no good angel in the New Testament asked such a thing. Demons clearly showed their intention to rule over mankind.

If the Bible is revisited as Zecharia Sitchin did, and the Annunaki put at the place of angels, something illogical emerges. If Annunaki were angels who created as a group, human beings to serve them, there is no way many angels would work for the good of humans the way they did as indicated in the Bible.

In the Bible, angels seem not to have businesses of their own apart from helping the Supreme God and humankind. The Bible does not clearly describe any negative or evil supernatural being before the creation of humanity, but the Babylonian creation myth does and the seeker seems forced to choose between one of these two scriptures.

At the analysis of the Babylonian creation myth and pantheon, one discovers that gods or the Annunaki and Igigi are not ashamed to be perceived as negative and evil in the sight of humans. This could be because Mesopotamians had similar values. On the contrary, the good angels of the Bible clearly show humanity that there are other supernatural beings like them who are evil. They made the effort to appear good and worked with the patriarchs and prophets to fight evil.

Which story is true? The Mesopotamian story that is silent about the All Pervading God and paints evilness as a natural way of being or the Bible which points to the Supreme Creator, to the Demiurge, to good angels and to demons? The tendency for human consciousness, mind, love, justice etc…, is to say that even though errors could be found in the Bible on other matters; concerning cosmogony, the Babylonian Story is the one that should be untrue. This poses a serious problem because the Mesopotamian and Sumerian story is supposed to precede the Biblical story. Even Abraham is acknowledged by the same Bible to have come from Mesopotamia.

A way to solve the problem could be that in reality the Babylonian story is theologically inaccurate, designed for deceptive purposes by the fallen angels and demons of the Bible, finally unmasked through the work of good angels and men who were looking for God unsatisfied with the demons. *Nevertheless, Annunaki and Igigi could have truly been beings with blood.*

This possibility finds support in the story of Atlantis as told by the Greek philosopher Plato in his *Critias*. In that story, the god Poseidon was the patron deity of Atlantis. With his wife [a mortal woman], he fathered ten sons who became each king of a part of Atlantis. After their death their sons inherited their thrones from generation to generation centered on the lineage of Atlas, the first son of Poseidon. With the trident scepter of Poseidon, these kings held sway over the inhabitants of Atlantis.

The clue is the transmission of the scepter of Poseidon from one king to his successor. It is very unlikely that a functional god would separate from the instrument and emblem of his power in that way. Only a man corresponds to that description.

For Ignatius Donnelly, the history of Atlantis is the key to Greek mythology[60]. He also affirms that there can be no question that the gods of Greece were human beings. To him the tendency to attach divine attributes to great earthly rulers is one deeply implanted in human nature. Donnelly justifies his declaration stating that *the deities of the Greek pantheon were not looked upon as creators of the universe but rather as regents set over it by its more ancient original fabricators.*

Hence, *Annunaki and Igigi could have been human beings of supernatural power taught and guided by demons to spread false ideas about the creation of man.*

Blavatsky agreed with this view when she said: '*Under the evil insinuations of their demon, Thevetat, the Atlantis people became a nation of wicked magicians[61].*'

This view of Greek and Sumerian gods can also explain why they resembled so much humans both on morphological and behavioral points. It shows how human beings with a certain spiritual knowledge, science, or magic could manipulate or try to manipulate the minds of their fellow human beings. This fact is well illustrated in the cartoon *Conan the Adventurer.*

---

[60] Hall, *The Secret Teachings of All Ages,* 83.
[61] Ibid.,85.

It is possible that those powerful Annunaki and Igigi who had physical bodies be from earth or another planet. A proof of the existence of powerful extraterrestrial beings will not contradict the existence of angels and demons. This will simply be a proof that physical life can exist elsewhere than earth with its own features which can appear supernatural to humans. The possibility of spiritual life would remain unaltered as argued in the chapter on epistemology.

So, real supernatural beings, fallen angels or demons, extraterrestrials and human magicians could have played gods in human history. Serious spiritual research as well as new archeological discoveries could specify if one, two, or the three theories are accurate.

The seduction of Gilgamesh, a Babylonian King, by the goddess Ishtar, the disappearance of ancient gods replaced by new ones, the death of the Mesopotamian gods Apsu and Kingu, the sons of God having children with women in Genesis: 1-8 could have been stories of only physical beings. It is also possible that spiritual beings were involved and in that case, some elements such as children being born from the relation between demons and women [the Nephilim] would have a symbolic meaning rather than a literal one.

In the research of truth concerning the past, there are three important limitations. Sometimes the text of an author who lived in ancient times is so cryptic, so symbolic, so mysterious that only he/she can unlock it. When a seeker of the present forces an interpretation from the text, there is an important risk of mistake and misdirection. Even in a dialogue between people facing each other, there is a risk of misunderstanding that one protagonist can remove by asking the other to be clearer.

In the study of an ancient text, the author is no longer there to make the necessary adjustment as Socrates mentions in *The Phaedrus*, one of Plato's dialogues. The situation is worse if the ancient writer had willingly encrypted or sealed the text. Of course there is the possibility of divine revelation; however all claims of revelation are not honest and the seeker must be careful. The revelation he/she should look for is not the one that its receiver alone understands but one that can enlighten others as well if they receive the proper teaching and/or training.

Most of the time, the understanding of an information requires prerequisites. A seer must make sure his/her audience has the experience and/or the mind power necessary to comprehend and withstand a revelation. If such is not the case, he/she must tirelessly and without dishonesty work to raise the audience to the level where it can bear the revelation. Once again, as Moses told Joshua in Numbers 11: 29, it is better that all receive the spirit of God.

Elementals and Jinns

In some occult systems, elementals are inhabitants of one of the four elements, especially any of the beings described by Paracelsus [1493-1541], an influential alchemist, esotericist, astrologer, and physician, as intermediate in corporeality between humans and spirits. Paracelsus also known as Philippus Aureolus Theophrastus Bombastus von Hohenheim described the earth elementals [gnomes], the water elementals [undines], the air elementals [sylphs] and the fire elementals [salamanders]. How Paracelsus came to his conclusions is not well known, but most of his biographies and the anime *Fullmetal Alchemist* portray him as interested in alchemy and esotericism from his adolescence.

His description of the elementals appeared credible in the sight Manly Hall who gives many details about it[62]. Hall also acknowledges

---

[62]Hall, *The Secret Teachings of All Ages*, 328-341.

the existence of demons and speaks of other kinds of spirits of ceremonial magic[63]. He mentions that the original science which was good has been corrupted by black magic and that for example there were many black magicians among the kabbalists of the Middle Ages who became enmeshed with demonism and witchcraft.

Hence, the famous esoteric scholar Hall also thinks that demons are real. To Him, the transcendentalism of the Kabbalists is founded upon the ancient and magical formula of King Solomon. Manly Hall describes the Baphomet as the mystic pantheons of those disciples of ceremonial magic, of the Templars who probably obtained it from Arabians. He states that the Baphomet is identical with the famous hermaphroditic Goat of Mendes who is a composite creature formu-lated to symbolize astral light.

According to Manly P. Hall, Napoleon Bonaparte [1769 - 1821] and the heads of the Medici [14th - 18th centuries] were served by elementals, while Socrates had a godlike, learned daemon who deserted him when the sentence for his death was passed. In the discourse of Plato, the *Apology*, Socrates admits to have been in frequent contact with a divine being who acted as his advisor but did not manifest during his trial[64].

For Hall, transcendentalism and all forms of phenomenalistic magic are but blind alleys, outgrowths of Atlantean sorcery; and those who forsake the straight path of philosophy to wander therein almost invariably fall victims to their imprudence. Man incapable of control-ling his own appetites, is not equal to the task of governing the fiery and tempestuous elemental spirits, he says. Hermes Trismegistus

---

[63]Ibid., 315.
[64] Plato and Warrington, *The Trial and Death of Socrates: Euthyphro, Apology, Crito, Phaedo,* 48, 49, and 61.

also mentioned, long before Paracelsus, the elementals of the air and the earth in the *Book of Thoth*[65].

The Secret Teachings of All ages mentions how dangerous the invocation of the spirits of dead humans could be and the ability of elementals to impersonate those who have passed on. It presents four premises of the theory and practice of black magic which are:

1.   The visible universe has an invisible counterpart, the higher planes of which are peopled by good and beautiful spirits; the lower planes, dark and foreboding, are the habitation of evil spirits and demons under the leadership of the Fallen Angel and his ten Princes

2.   By means of the secret process of ceremonial magic, it is possible to contact these invisible creatures and gain their help in some human undertaking. Good spirits willingly lend their assistance to any worthy enterprise, but evil spirits serve only those who live to pervert and destroy

3.   It is possible to make contracts with spirits whereby the magician becomes for a stipulated time the master of an elemental being

4.   True black magic is performed with the aid of a demonical spirit, who serves the sorcerer for the length of his earthly life, with the understanding that after death, the magician shall become the servant of his own demon. For this reason a black magician will go to inconceivable ends to prolong his physical life, since there is nothing for him beyond the grave.

The existence of elementals is also philosophically justifiable. As previously mentioned, *if the physical body [energy in high concentration] can carry consciousness, it is also possible that less concentrated bodies [subtle bodies] also carry consciousness.* It is possible that these beings specialize in the "life" and management of elements

---

[65] Hall, *The Secret Teachings of All Ages*, 96.

such as earth, water, air, and fire in the same way there are animals that live in water, on earth, in the air and in places of high temperature such as the desert.

The equivalent of elementals in Islam are Jinns; an invisible intelligent race lower than angels and related to elements [Qur'an 15: 27]. The Devil, Shaytan, also called Iblis is said to be a Jinn of the fire element [38: 76]. There is a debate in Islam whether Satan is a Jinn [elemental] or a demon [fallen angel].

Sylvia Browne declared that she does not believe anything said about elementals[66]. However, she acknowledged the existence of gnomes and other little creatures of the paranormal such as fairies and elves[67]. So, one can infer that Browne believes in the existence of creatures like elementals without giving them any specific association with the elements of fire, water, air, and earth. On the contrary, Sonia Choquette who is a theologian dealing with metaphysics and the paranormal joins Paracelsus, Hall, and many others in associating certain forms of subtle life with the four elements of nature[68].

Deified humans, messiahs, and godship

History and mythology talk about many pharaohs of Egypt who were considered as gods and some men in Greece and China who lived as mortal but were deified at their deaths. Jainism is remarkable by its strong attachment to the divinity of humans who should become gods after a growth period. To Hermes some men are gods[69].

---

[66] Browne, *Phemenon*, 112.
[67] Ibid., 302.
[68] Sonia Choquette, *Ask Your Guides: Connecting to Your Divine Support System* (Carlsbad, Calif: Hay House, 2006), 99-112.
[69] Salaman, *The Way of Hermes*, 58.

Judaism and Christianity also have in their scripture the idea that humans are gods [Psalms 82: 6, John 10: 34]. *By insisting on the fact that human beings who receive God's message are gods, Jesus gives a clue concerning his own humanity and divinity.* Jesus thereby justifies the sayings of Moses in Deuteronomy 18: 18 and those of Islamic theology and anthropology which assert that he [Jesus] is a prophet of God [Qur'an 4: 171]. Hence there is no contradiction in calling Jesus a divine being and a prophet.

In Jainism, the belief that humans are gods is exclusive of the Supreme Creator God and is the spiritual equivalent of the superhuman concept of Nietzsche which denies God and exalts man. If these two philosophies are admirable for the high value attributed to humans, they lack consistency when they deny God. If men are Gods and there is no God, then again, who is responsible for the existence of things that men themselves acknowledge not to have created?

That Jesus is Messiah cannot be denied when the word 'Messiah' is properly understood.

The idea of the messiah is not an original Christian idea. That idea is mentioned in the Old Testament or Hebrew Bible in several passages and a careful reading of it gives a perspective, different from the one given in Christianity.

Etymologically, 'messiah' means 'the anointed one.' In the history of ancient Israel, kings like Saul, David, and Jehu; priests like Aaron, and prophets like Elisha [1 Kings 19:16] have been anointed.

Many Old Testament prophecies are generally understood to be related to Jesus. But not all of them are.

The first one appears in Genesis 49: 10 in the last words of the patriarch Jacob to his sons. According to him, the scepter or the center of power shall not depart from the tribe of Judah, his fourth son, until Shiloh or Messiah comes [21st Century King James Version].

The Old Testament does not give any account of the development of Israel as a people in Egypt after the death of Jacob apart from its slavery. When the hour of liberation from Egyptian oppression came, the God of the Old Testament chose Moses, a man from the tribe of Levi [Exodus 2: 1-10] to lead his people as a political ruler, law giver, miracle performer, and prophetic guide.

Moses announced the coming of a prophet that will be like him [Deuteronomy 18: 15- 22].

There are two serious candidates for that position. The first is the prophet Samuel who was prophet, political leader, and law giver. However he did not perform miracles as Moses did. The second candidate is Jesus who was a prophet, a law giver, and miracle performer but not a political leader. Moreover, the God of Jesus was not the God of Moses and Samuel.

When Moses died, Joshua of the tribe of Ephraim [Numbers 13:8-9] became the political leader. Among the Judges of Israel, only Othniel, the first Judge, came from the tribe of Judah. Samuel was prophet and judge [1 Samuel 7: 3-6] from the tribe of Ephraim [1 Samuel 1] like Joshua. Even the first king of Israel, Saul was not from the tribe of Judah, but from the tribe of Benjamin [1 Samuel 10: 20-27].

Though the tribe of Judah has played a prominent military role in Ancient Israel from the time of the Exodus, it is only from King David that one can see it take over the political leadership.

The prophet Micah [5: 2-5] gives the information that a ruler and deliverer of Israel [from the Assyrians] will come from Bethlehem of Judah. Many Bible students and scholars from various Christian denominations consider that this prophecy of Micah is about Jesus. However, this way of taking the scripture is not correct.

Micah's prophecy talks about Assyrian threat which was no more at the time of Jesus eight centuries later. The deliverer of Israel mentioned in it should have lived at a time where Assyrians were a problem to the people of Israel, which disqualifies Jesus. As in the past of Israel, the deliverer would be a political leader like King David or a judge like Othniel. Those two leaders were saviors [not in the way Christians understand it] before Jesus. The identity of the Messiah-Savior of Micah will be revealed after a tour within the prophecies of Isaiah.

Isaiah was a contemporary and probably an elder of the prophet Micah.

In most of the biblical versions, Isaiah 9: 1-7 is entitled '*Hope in the Messiah.*' This prophecy is in general correlated to Jesus because of its supposed fulfillment in Matthew 4: 13-16. However, the person it directly points to is Prince Hezekiah, the future King of Judah, and contemporary of Isaiah. Isaiah In the passage mentioned above prophesied on the future of the prince and on that of the kingdom of Judah.

Indeed, the first verse of this ninth chapter of Isaiah tells that there will be no more gloom on those who were in darkness or anguish in the land of Zebulun and Naphtali in Galilee. Galilee was the northernmost region of ancient Israel where the five tribes of Issachar, Zebulun, Asher, Naphtali and Dan lived [Judges 18, Joshua 19: 47].

In older times, Galilee had been victim of alien [gentile] invasions. The first time was the Midianite invasion [Judges 7: 1-3] repelled by Judge Gideon. The second time was the invasion of Ben Haddad, King of Aram [Syria], when Baasha was King of Israel and Asa King of Judah [1 Kings 15: 16-20]. A third time was when Tiglath Pileser III, King of Assyria took many cities in Galilee [2 Kings 15: 29, 2 Chronicles 28] in the year 732 B.C.E. Isaiah remotely witnessed this third invasion which happened during his ministry [Isaiah 1: 1] (742-701 B.C.E).

So in Isaiah 9: 1-5, the God of the Old Testament promises to remember Galileans and free them again as he has done at the time of Gideon. That was a messianic hope or a hope for salvation.

But who is the messiah, the anointed one, the giver of freedom, the new born son who will break the rule of Assyria and bring back the independence of Galilee? Certainly not Jesus who will be born only several centuries later. At the time of the prophecy of Isaiah, Ahaz was King of Judah and father of Hezekiah. Hezekiah is said to have begun his reign in 715 B.C.E; therefore, it is very likely that he was born at the time of Isaiah's prophecy, about 17 years earlier.

Hezekiah was not the sign promised to his father Ahaz in Isaiah 7 precisely in the 14th verse. That sign was to be given to Ahaz as the promise of his God to deliver him from the attack of the Kings of Syria [not Assyria] and Israel [the tribes separated from the tribe of Juda]. This particular sign is Isaiah's own son Maher-Shalal-Hash-Baz [Isaiah 8: 1-4]. God assured Isaiah, and Ahaz through Isaiah's prophecy that before Maher-Shalal-Hash-Baz is old enough to say 'Papa' or 'Mama' [King James Version], the Kings of Syria and Israel, the enemies of Ahaz, will be vanquished by the King of Assyria.

Hence the significance of Hezekiah is different. If Maher-Shalal-Hash-Baz, son of Isaiah is a sign for the freedom of Judah, Hezekiah is a sign for the freedom of Galilee. Indeed as Prince and future King, Hezekiah was in position to lead military campaigns against the Assyrian occupants of Galilee and free the land as Gideon did.

Isaiah then appears to be on the same line with his younger colleague, Micah. Both prophets mutually confirmed each other's sayings that the problem is the Assyrian. Therefore Hezekiah is a better candidate as fulfiller of the prophecies of Isaiah than Jesus who again had nothing to do with Assyrians.

However, Hezekiah, though the best king the territory of Judah has ever known [2 Kings 18], and though he fulfilled the prophecy of Micah, did not fulfill the prophecy of Isaiah completely. He followed his God faithfully and his God was with him in everything he did to the point of defeating for him the King of Assyria, Shalmaneser [2 Kings: 19: 35].

Hezekiah who had rebelled against Shalmaneser for tax reasons [2 Kings 18: 7] and won battles against him did not push his advantage to liberate Galilee and reunite the northern kingdom and Judah as in the time of David. Hence, Hezekiah was an announced messiah, deliverer or savior who achieved a limited result.

Additionally Hezekiah can be easily proven to be a rod from the Stem of Jesse [Isaiah 11: 1] as asked by the prophecy of Isaiah [being a descendent of David son of Jesse] and to have come from Bethlehem [Micah 5: 1] as asked by the prophecy of Micah [Bethlehem is the city of origin of the house of David and Jesse which includes Hezekiah; see 1 Samuel 16: 1].

Several Christians do not pay attention to this last biblical verse and to others that are similar. They incorrectly believe that Bethlehem is a particular characteristic only of Jesus while in fact, that place was attached to the house of David long before its association with Jesus.

Without doubt Isaiah and Micah were far from talking about the Messiah Jesus as most Christians believe.

Another proof that Jesus could not have been a Messiah based on Davidic bloodline dwells in the fact that even though the God of the Old Testament promised eternal kingship to the house of David [2 Samuel 7: 12-16], the promise was assorted with the condition of faithfulness and obedience from that house [1 Kings 8: 25, 2 Chronicles 6: 16]. After several episodes of disobedience of the Davidic house to that God starting with King Solomon, kingship through Davidic blood line was terminated by the God of the Old Testament who used Nebuchadnezzar, King of Babylon as his instrument in that matter [2 Kings, chapter 24 and 25].

The prophet Daniel speaks of an Anointed One [Daniel 9: 24-27], a Messiah, a Prince, a Most Holy who will come after 7 and 62 weeks counting from the time the word went forth to restore and build Jerusalem. If one applies the rule of one day for one year of Numbers

14: 34, as the Jehovah Witnesses do, the time of the coming of this Messiah appears to be around the time of the birth of Jesus. But the later did not restore or rebuild Jerusalem.

Isaiah 53 and Psalms 22: 1 are two other pessimistic prophecies that many theologians and religious people link to Jesus.

Here, it is important to see how first Christians, especially some authors of the New Testament understood the messianism of Jesus. The first to consider is the author of the Gospel of Matthew who is known to scholarship as the Jewish Christian. There is an agreement that this author made much effort to justify Jesus' life and ministry to potential believers of Jewish origin. His first attempt appears immediately in the first chapter of the gospel, where he provides a lineage of Jesus that goes up to David.

Second, Matthew tried to present Jesus as the fulfiller of some of the prophecies of Isaiah [Matthew 3: 1-2/ Isaiah 40: 3, Matthew 4: 14/ Isaiah 8: 23 and 9: 1, Matthew 8: 16-17/ Isaiah 53: 4, Matthew 13: 14-15/ Isaiah 6: 9].

However, no matter the connections of Jesus with the bloodline of David, he could not be a Messiah based on that as demonstrated. That Jesus tried to give a second breath to the prophecies of the Old Testament emerges after a short analysis of those passages. Each of those old prophecies could have been about other events. Formal proofs of these possibilities have been found for Isaiah 8: 23 and Isaiah 9:1.

The sojourn of Jesus in Galilee shows that he gave a second meaning to the prophecy of Isaiah. Here, Jesus is trying to fulfill an old prophecy, but it has clearly been shown that the passage is directed toward Assyrian invasion that happened about 8 centuries earlier. Jesus had no Assyrian to get rid of.

Other scriptures that Jesus tried to follow [Psalm 22: 1, Isaiah 52: 13-15, and Isaiah 53] appear to be sayings for example of King David confronting his enemies. It is more reasonable to accept that Jesus repeated the word of David [*My God, My God, why have you forsa-ken me?*] on the cross [Matthew 27: 46] rather than affirming that David imitated his lord [Jesus] who was to come more than 800 years after him.

Jesus, during his ministry also kept in mind the prophecies of Da-niel [Matthew 24: 15]. From all this it is evident that Jesus tried to follow ancient scriptures, most of them primarily not related to him. If he indirectly admitted his connection with David [Matthew 22: 41-45], he made no attempt to become an earthly king and even turned down an opportunity offered to him [John 6: 15].This attitude is in accor-dance with the end of Davidic rule.

All along his ministry, especially from the moment he began an-nouncing his death, Jesus focused on a spiritual kingdom rather than a physical one. That is why he advised to give to Cesar what be-longed to him and to God what belong to God [Luke 20: 25] and that is why he said to Pontius Palate that his kingdom was not of this world [John 18: 36]. He also affirmed that his disciples were not of the world [John 17: 14] and he taught them various ways to deal with spiritual issues rather than earthly matters.

Furthermore, as stated by the Unification Movement, in his fight against sin, Jesus did not primarily adopt the crucifixion as answer. In the beginning of his work he emphasized teaching, education, belief in God, love, and so on. As previously mentioned, his words are spirit and life. But from a time right before or after his transfiguration, he began talking about his death as a way of salvation and about the earthly suffering for his followers. This was a major shift.

First he desired the renewal of the people through repentance, teaching, and obedience to that teaching. His laws and rules were different from what was in the law followed by Jews in some respects. Second he decided to go to the cross but in many occasions showed his unhappiness with that path [Matthew 23: 37] and even tried to avoid it [Matthew 26: 38-44].

The thing that is certain from the analysis of Jesus' ministry is that he viewed himself as a messiah, a Christ [John 4: 25] not in the Davidic sense but as the person who came to work for the people's spiritual growth and preparation for the afterlife. The author of 1 John 3: 8 summarizes well this view saying that the son of God has come to undo the works of the Devil. If Jacob, Moses, and many prophets envisioned the messiah as a political figure, and if a king like Hezekiah corresponds to that description, Jesus worked on the spiritual front. He saw himself as a spiritual leader.

He spoke of himself as the way, the truth, and the life [John 14: 6] because God is the Truth, the Way, and the Life. If Jesus was not a messiah, a savior, in the political sense, he was certainly one in the prophetic and spiritual sense.

But the God of the Old Testament was a political God. Jesus has not spoken about that God who appeared to Abraham, Isaac, Jacob, and Moses and who made Saul, David, Solomon, and Jeroboam kings. Jesus did not follow all the laws of that God. However his disciples still had several elements of the philosophy of that God in mind; which explains their difficulty to understand him asking him to show them God or reprimanding him for wanting to die on the cross. In fact, Jesus revealed only a part of what he had in mind by fear of not being understood even by his disciples as shown in John 16: 12.

It ought to be mentioned that Jesus did not draw all the consequences of his desire to relate without intermediary to the Universal All Pervading Supreme God. He understood that anybody can be the way, the life, and the truth through that Supreme God being able to do great things and work for the removal of evil including chasing demons out of possessed people. No one before Jesus tried to chase demons who were considered like angels as gods.

By understanding that the human potential is greater than that of angels, he not only avoided to be guided by the God of the Old Testament preaching non-violence, but he also went as far as to perform exorcism and dealt forcefully with fallen angels. Even Hermes did not go that way. Jesus achieved a level that helped him display a strong spiritual power and all humanity should learn his secret.

However, though the work of Jesus was spiritually more powerful than that of Hermes, it was not as philosophical or reasonable as his. Hermes was told that the Universal Mind supports his own mind in helping others. Though Jesus knew that the True God was in him, his mind could not decide for sure whether to die on the cross or not. So, he kept asking his God who is the Universal All Pervading God to give him an answer.

But the answer of the True God could only come through Jesus' own mind in contrary to the God of the Old Testament who gave direct answers based on his own nature received from the Universal Soul. Therefore, it was the responsibility of Jesus to freely decide the best way of helping humanity by putting his reason and power strongly into use. The crucifixion was his final choice resulting in him being disappointed thinking that the True God has abandoned him. He could have made a different choice with more satisfaction.

Any human, man or woman, who cares for humanity and the universe, can make the same claims as Hermes and Jesus learning respectively mental power and spiritual power like them while trying to go beyond their achievements. Jesus never asked to be worshiped. He considered people as his brothers and sisters, served his fellows humans, and tried to regulate the sphere of angels.

Chapter 17

Assessment of Evolutionary Religion, Monotheism, Pantheism, Panentheism, Polytheism, Deism, Dualism, Henotheism, Kathenotheism, Autotheism, and Monolatrism

T HE concept of evolutionary religion summarized in chapter 8 stimulates two opposite commentaries.

The first is positive. Because only fools do not learn from their mistakes, if religion has to evolve in order to provide better answers to the difficulties mankind faces, this can only be appreciated. But if it is to invent God and try to organize society around Him, evolutionary religion would mean that religion is deceptive and dishonest. No reasonable person can deny the crimes and mistakes of several religious people in history. However, religion has its positive sides and God is the most precious thing religion has.

Akhenaten did not "invent" monotheism just to win the war against the Hittites because his choice was philosophically grounded. Why should it be forbidden to Akhenaten to have the kind of thinking that leads to the conclusion that in reality, there is only one Supreme, Invisible God who has a close relationship with the Light and that the sun which emits light helps understand God?

By using the sun to meditate on God, Akhenaten simply did the same thing Hermes and Paul did: the use of the creature to understand the creator.

If Akhenaten's attitude was just a political maneuver to unite his people in order to defeat the Hittites, why would he take the risk of calling His God Aten instead of Amun-Re? Raising Amun-Re from his status of head of a henotheistic system to that of a monotheistic system would have proven more efficient. *Henotheism* is the belief in one god without denying the existence of the others in contradiction to monotheism to which there is only One True God.

 But everything discussed in this volume so far shows that this contradiction is not too strong and depends on the angle [angel] from which the question is considered. Indeed, Henotheism is right when one admits that angels and humans who are philosophically and spiritually advanced can be called gods; and *Monotheism* is correct when it considers above all creatures [gods or not] only One Supreme and Incomparable God.

Coming back to Akhenaten, let's suppose he was not a very wise person. At least he would have been wise enough to avoid internal division seeing the persistence of the priests of Amun-Re and those of the other gods to maintain their cults. His religious reform instead of uniting the people against the Hittites rather divided it profoundly. Nevertheless he maintained his position taking the great risk to have an opposite result to his expectations. Instead of the empowerment of the people to transcend itself and fight victoriously, there were anger, sadness, and dissatisfaction.

Why would Akhenaten's action necessarily be that of a capricious and stubborn ruler, while there is also the possibility that in fact he was a misunderstood visionary man and good religious philosopher? Why would Moses, Jesus, and Mohammed be great religious founders and not Akhenaten? In fact *if Akhenaten has used the methods of holy wars and inquisition like Ancient Israelites, Christians, and Muslims, it is possible that "Atenism" or "Akhenatism" be one of the great monotheistic religions of the present time.*

It is true that humans have something within that pushes them to look for a higher power. *Monotheism* is valid as are *pantheism, panentheism, polytheism* [hard and soft] *in certain forms*; especially when they consider creation as part of God and humans and angels as gods.

Deism is sometimes defined as the belief, based solely on reason, in a God who created the universe and then abandoned it, assuming no control over life, exerting no influence on natural phenomena, and giving no supernatural revelation. Other times it is explained as a religious and philosophical belief that a supreme being created the universe with the understanding that this affirmation and religious truth in general can be determined using reason and observation of the natural world alone, without the need for either faith or organized religion.

The second definition explicitly contrasts reason with faith. In fact, there cannot be true faith without a reason and reason gives birth to a kind of faith or confidence. Reason and faith, especially the faith centered on reason, generate hope.

In the science of physical things believed to be based solely on reason, faith is also present in the sense of 'yet to prove convictions.' Deism is right to emphasize reason but since reason is ultimately the base for faith or hope and since additional reason is found when hope or faith or hypothesis is confirmed by experience, faith cannot be completely separated from reason whether in dealing with Divinity, spirituality, or physicality.

How humans relate to the divine has been partially tackled in this work. However its theological stand rather than an anthropological one does not allow giving much more detail.

How the All Pervading God deals with the universe and its laws as well as with human beings could be broadened in an anthropological volume. It is in that kind of work that special revelation and the place of organized religion can be fully explored.

For the same reasons *henotheism, kathenotheism* and *Monolatrism* will not be fully discussed here since they imply worship which has a strong anthropological dimension and about which a lot of information need to be presented.

Autotheism, the deification of humans which is advocated by various religions is however confirmed and *dualism* has been proven groundless.

The point *monotheism* tries to make, inelegantly in many cases, is that no matter what god is considered; he or she originates from the Supreme All Pervading God, Invisible on earth and in heavens, the only one worthy of the supreme consideration. *True monotheism is not the primacy of an anthropomorphic god over others like in the Old Testament, but the acknowledgment of the Universal Soul*, the one that is part of the unconsciousness of gods, angels, demons, or humans and who keeps them alive and functioning even when they sleep. It is sad that some proponents of monotheism have had to resort to inhuman methods in some cases to prove their point. However, this can change for the better.

As Justin Barrett admits, monotheism is highly attractive. It has the power to move humanity to a brighter future. ***In a society in which there is religious tolerance associated with the respect of human rights by all; the real meaning of the universe will finally*** *appear to all*. Nevertheless, from some philosophical perspectives, many of the other spiritual "isms" are justified.

Conclusion

THE best way to know divinities is through authentic spiritual experiences such as those narrated in several religious and spiritual scriptures like the *Poimandres* and the Bible. Unfortunately, those experiences are not shared by all humans at the same time. This enables some to call those experiences myths or hallucinations and see 'out of body experience' with a very skeptic eye. *However, not all accounts are imagined stories.*

Even the Holy Spirit has not manifested, according to scriptures, to over more than 120 people at the same time and that kind of experience is quite rare. Those who believe that the manifestation of the Holy Spirit has to do with physiology are not wrong since there is a correspondence among all forms of energy, most of which are electrical in nature. But the physiology in question is of a high order.

It is true that the form of electricity that governs the physical heart and the nerves as medical science knows as well the Holy Spirit respond to the activities of human mind. However, the first is generated by and obeys to different laws than those that govern the second. Electricity in the heart and nerves, to name just those elements, is generated from the physical body and responds to the mind serving as mediator between that mind and the body through the brain, nerves, and some chemical substances called neuromediators.

The Holy Spirit is driven into a person through the activities of the mind which are of religious, spiritual, philosophical, and moral nature. Seeker has discovered based on his personal authentic spiritual experiences that religious and spiritual schools have given many accurate descriptions about that Energy while the science of physical things says nothing.

The fact that this science might someday give some explanations about the Holy Spirit removes nothing from the Divine nature of the later. The people of the world ought to remember that chemistry sprang out of alchemy and that many physical disciplines have their origin in spiritual schools of the past. The progress of the science of physical things which is desirable will only prove the unity of the cosmos, physical and spiritual.

Scientists of the physical things know that people do not see microorganisms with the naked eye. The same way, spiritual scientists speak of specific methods that will lead into the presence of supernatural beings such as angels.

The best way of experiencing the Supreme Invisible All Pervading God is through the Holy Spirit which is also light, power, or ultimate sacred fire. Some of the most amazing manifestations of divinities to people are described in the stories of Hermes Trismegistus and Jesus. Various ways to encounter supernatural beings or gods have been presented particularly in chapter 10.

Apart from direct experience with divinities [which needs to be scientifically confirmed], philosophy or theology is what contributes the most efficiently to the knowledge of their existence and nature. Philosophy or theology helps make sense of religious and spiritual scriptures and stories, physical science, as well as the experiences lived by people. It is that philosophy and theology, which has been at work in the body of this volume that enables the following cosmological and historical formulation.

In the beginning, there was the Supreme Invisible All Pervading God. The Supreme God was the Cosmic Mind dwelling in Light [Energy, Holy Spirit, or Divine Substance]. Light is the Abode of God. That Mind was the essence of all beings which were to come into concrete existence. It was the 'Male-Female' source of the Logos or Creative Divine Word [Thought, Reason, Laws], also plus and minus, and which served to perform the work of creation.

He-She took the time to think about the creation to come. At the end of that Divine Meditation or Thinking, the Logos or Word was ready. God knew all the beings He-She would create. But humans, the most important beings God envisioned, dreamed of, could not come into existence without the others elements of His-Her creation.

So, first God created the angels with divine light and gave them a variety of personalities, qualities, and powers. They can be collectively called the Demiurge, acting gods, sons of God, or representative of God including the powerful angel called God of the Old Testament. They are also the abode of God. Angels are spiritual beings made of light and mind. Their light, spiritual body, substance, or energy, was the result of the modification, condensation or concentration of the Original Divine Energy.

Finally humans were created from a denser and less subtle matter, substance, light, or energy plus the seed of consciousness and unconsciousness called mind, with the help of angels. Hence, undoubtedly, they are also the abode of God as are all physical and spiritual things. Humans are particular because they can relate to God understanding His-Her presence in all beings, physical and spiritual. This enables them to be the *natural* superintendents or managers appointed by God.

Because the human soul has to rise to the Divine Soul from the starting point of total unconsciousness like things; passing later through the stages of vegetal soul, animal soul, and angelic soul, it is for sometime inferior to the angelic soul. Therefore, before humans can reach their divine status, angels manage or guide the entire universe [energy, minerals, planets, stars, plants, animals, humans, etc...] as representatives of God.

One of the angels who was very intelligent decided to have ideas different from those of the powerful angel called God of the Old Testament and convinced many other angels not to follow him. This is the origin of evil and demons, who invented so many lies that only sanctification that leads to the direct presence of All Pervading God and good angels to some extent could bring true answers to the deep questions humans have.

Not willing to let humans grow naturally and surpass them, the angels who became demons deceived the human species for ages. They decided to have their abodes not only in the invisible realm, but also among men and women on earth. They dwell in temples both of stone and of flesh. They are the gods, sometimes manifest, sometimes hidden behind imaginary gods. They lied, tricked, misguided, and harmed immature and ignorant humans hiding the divine truth from them and corrupting them with false philosophy or wisdom. Finally, they posed as God and asked humans to worship them.

Demons continue their crimes even nowadays and humans are still falling into their traps listening to the voices of the rejection of wisdom and reason, indiscipline, loss of self-control, hatred of others which cause crimes, conflicts, and wars as one can see happening around the entire globe. Fortunately, a part of the population has kept itself from following demons and is trying to improve itself and build the welfare of all.

One angel called the Lord God despite his many qualities asked to be worshipped. This could be seen as a step toward true monotheism which is the acknowledgment of the All Pervading non-angelic Supreme God. Angels fought demons and tried to teach humans true divine knowledge the best they could. However, the good angels were not all wise as the Supreme God or as wise as mature humans could be. So they made mistakes which explain how they poorly managed some situations in the Bible easily accepting divisions and genocides as solutions to the problems caused by the unbalance of the spiritual world.

Representing God that none could see, angels walked with and talked to Adam and Eve, Enoch and Noah, Abraham and lot; they appeared to Isaac and Jacob, to the parents of Samson, to Isaiah, Ezekiel, Daniel, Jesus, Peter, John, Mohammad etc…; helping in the founding of various religions, spiritual schools, and philosophies to combat the work of demons who had their own religions, spiritual schools, and philosophies.

While God was using good angels at their best, He-She also supported humanity via the qualities and the strength that His-Her Holy Spirit can provide. Hence, some humans like Hermes, Jesus, and Paul started to question the management of all supernatural beings, good and bad, and began teaching that humans are to be gods even closer the Universal Soul than the best angels. Jesus especially called himself the Son of Man and was said to have become superior to angels. *Thus, the supremacy of astrotheology or the rule of gods via stars, planets, and other elements of nature met challengers. Jesus even started for the first time to expulse fallen angels from possessed people.*

But, though the Jesus of the Bible accomplished these great deeds, *his educational methods and teachings could not attract many people truly determined to undo the works of the Devil and demons beginning with the abandonment of their own sins and the gain of divine knowledge and wisdom.* The gap between him and them was so important!

But the Jesus of the Bible was also personally responsible for neglecting earthly matters and for thinking that he could save humankind anyway by dying on the cross using his blood as one definitive cleansing instrument, not to mention his unwillingness to listen to advice for example from Peter. The regrettable fact remains that the world, including Christians, has since been in deep trouble starting with the destruction of Jerusalem.

The typical Christian answer which consists in saying that the work of Jesus saved souls for Paradise is partially acceptable; but it is at the same time the recognition of a failure because *God did not create humanity to suffer on earth and then be saved in Paradise.* Moreover, ancient prophets and their followers suffered too on earth and went to heaven after death. Their prophecies were not only for a salvation after death but for a salvation and peace on earth first.

At first Jesus went exactly in that direction asking for repentance and the change of bad habits as well as the study and practice of the Divine Word or Wisdom. He even taught people to pray for the coming of the kingdom of God on earth. Something important must have happened for him to latter turn his focus only on spiritual salvation. The result is that the world is still in pain waiting for humanity to understand and occupy its true position.

If Christians could understand why Jesus remembered the people in John 10: 34 of the words of the Old Testament in Psalms 82: 6, words that he agrees with, then they would produce a new effort and place themselves better in the Divine Plan that wants to raise each human to have the status of god and unite humanity around great ideals.

John 10: 34: Jesus answered them: Is it not written in your law: I have said: You are gods?

Psalms 82: 6-7: I have said: You are gods, You are all the sons of the Most High. But you die like humans…

Jesus cited the Old Testament because some people could not understand why he called himself Son of God. His answer was not only a justification of his own divinity, but also that of other humans. That answer also shows that Jesus did not consider himself as a God who is member of some Trinity, but a god that any human can become. The verse drawn from the psalms expresses well what Jesus meant to teach asking: *'Why do you die as humans when you can die as gods?'*

Hence, everyone would be able to bring a personal stone for the building of a universal philosophy, science, and spirituality. Human geniuses would appear everywhere for the happiness of all.

Saint Paul who was very instrumental in founding Christianity and who displayed several qualities also made very important theological mistakes that this book has partially tackled. The works of Jesus and Paul will be more analyzed in the next volume that will be entitled *Divine Humanism: Creating the Happiest Society.*

This work has presented arguments that hopefully will encourage people to strengthen their relationships with the Universal Soul going beyond astrotheology or the rule of angels whether fallen or not.

Seeker agrees with Hermes that humans are at least the equals of angels but goes farther and affirms based on the state of the world and on some passages of scripture that the human potential is greater than that of angels. Humans and angels [good and bad] must learn to know each other for appropriate mutual respect.

Obviously, demons have a serious problem that they seem not to be able to get out of by themselves. They would gain to let humans and good angels help them even if this includes reparation of the crimes committed. They need care and remedies for their philosophical and bodily troubles as well as several other things.

The invention of dualism as the necessity of both good and evil is a big lie that they should abandon. Humans and good angels should never swallow that pill because it contains the justifications for all the crimes of demons.

They seem to have forgotten or fake to have forgotten that no evil was required for their own creation and that of the rest of the universe. Even humans make progress only through good. Suffering became necessary because of evil. So, demons would do better by no longer sending emissaries, teachers, internet blog animators, spiritualists, and so on to make people think that evil is necessary for the fast development of humankind or that it helps avoid annoyance.

Some people may be sensitive to the philosophical arguments brought forth, others to the scriptural ones, still others to the experiential ones [physical or spiritual], and finally others to all of them.

One needs to reflect on experiences, lived personally or by others, and also reflect on scriptures as well as to organize them into knowledge eliminating what is wrong and reserving what needs more investigation.

This book wants to encourage spiritual researchers to explain the various scriptures and practices of the world whether religious or secular in term of the generalities on God and the gods and in term of united and rational living experience. It is also desirable that new life enhancing scriptures about the rational and empirical God emerge to roll back the ignorance of human beings concerning the physical and the subtle worlds and to enable the emergence of the harmonious universe all long for.

Wars and conflicts in human individuals, families, societies, nations, and blocks are primarily due to the wars and conflicts among angels and demons as the book of Daniel in the 10th chapter [verses 20 and 21] shows.

One can only agree with Manly Hall when in the conclusion of *The Secret Teachings of all Ages*, he asserts that war is the irrefutable evidence of irrationality and can easily lead to the destruction of civilization. *When one considers the management of angels and demons marked by repetitive conflicts and wars until today, the fair conclusion that their rationality is not very high can be made.*

Humans therefore have the duty to stop being guided mainly by that intermediary rationality or astrology and need to find the philosophy and the practices that can enable them to cooperate and support one another while finding a way to help angels and demons solve their problems.

That is the objective of the next volume. That proposal should harmonize with what the Divine Soul want to teach through other human souls of the present time who have reached an appreciable level of development. Together, the human species can accomplish that task.

If it is true that no individual can succeed until he/she has developed a philosophy of life as Hall said in the same conclusion, it is also true that the human species cannot succeed and build everlasting peace on earth unless it develops a philosophy for the entire species, a general philosophy that will help individuals make up their specific philosophies so that they are in harmony with one another, do not destroy society or civilization, and improve the general philosophy.

Spiritual science also has to be reconstructed step by step so that the future generations escape the useless suffering caused by the barbaric man or woman under demonic influence or from his/her own will. Becoming good, better, more beautiful, more truthful, wiser, and more loving is what all should aim for no matter the starting point. Happiness for all is truly possible.

Appendixes

Appendix 1

Religious artifacts in history

Territory	Religious artifacts		Other artifacts	
Botswana			Tsodilo rock art[70]	Over 100.000 years
Malawi			Chongoni rock art[71]	Late stone age
Australia			Rock Painting in Kakadu[72]	18.000 B.C.E.
France			Rock art in Lascaux cave[73]	14.000 B.C.E.
Libya			Rock art sites of Tadrart Acacus[74]	12.000 B.C.E.
Papua New Guinea			Kuk early agricultural site[75]	5000 B.C.E.
Oman			Sites of Bat, Al-Khutm, and Al-Ayn[76]	3000 B.C.E.
Pakistan			Ruins of Moenjodaro[77]	3000 B.C.E.
Assyria	Ancient city of Ashur[78]	3000-2000 B.C.E.		
Egypt	Pyramid of Zoser at Saqara[79]	2800 B.C.E.		

[70]Unesco. World Heritage Convention.http:// whc.unesco.com/ (accessed April 1, 2010).
[71] Ibid.
[72]Grolier Educational (Firm), *Ancient Civilizations* Vol 1, (Danbury, Conn: Grolier Educational, 2001), 8.
[73]Unesco.
[74]Grolier Educational (Firm), *Ancient Civilizations*. Vol 1, (Danbury, Conn: Grolier Educational, 2001), 25.
[75]Unesco.
[76]Ibid.
[77] Ibid.
[78]Ibid.

Akkad			City of Elba[80]	2500 B.C.E.
Anatolia			City of Alaca Höyük[81]	2500 B.C.E.
Mesopotamia			Clay tablet[82]	2400 B.C.E.
Babylonia	Tiny bronze and gold statue of King Hammurabi in prayer[83]	1800 B.C.E.		
China	Oracle bone from the Shang Dynasty[84]	1766-1100 B.C.E.	Decorated bronze cooking vessel from the Shang Dynasty[85]	1766-1100 B.C.E.
Elam	Holy city of the Kingdom of Elam Tchongha Zanbil[86]	1250 B.C.E.		
Sudan	Gebel Barkal and the sites of the Napatan Region[87]	900-270 B.C.E.		

---

[79]Grolier Educational (Firm), *Ancient Civilizations*. Vol 1, (Danbury, Conn: Grolier Educational, 2001), 27.
[80]Ibid., 49 Ibid., 27.
[81]Ibid., 27.
[82]http://en.wikipedia.org/wiki/Modern_human_behavior (accessed April 1, 2010).
[83]Grolier Educational (Firm), *Ancient Civilizations*. Vol 3, (Danbury, Conn: Grolier Educational, 2001), 10.
[84]Ibid., 14.
[85]Ibid., 34.
[86]Ibid., 34.
[87]Ibid.

Senegambia	Stone circles of Senegambia[88]	300 B.C.E.		
Japan			Terracotta figurine[89]	500 C.E.
Afghanistan	Remains of the Bamiyan Valley[90]	100 C.E.		

---

[88]Ibid.
[89] Ibid.
[90] Ibid.

Timeline of civilizations according to four historical sources

Jane Mac Intosh[91]		Crane C. Brinton[92]		Grolier Educational[93 and 94]		Penguin[95]	
Civilization	Time-line	Civilization	Time-line	Civilization	Time-line	Civiliza-tion	Time-line
Jericho	7500 B.C.E.	Jericho	7800 B.C.E.	Jericho	10000 B.C.E.		
Çatal Höyük (Turkey)	7000-6000 B.C.E.	Çatal Höyük	6500 B.C.E.				
Temples in Mesopota-mia	5500 B.C.E.						
Megalithic tombs in Europe	5000 B.C.E.			Mesopota-mia	5000 B.C.E.	Chinese Yang Shao culture	5000 B.C.E.
		Jarmo in ancient Mesopo-tamia	4500 B.C.E.			Sumer	4500 B.C.E.
Uruk	4000 B.C.E.						

[91] Jane McIntosh and Clint Twist, Civilizations: ten thousand years of ancient history (London : BBC, 2001) 6-7.

[92] Brinton, Crane, John B. Christopher, and Robert Lee Wolff, *A History of Civilization* (Englewood, Cliffs, N.J.: Prentice-Hall, 1976) 10,11,14,16, 20, 21, 23, 25, 28, 38, and 59.

[93] Grolier Educational (Firm), *Ancient Civilizations*. Vol 1 (Danbury, Conn: Grolier Educational, 2001), 10, 27, 29, 32, 40, 49, 50, 53, and 56.

[94] Grolier Educational (Firm), *Ancient Civilizations*. Vol 2 (Danbury, Conn: Grolier Educational, 2001), 4, 14, 15, 38, 53, 55, and 68-71.

[95] Arthur Cotterell, *The Penguin Encyclopedia of Ancient Civilizations* (London: Penguin, 1988) 22, 61-2, 72, 84, 89, 102, 109, 111, 118, 130, 135, 144, 147, 176, 214, 245, 288, 318, 325, 332, and 343.

Temple pyramids in Peru	4000 B.C.E.							
Trade towns in Iranian plateau	4000 B.C.E.			First Mesopota- mian Temples	4000 B.C.E.			
First writings in Mesopota- mia	3500 B.C.E.	Uruk	3550 B.C.E.					
Walled towns in Egypt	3400 B.C.E.							
Earliest hieroglyphic writings in Egypt	3200 B.C.E.						Egypt	3100 B.C.E.
Cuneiform writing	3100 B.C.E.			Sumer	3000 B.C.E.			
Permanent settlements on Peruvian coast	3000 B.C.E.			Troy	3000 B.C.E.			
				Cycladic culture	3000 B.C.E.			
				Minoan civilization	3000 B.C.E.			
				Step pyramid of Zoser at Saqara	2800 B.C.E.			
Pyramid of Djoser at Saqara	2700 B.C.E.			Egyptian Old Kingdom	2650 B.C.E.			
Indus script fully developed	2600 B.C.E.	Cretan or Minoan civilization began	2600 B.C.E.	Indus civilization	2600 B.C.E.			
U-shaped shrines in Peru	2600 B.C.E.			Nubian Kush	2500 B.C.E.			
Great pyramid of	2550 B.C.E.			City of Elba in Akkadian	2500 B.C.E.		Indus	2500 B.C.E.

Khufu at Giza				Empire			
Sumeririan script modified for writing Akkadian	2500 B.C.E.					Akkad	2340 B.C.E.
				Akkadians	2334 B.C.E.	Troy	Before 2200 B.C.E.
Minoan civilization	2000 B.C.E.			Ziggurat of the god Mar- duk at Babylon	2000 B.C.E.	Babylon	2000 B.C.E.
				Old Assyrian and babylonian Empire	2000 B.C.E.	Assyria	2000 B.C.E.
Cretan script began	1800 B.C.E.			Statue of King Hammurabi in prayer	1800 B.C.E.	Minoans	2000 B.C.E.
Code of Hammurabi	1760 B.C.E.					Maya	2000 B.C.E.
First alphabetical signs in the Levant	1700 B.C.E.	Hittite capital Hattusas	1700 B.C.E.	Hittites	1700 B.C.E.	Hittites	1700 B.C.E.
Mycenaean civilization	1650 B.C.E.	Hyksos	1600 B.C.E.			Myce- naean	1600 B.C.E.
Chinese Writings on oracle bones	1600 B.C.E.			Polynesian Lapita culture	1600 B.C.E.		
Mitanni Empire	1600 B.C.E.	Myce- naean civilization	1600 B.C.E.	Mycenaean civilization	1600 B.C.E.	Mitanni	1595 B.C.E.
		Mitanni [Hurrian State]	1500 B.C.E.				
		Phoenicia	1400 B.C.E.			Uratu and Armenia	1350 B.C.E.

Olmec	1200 B.C.E.			Olmecs	1200 B.C.E.	Israel	Before 1223 B.C.E.
Chavin Civilization in the Andes	1200 B.C.E.			Phoenicia	1100 B.C.E.	Phrygia and Lydia	1200 B.C.E.
						Olmecs	1200 B.C.E.
				Adena culture	1000 B.C.E.	Phoenicia	1000 B.C.E.
		Dark Ages	1100-800 B.C.E.	Etruscans	900 B.C.E.		
		Homer's Iliad and Odysseus	850-750 B.C.E.	Chavin culture	900 B.C.E.	Persia	900 B.C.E.
Phoenicians trading empire spreads throughout Mediterranean	800 B.C.E.			Celts in Central and Western Europe	800 B.C.E.	Etruscans	800 B.C.E.
Greek states	800 B.C.E.			Greece	800 B.C.E.	Rome	753 B.C.E.
		Medes cooperated with Babylonia	612 B.C.E.	Persian Empire	550 B.C.E.	Greece	700 B.C.E.
		Persians destroyed Babylon	538 B.C.E.	Temple to Zeus in Greece	510 B.C.E.		
Simple writing system in Mesoamerica	500 B.C.E.			Roman Republic	509 B.C.E.		
Tehoutihuacan	400 B.C.E.			Anuradhapura (Sri Lanka)	400 B.C.E.		
Nazca culture in southern	250 B.C.E.			Teotihuacan	200 B.C.E.		

Peruvian coast							
				Hopewell culture	100 B.C.E.		
		Poet Virgil	70-19 B.C.E.	Roman Empire	27 B.C.E.	Teotihua-can	100 B.C.E.
Jesus	4 **B.C.E.** **-30** C.E.	Jesus	8 or 4 B.C.E. 29 or 30 or 33 C.E.	Mayans	250 C.E.		
Classic Maya	300 C.E.			Korean Three Kingdoms period	300 C.E.		
Korea and Japan adopt many elements of Chinese culture including Buddhism	336 C.E.			Nubia, Meroe, and Aksun	350 C.E.		
Tiwanaku state	400 C.E.						
				Anglo Saxons invaded Britain	500 C.E.		
				Khmer Empire	600 C.E.		
				African Kingdom of Ghana	750 C.E.		
				Japan Heian period	794 C.E.		
Mississipian towns	800 C.E.			Vikings	800 C.E.		
				Toltecs	900 C.E.	Toltecs	900 C.E.
				African Kingdom of	1000 C.E.		

				Benin			
				African Kingdom of Mali	1200 C.E.		
				Great Zimbabwe	1270 C.E.		
Mixtecs gain control of Oaxaca Valley	1350 C.E.			Aztecs	1325 C.E.	Aztecs	1375 C.E.
Inca Empire	1410 C.E.			Incas	1438 C.E.	Incas	1438 C.E.

Appendix 3

Appearances of religious texts in history

Minian Smart[96]		Sacred-texts online[97]	
Text	Civilization and age	Text	Civilization and age
		Pyramid texts	3100 B.C.E. Ancient Egypt
Prophecy of Neferti	2600-2450 B.C.E. Ancient Egypt	I Ching	2953-2838 B.C.E. Ancient China
Lamentation over the destruction of Ur	2500-2000 B.C.E. Sumer		
Pyramid texts	At least 2300 B.C.E. Ancient Egypt		
Enuma Elish	2000 B.C.E. Babylon	Enuma Elish	1800 B.C.E. Babylon
Law code of Hammurabi	1728-1686 B.C.E. Babylon	Code of Hammurabi	1792 B.C.E. Babylon
		Gilgamesh epic	1760 B.C.E. Babylon
		Egyptian Book of the Dead	1600 B.C.E. Ancient Egypt
		Rig Veda, Sama Veda, and Yayur Veda	1550-1450 B.C.E. Ancient India
		Avesta	1500 B.C.E. Ancient Iran [Persia]
Stelae of Amenmose	1550-1305 B.C.E. Ancient Egypt		
Akhenaten's Great Hymn to Aten	1370-1353 B.C.E. Ancient Egypt		
		Torah	1200 B.C.E . Ancient Israel
		Iliad/Odysseus of Homer	1194 B.C.E. Ancient Greece
		Atharva Veda	1000 B.C.E. Ancient India
		Shih Shing [Book of Odes]	1000-500 B.C.E. Ancient China

---

[96] Ninian Smart and Richard D. Hecht, *Sacred Texts of the World: A Universal Anthology* (A Herder & Herder book. New York: Crossroad, 2003), 6, 9-10, 12, 15, 17-18, 20, 22, 29, 31, 33, 35, and 38-39.
[97]http://www.sacred-texts.com/time/timeline.htm (accessed April 1, 2010).

		Song of songs [Bible]	950 B.C.E. Ancient Israel
		Brihad-Aranyaka and Chandogya Upanishads	800-700 B.C.E.
Creation according to Hesiod	750 B.C.E. Ancient Greece	Hesiod: Works and Days, Theogony	800 B.C.E. Ancient Greece
		Book of Isaiah [Bible]	740 B.C.E. Ancient Israel
		Books of Deuterono-my, Joshua, and Samuel [Bible]	700 B.C.E. Ancient Israel
		Ramayana	700 B.C.E. Ancient India
Timaeus of Plato	360 B.C.E. Ancient Greece	Tao Te Ching	650 B.C.E. Ancient China
		Mahabharata	540 B.C.E. Ancient India
		Book of Zecharia [Bible]	530 B.C.E. Ancient Israel
		Confucian canon	409 B.C.E. Ancient China
		Books of Proverbs and Job [Bible]	400 B.C.E. Ancient Israel
		Critias by Plato: contains the story of Atlantis	360 B.C.E. Ancient Greece
		Writings of Chuang-Tzu	340 B.C.E. Ancient China
		Book of Jonah [Bible]	300 B.C.E. Ancient China
		Septuagint, first Greek translation of the Old Testament	285 B.C.E. Ancient Greece
		Abhidharma, part of the Tripitaka	250 B.C.E. Ancient India
		Dhammapada canonized by Asoka	240 B.C.E. Ancient India
		Early Mishnah	200-120 B.C.E. Ancient Israel
		Book of Daniel [Bible]	164 B.C.E. Ancient Israel
		Apocrypha: Tobit,	160 B.C.E.

		Esdras, Enoch, others	
		Yoga Sutras of Patanjali	150 B.C.E. Ancient India
		Dead Sea Scrolls	150 B.C.E.
"Messianic" ecologue of Virgil	40 B.C.E.		
		Kojiki, Nihongi	1 C.E. Ancient Japan
		Colossians, Philemon, Ephesians, Philippians	0-63 C.E. Roman Empire
		Gospel of Mark	70 C.E. Roman Empire
		Gospels of Matthew and Luke	80 C.E. Roman Empire
		Gospel of John	90 C.E. Roman Empire
		Revelation of St John	81-96 C.E. Roman Empire
		Nag Hammadi Scriptures	100 C.E. Roman Empire
Metamorphoses [Manifestation of Isis] by Apuleius	2nd Century C.E.		
Buddacarita by Asvaghosa	2nd Century C.E.		
Enneads of Plotinus	205-270 C.E.		
On the Mysteries of Iamblicus	250-325 C.E.	Christian Bible	325 C.E. Roman Empire
		Confessions of St Augustine	401 C.E. Roman Empire
		Vulgate [Latin Bible] by St Jerome	404 C.E. Roman Empire
		Qur' an	610 C.E. Arabia
		First Hadith	630 C.E. Arabia
		Necronomicon of Abdul Alhazred	950 C.E.
		First Latin translation of the Corpus Hermeticum	1463 C.E.
		Luther' s 95 theses	1517 C.E.
		Nostradamus	1503-1566 C.E.

		NT translated into German by Luther	1522 C.E.
		NT translated into English by W. Tyndale	1525 C.E.
		Entire Bible in German by Luther	1534 C.E.
		Bible in English by Miles Coverdale	1535 C.E.
Popol Vuh	Recorded in the 16th Century C.E. Maya		
		Rosicrucian Fama Fraternitatis	1614 C.E.
		Sacred Books of the East by Max Müller	1879-1910 C.E.
		Atlantis, The Antediluvian World by Donnelly	1882 C.E.
		The Secret Doctrine by H.P. Blavatsky	1888 C.E.
		Aradia, Gospel of the Witches by C. Leland	1899 C.E.

References

Adams, David L., and Ken Schurb.*The Anonymous God: The Church Confronts Civil Religion and American Society*. St. Louis, MO: Concordia Pub. House, 2005.

Allen, James P., and Peter Der Manuelian.*The Ancient Egyptian Pyramid Texts*. Atlanta: Society of Biblical Literature, 2005.

Aristotle, *The Nichomachean Ethics*.

Armstrong, Karen. *A History of God: The 4000-Year Quest of Judaism, Christianity, and Islam*. New York: A.A. Knopf, 1993.

Ascalone, Enrico. *Mesopotamia*. Milano: Electa, 2005.

Barrett, Justin L. *Why Would Anyone Believe in God?* Cognitive science of religion series. Walnut Creek, CA: AltaMira Press, 2004.

Bartlett, Robert C. "Aristotle's Introduction to the Problem of Happiness: On Book I of the Nicomachean Ethics." *American Journal of Political Science* 52, no. 3(2008): 677-687.

Blavatsky, Helena Petrovna. *Isis Unveiled: a Master-Key to the Mysteries of Ancient and Modern Science and Theology,* 1972.

Blavatsky, Helena Petrovna. *The Secret Doctrine: the Synthesis of Science, Religion, and Philosophy.Second Edition*, 1888.

Brinton, Crane, John B. Christopher, and Robert Lee Wolff.

A History of Civilization. Englewood, Cliffs, N.J.: Prentice-Hall, 1976.

Bromley, David G. *Teaching New Religious Movements.* Oxford: Oxford University Press, 2007.

Brown, Dan. *The Lost Symbol: A Novel.* New York: Doubleday, 2009.

Browne, Sylvia, and Lindsay Harrison.*Phenomenon: Everything You Need to Know About the Paranormal.* New York: Dutton, 2005.

Browne, Sylvia. *Exploring the Levels of Creation.* Carlsbad, Calif: Hay House, 2006.

Browne, Sylvia. *If You Could See What I See: The Tenets of Novus Spiritus.* Carlsbad, Calif: Hay House, 2006.

Campbell, Jeremy. *The Many Faces of God: Science's 400-Year Quest for Images of the Divine.* New York: W.W. Norton & Co, 2006.

Choquette, Sonia. *Ask Your Guides: Connecting to Your Divine Support System.* Carlsbad, Calif: Hay House, 2006.

Chryssides, George D., and Margaret Wilkins.*A Reader in New Religious Movements.* London: Continuum, 2006.

Clark, Lynn Schofield. *From Angels to Aliens: Teenagers, theMedia, and the Supernatural.* Oxford: Oxford University Press, 2003.

Cotterell, Arthur. *The Penguin Encyclopedia of Ancient Civilizations.* London: Penguin, 1988.

Culianu, Ioan P. *The Tree of Gnosis: Gnostic Mythology from Early Christianity to Modern Nihilism.* [San Francisco]: HarperSanFrancisco, 1992.

Daniélou, Alain. *The Myths and Gods of India: The Classic Work on Hindu Polytheism from the Princeton Bollingen Series.* Rochester, Vt: Inner Traditions International, 1991.

Danti, Michael D., and Richard L. Zettler.*Sumer and Its City-

*States.*Calliope. Peterborough, N.H.: Cobblestone Pub, 2003.

Davidson, Gustav. *A Dictionary of Angels.* New York: The
Free Press, 1967.

Dhammarama, Ahangama. *Gods and Their Origin in Sri Lanka:
The Buddhist and the Concept of Divinity.* Sri Lanka:
Ahangama Dhammarama Nayaka Thera], 2005.

Descartes, René, Elizabeth Sanderson Haldane, G. R. T. Ross.
*Discourse on Method and Meditations.*Dover philosophical clas-
sics. Mineola, N.Y.: Dover Publications, 2003.

Drury Nevill. *The New Age: Searching for the Spiritual Self.* New
York: Thames & Hudson, Inc, 2004.

Dunderberg, Ismo. *Beyond Gnosticism: Myth, Lifestyle, and
Society in the School of Valentinus.* New York: Columbia
University Press, 2008.

Ehret, Christopher. *The Civilizations of Africa: A History to 1800.*
Charlottesville: University Press of Virginia, 2002.

Fisher, Leonard Everett. *The Gods and Goddesses of
Ancient Egypt.* New York: Holiday House, 1997.

Freud, Sigmund, and Katherine Jones.*Moses and Monotheism.*
New York: Knopf, 1939.

Grolier Educational (Firm).*Ancient Civilizations.* Danbury,
Conn: Grolier Educational, 2001.

Hall, Manly P. *The Secret Teachings of All Ages: An Encyclopedic
Outline of Masonic, Hermetic, Qabbalistic, and Rosicrucian
Symbolical Philosophy : Being an Interpretation of the Secret
Teachings Concealed Within the Rituals, Allegories, and Myste-
ries of the Ages.* New York: Jeremy P. Tarcher/Penguin, 2003.

Hinnells, John R. *Persian Mythology.* London: Hamlyn, 1973.

Irwin, Harvey J. *An Introduction to Parapsychology.*
Jefferson, N.C. [u.a.]: McFarland, 1999.

*Japanese Gods and Myths.*Ancient cultures.Hoo, nr. Rochester,
Kent: Grange Books, 1998.

Jemiriya, Timothy F. *The Yoruba God and Gods*. Ado-Ekiti [Nigeria]: Petoa Educational Publishers, 1998.

Jonas, Hans. *The Gnostic Religion: The Message of the Alien God & the Beginnings of Christianity*. Boston: Beacon Press, 2001.

Jordan, Michael. *Dictionary of Gods and Goddesses*. Facts on File library of religion and mythology. New York: Facts on File, 2004.

Jung, C. G. *Psychology and Religion*. The Terry lectures. New Haven: Yale University Press, 1938.

Jung, C. G. *The Archetypes and the Collective Unconscious*. Bollingen series, 20. [Princeton, N.J.]: Princeton University Press, 1968.

Karma-glin-pa, Padma Sambhava, Gyurme Dorje, Graham Coleman, Thupten Jinpa, and Bstan-dzin-rgya-mtsho.*The Tibetan Book of the Dead [English Title]: The Great Liberation by Hearing in the Intermediate States [Tibetan Title]*. New York: Penguin, 2007.

Kelly, Karen. *The Secret of the Secret: Unlocking the Mysteries of the Runaway Bestseller*. New York: Thomas Dunne Books/St. Martin's Press, 2007.

Kirsch, Jonathan. *God against the Gods: The History of the War between Monotheism and Polytheism*. New York: Viking Compass, 2004.

Küng, Hans. *Does God Exist?: An Answer for Today*. Garden City, N.Y.: Doubleday, 1980.

La Due, Francia A., and William H. Dower. *Teachings of the Temple*. Halcyon, Calif: The Temple of the People, 1925.

Lainé, Daniel, Tobie Nathan, Anne Stamm, and Pierre Saulnier.*African Gods: Contemporary Rituals and Beliefs*. Paris: Flammarion, 2007.

Lurker, Manfred.*The Gods and Symbols of Ancient Egypt: An Illustrated Dictionary*. New York, NY: Thames and Hudson, 1980.

Martin, Michael, and Ricki Monnier.*The Improbability of God*.
Amherst, N.Y.: Prometheus Books, 2006.

Matczak, Sebastian A. *God in Contemporary Thought: A Philosophical Perspective : a Collective Study*. Philosophical questions series, 10. New York: Learned Publications, 1977.

Matthews, Caitlin and John Matthews.*Walkers between the Worlds:The Western Mysteries from Shaman to Magus*. Rochester, Vt: Inner Traditions International, 2003.

McIntosh, Jane, and Clint Twist.*Civilizations: Ten Thousand Years of Ancient History*. New York: DK Pub, 2001.

Moon, Sun Myung.*Exposition of the Divine Principle*. New York: The Holy Spirit Association for the Unification of World Christianity, 1996.

Moss, Carol. *Science in Ancient Mesopotamia*.Science of the past. New York: F. Watts, 1998.

Ouspensky, P. D. *In Search of the Miraculous: Fragments of an Unknown Teaching*. New York: Harcourt, Brance & World, 1949.

Pascal Blaise, and Roger Ariew, *Pensées*. Indianapolis, IN: Hackett Pub. Co, 2005.

Pick, Fred L., G. Norman Knight, and Frederick Smyth. *The Pocket History of Freemasonry*. London: Hutchinson, 1992.

Plato, and John Warrington. *The Trial and Death of Socrates: Euthyphro, Apology, Crito, Phaedo*. London: Dent, 1963.

Plato and William S. Cobb.*The Symposium ; Plato's Erotic Dialogues ; and the Phaedrus*. New York: State University of New York Press, 1993.

Rajinder Kaur. *God in Sikhism*. Amritsar: Sikh Itihas Research Board, Shiromani Gurdwara Parbandhak Committee, 1999.

Salaman, Clement, and Hermes.*The Way of Hermes: Translationsof The Corpus Hermeticum and the Definitions of HermesTrismegistus to Asclepius*. Rochester, VT: Inner Traditions, 2000.

Saliba, John A. *Understanding New Religious Movements*. Grand Rapids, Mich: W.B. Eerdmans, 1996.

Sanders, Tao Tao Liu.*Dragons, Gods & Spirits from Chinese Mythology*.World mythologies series. New York: Schocken Books, 1983.

Sikh Missionary Center.*Pearls of Sikhism: [Peace, Justice & Equality]*. Phoenix, Ariz: Sikh Missionary Center, 2008.

Slosman, Albert. *La vie extraordinaire de Pythagore*. Les Portes de l' étrange. Paris: R. Laffont, 1979.

Smart, Ninian, and Richard D. Hecht. *Sacred Texts of the World: A Universal Anthology*.A Herder & Herder book. New York: Crossroad, 2003.

Stevens, Keith G. *Chinese Mythological Gods*. Images of Asia. Oxford: Oxford University Press, 2001.

Steiner, Rudolf. *Knowledge of the Higher Worlds and Its Attainment*. New York: Anthroposophic Press, 1947.

Stephenson J. "Ancient, modern, and accurate: a reflection on theological method." *Lutheran Theological Journal* (2009):125-131.

Swedenborg, Emanuel. *Heaven and Hell, Also the World of Spirits or Intermediate State from Things Heard and Seen by Emanuel Swedenborg*. Boston: Swedenborg Printing Bureau, 1907.

Temple of the People.*Teachings of the Temple*. Halcyon, Calif: The Temple of the People, 1948.

Urantia Foundation. *The Urantia Book*. Chicago: Urantia Foundation, 1955.

van't Spijker, I., & Coulter, D. "Per visibilia ad invisibilia. Theological method in Richard of St Victor (d. 1173)."*The Journal of Ecclesiastical History* (2008):122-123.

Wallis, Glenn. "The Buddha Counsels a Theist: A Reading of the Tevijjasutta (Dighanikaya 13)." *Religion*.38, no. 1 (2008): 54.

Watt-Evans, Lawrence.*The Summer Palace*. New York: Tor, 2008.

Watt-Evans, Lawrence.*Touched by the Gods*. New York: TOR, 1997.

Wells, Susan E., and Harriet H. Carter.*Guided Tour to the Afterlife:The Remarkable First-Hand Account of One Woman's Death and Her Adventures in a New Life After Death*. San Diego, Calif: Hillbrook, 2000.

White, Daniel Ernest. *"... so help me, God": the US presidents in perspective*. New York, NY: Nova Science Publ, 1996.

Wilkinson, Philip, and Neil Philip.*Mythology*. Eyewitness companions. London: DK Pub, 2007.

Wilkinson, Richard H. *The Complete Gods and Goddesses of Ancient Egypt*. New York: Thames & Hudson, 2003.

Yip K. S. "Traditional Chinese Religious Beliefs and Superstitions in Delusions and Hallucinations of Chinese Schizophrenic Patients."*The International Journal of Social Psychiatry*.49, no. 2 (2003): 97-111.

Zindell, David. *Lord of Lies*. New York: Tor, 2008.

Index